Evangelizing the South

Recent titles in

RELIGION IN AMERICA SERIES
Harry S. Stout, General Editor

NATHANIEL TAYLOR, NEW HAVEN THEOLOGY, AND THE LEGACY OF JONATHAN EDWARDS
Douglas A. Sweeney

BLACK PURITAN, BLACK REPUBLICAN
The Life and Thought of Lemuel Haynes, 1753–1833
John Saillant

WITHOUT BENEFIT OF CLERGY
Women and the Pastoral Relationship in Nineteenth-Century American Culture
Karin E. Gedge

A. J. TOMLINSON
Plainfolk Modernist
R. G. Robins

FAITH IN READING
Religious Publishing and the Birth of Mass Media in America
David Paul Nord

THE FAITH OF THE COMMON PEOPLE
Protestant Fundamentalism in Boston, 1885–1950
Margaret Lamberts Bendroth

A PARADISE OF REASON
William Bentley and Enlightenment Christianity in the Early Republic
J. Rixey Ruffin

EVANGELIZING THE SOUTH
A Social History of Church and State in the Upper South
Monica Najar

Evangelizing the South

*A Social History of Church
and State in Early America*

MONICA NAJAR

2008

OXFORD
UNIVERSITY PRESS

Oxford University Press, Inc., publishes works that further
Oxford University's objective of excellence
in research, scholarship, and education.

Oxford   New York
Auckland   Cape Town   Dar es Salaam   Hong Kong   Karachi
Kuala Lumpur   Madrid   Melbourne   Mexico City   Nairobi
New Delhi   Shanghai   Taipei   Toronto

With offices in
Argentina   Austria   Brazil   Chile   Czech Republic   France   Greece
Guatemala   Hungary   Italy   Japan   Poland   Portugal   Singapore
South Korea   Switzerland   Thailand   Turkey   Ukraine   Vietnam

Copyright © 2008 by Oxford University Press, Inc.

Published by Oxford University Press, Inc.
198 Madison Avenue, New York, New York 10016

www.oup.com

Oxford is a registered trademark of Oxford University Press

All rights reserved. No part of this publication may be reproduced,
stored in a retrieval system, or transmitted, in any form or by any means,
electronic, mechanical, photocopying, recording, or otherwise,
without the prior permission of Oxford University Press.

Library of Congress Cataloging-in-Publication Data
Najar, Monica.
Evangelizing the South : a social history of church and state in the
Upper South / Monica Najar.
     p. cm.—(Religion in America series)
Includes bibliographical references and index.
ISBN 978-0-19-530900-3
1. Southern States—Church history.   2. Church and state—Southern States.
3. Southern States—Social conditions.   I. Title.
BR535.N35 2007
277.5'081—dc22   2007001260

9 8 7 6 5 4 3 2 1

Printed in the United States of America
on acid-free paper

*For Margaret Rosalie Najar
and Phoebe Rosalie Liskin*

Acknowledgments

It is a pleasure to acknowledge the generosity and expertise of the many individuals who assisted in the creation of this book. In this project, and the projects to come, I owe a happy debt to Jeanne Boydston. With a gift for posing piercing questions and with the clarity to discern patterns and arguments, she enriched my training and immeasurably aided this project. Her good humor and graciousness throughout the years will always be appreciated. Charles Cohen read many drafts of this project and generously gave of his time and expertise, offering his sharp insights and sharper wit. I have been blessed too to have wonderful colleagues at Lehigh University, many of whom have shared time, ideas, and very useful suggestions. In particular, Jean Soderlund has been a font of wisdom, and John Pettegrew carefully reviewed the manuscript and offered valuable suggestions. I am also grateful to the wonderful people at Oxford University Press. Cynthia Read has been a kind and wise editor, and Stacey Hamilton, Daniel Gonzalez, and Merryl Sloane have expertly guided this manuscript through the editorial process.

Other individuals generously read this book in part or in whole. Sarah Fatherly and Ellen Baker closely read drafts of the manuscript, offering their extensive expertise and unwavering support. Tracey Deutsch and Bethel Saler gave sage advice to improve this work. I am also grateful for the valuable suggestions of Jonathan Sassi, Cynthia Kierner, Anne Boylan, John Lauritz Larson, Sylvia Frey, Kirsten Fisher, Stephen Kantrowitz, Natasha Larimer, Anne Lewis-Osler,

David Chang, Ceci Najar, Simone Najar, Peter Russell, Michael Fitzgerald, Gail Cooper, Jan Fergus, Elizabeth Dolan, Benjamin Wright, Hannah Stewart-Gambino, and the anonymous readers for Oxford University Press. Gregory A. Wills kindly shared his own extensive research. Portions of the manuscript also benefited from comments by the members of the University of Minnesota's Comparative Women's History Workshop, the University of Wisconsin's Early American Colloquium, and the UW women's history community. A number of undergraduate and graduate student assistants provided various kinds of help throughout this project, particularly Meredith Gee, Courtney Smith, Seth Fertenbach, Christianne Gadd, and Silas Chamberlin. Kathryn Erb was a superb assistant who handled any number of tasks and managed an unwieldy database. The manuscript has been greatly improved by Holly Kent's keen eye and graceful prose.

I am also grateful to the archivists and librarians at a number of institutions. In particular, I would like to thank the staffs at the Library of Virginia, Virginia Historical Society, North Carolina Baptist Historical Collection at Wake Forest University, North Carolina State Archives, Southern Baptist Historical Library and Archives, Kentucky Historical Society Library, Tennessee State Archives, Margaret I. King Library at the University of Kentucky, Lehigh University, and Southern Baptist Theological Seminary. Darlene Slater Herod and her colleagues at the Virginia Baptist Historical Society have been generous with their time and expertise. Finally, I would like to thank the librarians and staff at the State Historical Society of Wisconsin, in particular, Michael Edmonds, who was always willing to offer assistance.

A number of institutions provided me with support to research and write this project. I am very grateful to the Committee for Institutional Cooperation; the Virginia Historical Society for Mellon research funds; the Department of History at the University of Wisconsin, Madison; the Graduate School of the University of Wisconsin, Madison; the Colonial Dames of Wisconsin; Lehigh University; the Southern Baptist Historical Library and Archives; and the Lawrence Henry Gipson Institute for Eighteenth-Century Studies. I also want to thank the Center for the Study of Religion at Princeton University, which provided not only the financial and physical space for a year of writing, but also wonderful colleagues and exciting conversations. Parts of chapter 4 were published in an earlier form in *American Baptist Quarterly* 16 (Sept. 1997) and are reprinted here with permission of the American Baptist Historical Society. A version of chapter 6 was published in the *Journal of the Early Republic* 25 (Summer 2005). My thanks go to the editors and the anonymous readers.

Finally, my family provided all kinds of support to enable me to complete this project. My mother, Margaret Najar, raised the questions that have become the foundation of my work and gave me all the tools to investigate them, and my father, Leopoldo Najar, remains an enthusiastic supporter of my choices. I am enormously grateful to both of them.

A note about quotations: I have kept the original spelling, capitalization, and punctuation as much as possible without the distracting use of [*sic*], and I have introduced corrections only when necessary for clarity.

Contents

Introduction, 3

1. The Manly Voice of Orthodoxy, 13
2. We, the Male and Female, 35
3. Our Domestic Peace, 65
4. On a Scale of Justice, 89
5. Unusual Strugglings of Mind, 115
6. The Equity of Hereditary Slavery, 137

   Conclusion, 163

   Appendix, 169

   Notes, 181

   Selected Bibliography, 223

   Index, 245

Evangelizing the South

Introduction

In January 1786, nearly ten years after Thomas Jefferson drafted it, the Bill for Establishing Religious Freedom finally became law in Virginia, delivering a mortal blow to the idea of state-supported religion. Disestablishing Virginia's Church of England was no easy task. Accomplishing it required over 100 petitions with more than 11,000 names, grand showmanship, anonymous editorials, raucous debates, alliances between deists and evangelicals, and even some well-timed blackmail. After what Jefferson called one of "the severest contests in which I have ever been engaged," the partisans may well have wanted to consider the matter closed.[1] But the bill was a legislative expression of what was a wider, and ongoing, reorientation of the place and function of religion. Disestablishment of the church was one stage, not the endpoint, in a cultural transformation of the relationship between religion and civil society in the Upper South that began in the decades before the Revolution and stretched into the early national era.

As Americans constructed new national and state structures in the late eighteenth and early nineteenth centuries, they reorganized the relationship and boundaries between the religious and civil realms on both the national and local levels; this reorganization determined the appropriate responsibilities and limits of government and religious bodies, as well as shaped the extent of civil and religious authority in the new nation. Much of this political and cultural reorganization occurred neither in statehouses nor courthouses, but in neighborhoods, churches, and taverns. Solidified by legal changes, the transformation was first and foremost a product of people's changing religious choices, a shift made visible in the 1750s and 1760s when the Separate and Particular Baptists began to evangelize the southern population. Their efforts acted less as a revival for those whose faith and commitment had wavered than as a missionary movement that appealed directly to the "unchurched"—those who belonged to no particular faith or congregation—a group that included both European Americans and African Americans. Within just a few years, these evangelicals began to spread their beliefs and their fervor, gaining converts and building churches throughout Virginia and North Carolina and into the western regions. The growth of the Baptists—the fastest growing sect in the revolutionary and early national Upper South—marked a shift in religious culture: the rapid numerical and geographic expansion of converts and churches signaled the start of the transformation of the South into a manifestly evangelical society.

Analyzing the Baptist churches in Virginia, North Carolina, Kentucky, and Tennessee, this book argues that eighteenth-century evangelicals left their mark on southern society less through the volume of their conversions than through the institutional structures that they introduced into the region's civil and religious life. These institutions and, in particular, the church structure positioned the evangelicals as the primary arbiters of affairs both civil and domestic. In their churches, Baptists hoped to create pure covenanted communities that could guide members to live God's commands and that could shine as beacons to unbelievers. To accomplish this, they empowered their churches with great authority over the lives of church members, exercising this authority in their neighborhoods, business places, courthouses, and homes. Through their interventions in such matters as marriage, slavery, and commerce, Baptist churches reshaped gender and race—two of the central elements of authority in southern society—and claimed many of the functions of a civil government. Churches, then, acted as both civil and religious bodies, creating institutions that drew settlers together, galvanized their loyalties, and schooled them in the structures of community—all in a culture that deeply distrusted institutions. In so doing, they assisted in reformulating the lines between the "religious" and "secular" realms with significant consequences for religion, slavery, and the emerging nation-state.

In studying the relationship between civil and religious society, this project constructs a social history of church and state. Although the phrase "church and state" has traditionally signaled the relationship of institutionalized religion to government, this study interposes the categories of gender and race in order to destabilize and rethink that relationship, a model that requires us to broaden our understanding of the interplay between churches and governmental bodies. The revolutionary era breakdown of colonial religious establishments and the subsequent reconstitution of a relationship between religion and government have been the focus of numerous works by historians and political theorists. Whether raised as a question of the historical evolution of church-state relations or as a question of the intentions of the "founding fathers," these developments have occupied scholars and political commentators for some time.[2] Although the extensive literature on such issues fixes on the relations of church and state, the phrase itself can be problematic and can hide more than it illuminates. "Church and state" suggests a coherence and stability of meaning that neither religious nor governmental bodies could claim in the 1770s and 1780s. The word "church" seems at odds with the various self-styled "religious societies" that became vocal participants in the debates about religious toleration and liberty, such as the Baptists, the Mennonites, and the Society of Friends, groups that eschewed many of the centralized institutional structures associated with the term "church." And "state," too, is a rather grandiose term for the nascent governmental bodies still very much contested and rudimentary. Moreover, the terminology of church and state has fostered an emphasis on legal developments and on the politics of the state.

Certainly, many of the contestations over religion concerned legal matters; these debates, however, must be understood in the broader context of the religious and political cultures of the era. During the revolutionary era and the decades immediately following, southerners were in the process of redefining the "proper" relationship between religion and civil society. As we will see, this was more than a question of the legal place of religion and churches, but also a question of determining what belonged to the secular realm and secular leaders and what belonged to God and the churches. After all, "sacred" and "secular" are social constructs that change and assume varied meanings in historical contexts. As R. Laurence Moore points out, "'secular' as a category for understanding historical experience depends for its meaning on the existence of something called 'religion,' and vice versa."[3] This is not to say that they are rigid categories that cannot overlap. But, by standing in relation to each other in binary tension, they mark boundaries and give meanings to time, space, and behavior. Sacred time, for instance, might include Sundays or annual religious festivals, designations that create a secular calendar as well. These culturally defined lines between the religious and secular arenas— between what is defined as the province of churches and what is defined as the province of secular authorities—also shape legal codes and constructions of social authorities and power.

In the late eighteenth-century Upper South, the traditional consensus of the boundaries of the sacred and secular realms broke down. With the rapid growth of the evangelicals and the dismantling of the religious establishment, the lines between religion and the civil arena (never completely fixed) were undermined. Evangelicals and nonevangelicals, often in bitter conflict, sought to redefine those markers. For Baptists, the solution was clear. Baptist churches consistently claimed authority over *all* aspects of their members' lives, including marriage, slavery, business practices, child rearing, and leisure activities. No issue, decision, or behavior was defined as private or outside of the purview of the church. At times, Baptists deliberately sought to supplant civil authority and, at other times, they filled a vacuum in arenas in which the state could not or did not claim jurisdiction. In doing so, they extended religious influence into traditionally secular arenas, expanding the reach of the sacred realm.

In directing attention to changing definitions of religious behavior and authority, this book reevaluates the social significance of the southern evangelical movement, a subject that has long occupied southern and religious historians and that continues to be hotly debated in the historiography of American religion and culture. Pointing to the rapid growth of converts and churches, historians such as Rhys Isaac and Donald Mathews have identified evangelicalism as one of the most important social movements of the late eighteenth-century South. They argue that evangelicals not only successfully converted southerners but also introduced a culture with distinct values and codes of behavior, which challenged traditional gentry culture, social norms, and social and political hierarchies. Other historians dispute this assessment, arguing that the historical visibility of the evangelicals was less a result of their ability to convert the "irreligious" and transform the revolutionary era South (as late as 1800, only one in seven white southerners and one in twenty-five black southerners belonged to an evangelical church) than of their ability to dominate the subsequent historical narrative. In her work *Southern Cross: The Beginnings of the Bible Belt*, Christine Leigh Heyrman argues that what was most remarkable about the evangelicals was less their rise to cultural dominance than how long they remained outsiders within southern society and objects of suspicion and hostility. In her study, Heyrman finds a deep cultural mistrust of evangelicals that continued well into the nineteenth century, limiting their ability to gain converts before the antebellum era.[4] Other works on nineteenth-century evangelicals support Heyrman's conclusions, emphasizing limited membership numbers relative to the southern population and using these numbers to measure the strength (or lack thereof) of evangelical groups. But looking at numbers or at critiques of evangelicals tells only parts of the story. The transformation of southern society into an evangelical culture began in more subtle ways and was well under way by the turn of the nineteenth century. It came neither with overwhelming membership numbers nor with a great wave of evangelical churches sweeping across the southern landscape. Instead, it began with the early evangelicals' ability to change and then dominate the relationship between religion and society, long before they had the numbers to achieve such a powerful transformation.

We can begin to understand how the Baptists achieved this transformation by studying their institutional bodies. At the foundation of the Baptist evangelical movement was a church theology and structure that empowered each member to be an active participant. A "church" referred not to a building set aside for religious worship but to the baptized individuals who covenanted together as a body.[5] Far more than a geographic unit of believers, the church was a group of members covenanted with one another and with God. Its role was to assist believers to live divine precepts by providing a collection of spiritual brothers and sisters to watch over each other, arouse them to perform their duty, and warn them away from sin. Its purity was then both a goal in itself as a fulfillment of members' promises to God and a path to the salvation of each member. The premise of Baptist theology was the belief in the equality of all souls, unalterable by earthly conditions; membership (versus nonmembership), then, was to be a more important distinction than gender, race, and status. This belief eliminated the need for a ruling minister or body and instead allowed the whole church to make decisions, instigate discipline, and vote on church matters. The church structure allowed the whole religious community to define its values and norms and, more specifically, gave voice to those who lacked such power in civil society, such as white women and slaves of both sexes. Participation in churches proved meaningful because churches claimed an expansive authority over all their congregants.

Baptists insisted that each member was responsible to the covenanted community, and they, therefore, created and enforced distinct codes of behavior concerning marriage, gender roles, work, leisure, and race relations. These codes, and their zealous efforts to enforce them, positioned evangelicals to be a powerful force in the construction of southern communities. Baptists seized that authority, claiming a broad jurisdiction over their members' lives. As the Baptists sought to create a godly religious community, they were determined to scrutinize all aspects of their congregants' lives. They, therefore, deliberately constructed an all-encompassing code that was explicitly intrusive in intent and practice. This was, in fact, how they defined their mission. Church covenants insisted that members must keep a "watchcare" over each other—that is, members had a right and a duty to watch over and judge each other's conduct. And they did so with an almost alarming vigor. Baptist churches came to rule on everything from the most public behavior to the most private relationships. Consequently, churches found themselves facing the most intimate and complicated issues in eighteenth-century southern society. Far from simply concerning themselves with matters of theology, churches embroiled themselves in the everyday concerns of members' lives and mediated matters that were increasingly defined in the late eighteenth century as under the sole purview of the white, male head of household.[6]

The sweeping powers of the local churches also allowed the Baptists to provide order for their religious communities and, more widely, for southern settlements in very concrete ways. The web of evangelical Baptist churches spreading throughout the Upper South in the late eighteenth century increasingly took on a variety of activities associated with civil rather than religious bodies. Specifically, the churches engaged in many of the functions of a southern county court, the basic unit of local government in the Upper South. Baptist churches not only disciplined members for moral transgressions, but also mediated contract disputes, supervised debt repayments, and ruled on the equity of trade disputes; in essence, the churches acted as a type of local government for their members. These civil functions enabled the churches to play a significant role in the creation of order in new settlements in the backcountry. However, they were not simply a temporary response to struggling or absent local governments; instead, these civil functions became an integral part of the developing Baptist institution. Moreover, Baptists' insistence on their own jurisdiction over disputes of all kinds between their members allowed churches to offer a form of "citizenship" to their members, which included people excluded from definitions of citizenship at the formation of an independent American nation, notably African Americans and white women.

Baptists' intense desire to maintain discipline and conformity also motivated them to structure communal order from the ground up. Turning their attention to the ongoing migration of settlers into western regions, churches worked to track and monitor dislocated individuals. During the revolutionary and early national eras, southerners swept westward into the Piedmont and across the Appalachians, creating a culture of migration and new, dispersed settlements. The constant migration, short-term residents, and weak or absent local governments in the backcountry created concerns among both coastal authorities and backcountry residents about dislocation and disorder. Baptist churches mitigated these concerns and even assisted in the migration and resettlement processes. Churches developed procedures for those wishing to migrate, which included informing their community and creditors of their intentions, settling outstanding contracts, and maintaining contact with a church community. Church networks kept track of migrating members not yet connected to a new community and also provided certification of past good conduct (or warned of misconduct). Church covenants also assisted in this migratory process by creating a community out of scattered settlers, by articulating each congregation's set of shared values, and, ultimately, by binding members together. Allaying fears of unsupervised, wandering individuals disconnected from family and social ties, Baptist churches carved a space for themselves as a source of communal (not simply religious) authority.

The evangelicals' close involvement in communal formation and the creation of order in new white settlements allowed these churches to remain intertwined with southern social structures. In effect, the evangelicals were able to powerfully affect southern society because they effectively wed Christianization to the colonization process. Historians have long recognized the crucial role of religion in North American colonization efforts. These studies reveal that when religious belief and church structure jointly played a significant role in the colonization of land and the construction of new communities, religion retained, often to a remarkable degree, an influence within the social, political, and economic structures in those settlements. While historians have examined these interconnections in the Mid-Atlantic and New England colonies, it is a model that, by most historians' accounts, does not fit the Chesapeake or Lower South, where the Church of England predominated.[7] The Church of England—lacking sufficient ministers, churches, or an organizational structure that was adaptable to dispersed southern settlements—was not a significant force in the motivations of early colonists or in the early settlements. The eighteenth-century evangelicals, however, focused much of their efforts and found their greatest successes in the backcountry, in part because they had a simple church structure that was easily (and cheaply) transplanted to new settlements. As migrants trekked into the western regions of Kentucky and Tennessee in the 1780s and 1790s, for instance, evangelical itinerant preachers journeyed with them, founding churches before residents built courthouses, signing covenants before they signed deeds, and constructing religious communities before there were neighborhoods. Evangelical churches were not only the first religious institutions in the western regions, they were the first institutions of any kind in these settlements. As the case of the Baptists demonstrates, this enabled evangelicals to integrate their churches and their beliefs into the very foundation of southern settlements, providing them with a crucial means to affect civil and social norms well past the founding of the nation-state.

Throughout the expanding Upper South, Baptists thus intervened in matters that ranged from intimate behavior in the bedroom to civil disputes over prices and debts, acting in what we might call both "private" and "public" arenas. Then, as now, those were complex terms that people used in a variety of ways, at times intending to convey fundamental categories that organize human behavior and social space. These are tricky terms for historians to use because some things (including churches) defy easy categorization, and they can lead to overly rigid models of behavior and social space. And yet we return to these terms (like "church and state"), despite their messiness and overlap, because of their significance to how Americans talked about the home, labor, and gender. Historians have found that in the late eighteenth and early nineteenth centuries, Americans constructed an increasingly sharp divide between domestic concerns and the economic and political worlds. They did so in a myriad of ways from architectural design to rhetoric. The public-private dichotomy was, in many ways, arbitrary in how it defined each sphere, and it served to erase women's participation in politics and their productive labor while associating them with the home, family, and Christianity. At its best, a historiographic model of nineteenth-century definitions of the public and private realms explains *ideological* categories that Americans used to understand or organize their world, rather than actual descriptions of behaviors and spaces (which confounded the very terms that people used).[8] Like their fellow Americans, Baptists found this dichotomy of public and private of great use. Yet they used it in distinct ways, ways that would serve as a countercurrent to the stability of these cultural categories in the region. For Baptists, "private" referred not to a sphere of behavior, but rather to *any* activity of the church or church members. "Public," then, referred to the realm outside of the church, which, as we will see, centered on individuals (nonmembers), rather than to a designated set of issues or physical spaces.

This book traces the nature, extent, and meanings of Baptist authority in a variety of arenas. The structure of the book is primarily thematic, though the chapters follow a loose chronology. The first chapter maps the social and spiritual landscape in Virginia and North Carolina in the mid-eighteenth century, charting the concurrent processes of the stabilization of the Church of England and the rise of dissenting sects. The subsequent chapters evaluate the authority of Baptist churches within a series of concentric circles from the individual, to the family, to the neighborhood, to a relationship with the state, and, finally, to the institution of slavery. Chapter 2 argues that, during the 1760s and 1770s, distinctly evangelical visions of manhood and womanhood emerged which became structured into early church membership. Examining the revolutionary and postrevolutionary eras, chapter 3 contends that, in an era of increasing autonomy for white male householders, churches nonetheless intruded into the relations of the household, reconfiguring them according to an evangelical model. Chapter 4 contends that Baptist churches met civil as well as spiritual needs for their membership, acting alongside or, at times, in lieu of county courts. In acting as a civil body, the Baptists offered a type of ecclesiastical citizenship to their members, including those members who were denied citizenship by the nascent state. Considering religion and politics in the early national era, chapter 5 explores the vital paradoxes in Baptists' understanding of the relationship between religious and political authority. Chapter 6 argues that, in the Baptists' ongoing efforts to mark the boundaries between the sacred and the secular realms, slavery came to be the defining issue, one that would determine the extent of, and limits to, Baptists' reach. As Baptists sought to preserve the unity of their churches in the early nineteenth century, they sacrificed their authority over slavery and yielded it to the civil realm, and in doing so, they helped to define the boundaries of religion and the new nation-state.

I

The Manly Voice of Orthodoxy

In 1754, a handful of missionaries traveled from their evangelical New England churches to the Upper South. They were Separate Baptists, a sect that originated in the northern revivals of the 1740s, embraced an enthusiastic style of preaching and worship, and required a conversion experience for membership. Lacking money, education, or a network of churches, these fervent missionaries had few resources with which to spread the gospel, save their powerful exhorters and passionate beliefs. After a brief stop in northern Virginia, the party—now grown to fifteen—traveled to northwestern North Carolina, where they established a small church and preached to any who would listen. Within three years, they had founded three churches with 900 members and soon had ministers and converts spreading throughout North Carolina and Virginia. As the Separate Baptists swept through the Upper South, a second, unrelated sect of Baptists began its own period of remarkable growth in Virginia. Known as Particular Baptists, they shared with the Separates only a belief in the necessity of a conversion experience and adult baptism by immersion, and they too experienced increased zeal and growing numbers of converts. Together, these two sects were able to create more Baptist churches in the ten years following 1755 than had collectively existed in the entire colonial South before that date. The rapid growth of these two sects signaled the start of the transformation of the South into a manifestly evangelical society.

Mapping the religious landscape of the late colonial Upper South, this chapter examines the patterns of religious practice of the state-established Church of England, which opened the door for competition from the small dissenting sect of the Baptists. While envisioning a church structure that included all residents of Virginia and North Carolina, the Church of England was forced to live, at times uneasily, with dissenters and those unaffiliated with a particular faith or church. The presence of dissenters did not persuade Anglican civil and religious leaders to rethink their vision of the relationship between church and state; far from it: Anglican clergy and lawmakers worked diligently to fulfill the promise held out by a state-established church. But that effort faced nearly insurmountable challenges in the late colonial era. With the southern population rapidly expanding both numerically and geographically during this period, the ability of a religious body to create new churches would prove vital to the established church. The Church of England did not need to be universal, but it did need to sustain the fiction that it served Virginia and North Carolina as a whole. The rapid growth of the Baptists after the 1760s exposed the fragility of that fiction. While Baptist churches grew exponentially, the Church of England labored to gain the lay adherence necessary even to support existing churches, let alone to create new ones. The Anglican Church's difficulty in keeping pace with the population of the Upper South opened the door for competing sects to recruit unchurched populations. This contest between established and dissenting churches introduced a new and compelling definition of "church" and religiosity that would ultimately reshape the religious landscape in the region and alter the concept of the state's place in the religious realm.

Virginia's late colonial church establishment was secured by a longstanding and complex web of legislation and emergent colonial practices. The origins of its legal establishment dated from the earliest years of the colony. King James's 1606 instruction for the government of the colony required that "true" Christianity be "preached, planted, and used...according to the doctrine, rights, and religion now professed and established within our realme of England." In response, the governor dutifully mandated Anglican worship and the colonists' attendance at church. The Virginia Company provided for the Anglican ministry through the creation of glebe lands, property set aside specifically for the use and support of the clergy. Upon its establishment in 1619, the House of Burgesses took over much of the responsibility for maintaining the established church. The civil authorities of Virginia ultimately became responsible for the basic structure of the Church of England in the colony. The House of Burgesses established parishes, determined when new parishes should be formed out of existing parishes, and set their boundaries.

It defined ministers' services and set their salaries. It created vestries (the local ruling bodies of the church and parish) and determined their structure and responsibilities. This power over the vestries continued to rest with the legislature; thus when colonists were dissatisfied with their vestry, they brought their complaints to the legislature, which had the power to dissolve the existing body and call for new elections. The governor also assumed responsibilities for the maintenance of the established church. These responsibilities often mimicked those of a bishop since the American colonies did not have a resident bishop, and instead fell under the jurisdiction of the bishop of London. Thus, for the purpose of the immediate and local business of the church, the governor served as the temporal head of the Virginia church, performing religious duties such as appointing a minister to a parish if the vestry did not do so within one year and suspending misbehaving ministers. Furthermore, all Anglican ministers and missionaries had to be presented to the governor before assuming their position in a parish. Civil authorities' extensive involvement in ordering the Church of England created a strong church establishment in Virginia and closely united the colonial government with the established church.[1]

In North Carolina, the road to establishment was neither as smooth nor as successful as in its northern neighbor. The proprietary charter of 1663 allowed the free exercise of any Christian religion but decreed that the Church of England alone could receive the support of the government. The legislation necessary to build a religious establishment, however, was not forthcoming. The offer of free exercise of religion drew a number of Quakers to North Carolina, as did Virginia's increased opposition to dissenters in the 1660s and 1670s. The Quakers formed a powerful minority and, at times, dominated the colonial assembly as well as other prominent posts in the government, proving vocal and resolute opponents of any effort to create an Anglican establishment. Anglican lawmakers were not able to pass the first church law until the Vestry Act of 1701, which attempted to create the basic structures of the church such as parishes and vestries. Even then, the proprietors disallowed the act because they felt it set ministers' salaries too low. The Carolina legislature passed yet another Vestry Act in 1715, which provided for many of the basic needs of the Anglican Church. In 1741, the North Carolina legislature passed another vestry law to improve and protect the Church of England, but the king disapproved of one of its provisions and disallowed it. Subsequent efforts to create and implement church policies met with similar royal disapproval, and English authorities did not allow another vestry act for more than twenty years. The act of 1765 increased ministers' salaries and established procedures for hiring and removing ministers, providing the most stable legal structure yet for the colonial North Carolina church. At long last, it provided the North Carolina Church of England with many of the same rights and responsibilities that it had in Virginia.[2]

Even with the occasional support of the colonial government, the Church of England faced tremendous difficulties gaining even a foothold in North Carolina. The religious and ethnic diversity of the settlers—by the 1740s, the colony had significant populations of English Quakers, Scots-Irish Presbyterians, and a number of German sects—ensured that, during the early eighteenth century, no single church could dominate the religious life of the colony. In 1729, when North Carolina became a royal colony, it did not have a single Anglican minister. The climate, the unhealthiness of the region, the vast size of the parishes, and the poverty (or stinginess) of the residents all conspired to ensure that even the most adventuresome missionary longed to make his stay in North Carolina a short one. Ultimately, however, the persistence of the missionary arm of the Church of England, the Society for the Propagation of the Gospel in Foreign Parts (SPG), and the support of the colonial government paid off: although the Anglican Church continued to suffer from a dearth of clergymen, churches, and chapels, by the 1760s it enjoyed an improved situation with more congregants, more functioning vestries, more churches, and more ministers.

As established by the Virginia and Carolina colonial legislatures, the colonial Anglican Church relied on a vestry system to run the parishes and churches. Vestries were made up of twelve men who had broad powers over church and parish business—including the power to contract with and pay ministers, set the parish tithe or tax, maintain the churches and chapels, and determine seating in the churches. The colonial vestries amassed more power over the colonial parishes and ministers than did their English counterparts. Their efforts to exert this power provoked frequent struggles between individual ministers and vestries over such issues as ministerial salaries and methods of payment. Even the location of the pulpit could provoke a conflict, as one Virginia minister found when he became embroiled in a dispute which became so heated that he eventually resigned his parish and left for Maryland.[3]

For the southern vestries, "parish business" involved much more than spiritual matters. The colonial Anglican vestries had many civil functions and acted as an important component of local government. The Anglican parish was a vital part of colonial Virginia's government and, to a lesser degree, of North Carolina's. The colony, county, and parish acted as the three primary arenas of government, though the boundaries—particularly between county and parish—were often unclear, and jurisdictions occasionally overlapped. Virginia vestries commonly collected money for the church and minister, assisted the poor, bound out orphaned and poor children when necessary, oversaw the reestablishment of property boundaries, and presented local allegations of wrongdoing to the county courts. In eastern counties, where power was centralized in the hands of a small group of elite men, county and parish jurisdictions further overlapped, in that magistrates were often vestrymen. Despite the far weaker condition of North Carolina's established church, it too performed a host of civil functions. Like Virginia parishes, North Carolina parishes had responsibility for supporting ministers, building churches and chapels, determining land boundaries, providing poor relief, and levying parish taxes. At some points in the eighteenth century, North Carolina parishes also maintained weights and measures standards for the colony and paid bounties for the destruction of predatory animals. Unlike in Virginia, though, many parishes lacked even the basic elements needed, such as ministers and vestry elections, for the church government to perform these tasks effectively and consistently.

The Virginia and North Carolina church establishments and the vestry systems led to some astonishing overlaps of church and state. The vestries had civil functions, and local officials often served as vestrymen. The governor could assign a minister to a parish when the vestry failed to do so. The colonial assemblies established parishes and dissolved vestries. Church wardens presented offenders to the county courts; the county courts prosecuted those who failed to attend church. The county clerk compiled a list of tithables for parish taxes; vestries kept the vital statistics of the community. Parishes taxed residents for the support of the church, ministers, and the poor, and the county sheriff often acted as the parish tax collector. Church and government, it was expected, would work jointly to govern the colonial population.

The close connection between the church and the civil institutions was in keeping with Anglicanism's practical theology. In the eighteenth-century Atlantic world, Anglicanism was greatly affected by the religious conflicts in England during the previous century. Seventeenth-century England, while living under a state church, included many groups along a spectrum of Christian theology, from the Calvinist, primitivistic Puritans to Arminian, ritualistic Catholics. These divisions were not confined to the populace: even the monarchs and bishops were scattered along the religious spectrum. After the beheading of a king, and more than a century of squabbling, dissension, and schisms, the English were ready for a moderate, uncontroversial faith. With the Glorious Revolution, they arrived at a set of practical compromises, retaining the Book of Common Prayer and the Thirty-Nine Articles and adopting an act for religious toleration. These compromises ended the intense conflicts, produced a less doctrinal religion, and created a framework in which the state-protected church coexisted with dissenting sects. Concurrent with this development of a moderate religion, Anglican theology became wedded to rationalism as another way to eliminate religious disputes. The Church of England was to embody "a reasonable faith consistent with the laws of nature." Supporting the compromise within the Glorious Revolution, the Latitudinarian bishops strengthened the post-1689 church trend of combining religion and reason. They stressed practical morality rather than doctrinal disputes and argued for a broader toleration of Christian sects. The eighteenth-century English colonists felt the effects of the movement toward a moderate, rational faith. With the church steeped in rationalism, southern Anglicanism deemphasized "sin, redemption, and salvation" in favor of "duty, obedience, goodness, and character."[4]

Colonial elites further tied civil and church authority, acting in leadership positions in both arenas. Vestrymen were usually drawn only from the elite ranks of the laity. These men often held positions in civil government as well as their parish office, commonly serving as sheriffs, justices, and even burgesses. Elite control of the vestries was reinforced by the religious bodies' election procedures. Vestries were usually required to hold elections only at the time the parish and vestry were created. Thereafter, vestrymen could serve for life, and the vestries themselves had the right to appoint their new members when necessary, insulating themselves from the opinions of the parishioners. There were occasions when elections were called, but most vestries served for extended and indefinite periods of time between rare and exceptional elections. Only in the backcountry—where an elite class had not yet solidified—were vestries more likely to include non-elites. Even in these regions, the formation of an elite class was announced through control of the vestries and civil offices.[5] Thus, while the Anglican Church was largely controlled by the laity, only a small group of them actively influenced church policy and practices.

Given the church's close connection to civil authority, it is perhaps no surprise that colonial elites were deeply invested in the Church of England. The gentry themselves used the churches to display and emphasize their privileged and elite status. At Sunday services, while the rest of the congregation entered the church, elite men hung back and remained in the church courtyard. With the congregation seated, the front pews remained empty as the elite remained outside, at times even through the beginning of the services until the minister began his sermon. The procession of the elite men into the church and into their front private pews dramatically distinguished them from the lower orders. Even the physical characteristics of Anglican churches separated and privileged the elite class. In his study of Anglican churches in Virginia, Dell Upton reveals how physical spaces in and around churches were ordered in accordance with the southern social hierarchy. Within the building, congregants' status was indicated by both where they sat and in what kind of seating. Closest to the pulpit were private pews, which were closed off and had seats with backs. These reserved pews were used by the vestrymen, their families, and members of the gentry. Behind these great pews would be people of lesser rank in smaller pews with no backs. Farther still from the pulpit were simple benches on which poor whites would sit. Black congregants (often few in number) would stand behind these benches. The gentry's efforts to differentiate themselves from the other parishioners increased after 1720, according to Upton, when the elite began to pay for and use "hanging pews" (pews above the rest of the church body) and, later, private galleries and private staircases.[6]

With the aid and support of the government and the investment of colonial elites, the Anglican Church was well positioned to define the religious culture of the South, but the social geography produced a number of obstacles for any religious body seeking to church the population. By the mid-eighteenth century, Virginia and North Carolina had grown to encompass different cultures. Home to a number of bustling river ports and plantations of all sizes, the Virginia Tidewater was overwhelmingly rural with few urban centers, and even the capital of Williamsburg and shipping centers like Norfolk remained considerably less populated than similar areas in the northern colonies. The tremendous success of slave-produced tobacco and grain had fostered the creation of extreme wealth concentrated in the hands of a relatively small and stable elite class by the early eighteenth century. By the middle of the century, some wealthy planters had amassed land holdings of thousands of acres and considerable numbers of slaves. Even in the North Carolina Tidewater, where the settlements were neither as old nor as prosperous as in Virginia, some planters had managed to acquire sizable estates, and by midcentury, that region, too, had benefited from a growing population and an increasingly stable economy. While North Carolina's economic development lagged behind its neighbors, a diversified economy developed by midcentury that included tobacco production in the northern Albemarle region, rice in the Cape Fear region, as well as grains and naval stores. Throughout the Upper South, the land and agricultural systems encouraged dispersed, rural settlements. Even in coastal communities, colonists tended to live on farms distant from one another, averaging only 24.5 people per acre in the Tidewater region.[7]

The Piedmont, the hilly region between the Fall Line and the Appalachian Mountains, by midcentury contained settlements that were more than a generation old and differed in many ways from the Tidewater. Undeterred by the small Native American presence in the region, white settlement of the Virginia

Piedmont began as early as the turn of the eighteenth century, developing first along rivers and their tributaries. Intrepid individuals looking for good land or trading opportunities built homesteads and trading posts in the region long before either the colonial government or the colonial church made their presence felt. Much of the early migration into the Piedmont came not from the Tidewater but from Pennsylvania, as Germans and Scots-Irish, trekking southwest in search of good and cheap land, settled largely in ethnic enclaves. Emigrants from the coastal settlements also arrived to claim and farm Piedmont lands. The organization of western Virginia into counties followed the coming of white settlers, and, by 1730, a number of large western counties extended across the Piedmont and off the western edges of colonial maps. With the creation of western counties came the rudiments—but only the rudiments—of Virginia colonial governmental services, including the creation of local courts with the authority to provide for roads, ferries, and law enforcement. Colonial expansion in North Carolina followed a similar pattern, though it grew more slowly and a few decades later. A smaller population and a weaker economy in North Carolina kept European settlements close to the coast in the early eighteenth century. Increasing immigration to the colony after 1740, however, placed new demands on land, and Piedmont settlements began to develop in the 1740s followed by the establishment of counties and skeletal governmental services within a few years.[8]

By the mid-eighteenth century, migrants were spreading steadily throughout the Piedmont, moving west from Tidewater counties and south from central Pennsylvania through central Virginia and North Carolina. Even after decades of white settlements, however, the region continued to be characterized by dispersed, even isolated homesteaders, few churches of any denomination, and only the most elementary governmental services. Relying on a mix of crops and livestock, Piedmont settlers grew tobacco and wheat as commercial crops where possible, corn as a subsistence crop when necessary, and kept hogs and cattle to supplement their families' diets and their cash crops.[9] By the 1770s, the steady stream of migrants began to create pressure for more, cheaper, and better lands, and, during the American Revolution, migrants increasingly pushed farther westward, moving the backcountry into the mountain regions and into what would later become Kentucky and Tennessee.

Although there were significant differences between these different territories, there were also important characteristics that the Upper South shared as a region. Whether a merchant in the port town on the James River, a tenant farmer in North Carolina, or a German-speaking immigrant in the Virginia Piedmont, virtually all people in the Upper South were affected by the structures and culture of tobacco. As the dominant cash crop of Virginia and substantial parts of North Carolina, tobacco shaped land use, settlement patterns, labor, financial exchange, and class systems. There were other cash crops as well, including Virginia's exports of corn and wheat, which grew considerably in the mid-eighteenth century, and North Carolina's profitable exports of naval stores. But tobacco continued to be the economic foundation of the Upper South. Between 1725 and 1775, tobacco "rose by more than 250 percent in total volume." Even as production rose and prices fell in the mid-eighteenth century, planters' profits continued to rise.[10]

The tobacco culture dramatically affected land use and labor patterns. Planters bought large amounts of land and typically turned much of it over to tobacco cultivation. When tobacco lands were depleted, larger land owners were able to rotate to new lands. The profitability of tobacco and expansion of the population brought many of the wealthy to buy large amounts of western land, sometimes intending it for their sons and sometimes planning to sell as the population and prices rose. With their profits tied up in a labor-intensive crop and the supply of white servant labor dwindling in the final decades of the seventeenth century, planters turned decidedly to slave labor to maintain and maximize their profits. By 1720, slaves were already one-quarter of the population in the Chesapeake and increasing rapidly; by 1760 that proportion had risen to almost 40 percent.[11] Much of that slave population was located in the Tidewater region, and the proportion of slaves was much smaller in the Piedmont until the years prior to the Revolution and in the western territory until the 1780s.

It was these very conspicuous elements of society in the Upper South— the tobacco culture, dispersed settlement patterns, and an increasingly biracial population—that proved to be among the most significant obstacles to the Church of England and, indeed, to any competing church's efforts in the region. Although the Anglican Church strengthened its position in the eighteenth-century Upper South, especially in the Tidewater areas of Virginia and North Carolina where it had developed a solid base of ministers, churches, and congregants, it had difficulty extending its influence beyond this region. Ministers reported again and again throughout the seventeenth and eighteenth centuries that the people in the region were indifferent to the concerns of the church and rarely attended services or sought to have their children baptized. Some of these complaints, however, said less about the colonists' spiritual inclinations than about the sparse settlements that characterized the colonial Upper South.

The diffused settlements in particular created great difficulties for the Church of England because of how it defined a "church" and right religious practice. For the Anglicans, a church referred to a consecrated building that was suitable for dignified worship, which often required an expensive investment. The church building itself was a statement of faith, signaling respect for and commitment to the worship of God. Whereas in some religions (such as the congregationally organized Puritans and Baptists), individual congregations wrote out a declaration of faith or a church covenant, the Anglicans came closest to such a communal text in their church building, which served as a physical, visible, and local affirmation of their commitment. They expected it to be larger and grander than other public buildings, built with the best materials the community could afford. The design was carefully chosen and meticulously executed over a number of years (and, in some cases, decades). This meant that some churches were no sooner finished than they required repairs and renovations. Worship too required some outlay of money: a hired minister (ordained in England), copies of the Book of Common Prayer, and communion vessels (often gold). With these requirements for worship, parishes had to be geographically large enough to include sufficient tithables to meet the costs incurred by hiring a minister and by building and maintaining a church. But large parishes also made communal worship difficult, particularly in light of the poor roads, which hindered transportation. This was especially true in North Carolina, where the poverty of the inhabitants resulted in very large parishes and where the roads, even in the mildest seasons, were nothing short of daunting. Balancing church expenses with the parishioners' needs and wants proved a difficult task. Parishioners who had gone to great lengths to pay a minister's salary were dismayed when services occurred infrequently because the minister traveled through large parishes. Yet those colonists on the distant edges of the parish also expected services, baptisms for their children, and clerical officiation at their marriages. These competing demands created plentiful opportunities for misunderstandings, hurt feelings, and conflicts between the laity and clergy. Ministers often complained of the difficulties in getting their salaries paid, and the laity complained of ministers too lax in the performance of their duties.[12]

The Anglican Church, then, was faced with the dilemma of parishes that were too large for a minister to serve effectively or too small to afford a minister and the other costs of worship. In a joint letter to the bishop of London, the Maryland clergy described many of the hardships of their southern service: "The extent of our Parish is generally very large, some of them being about 20 from 30 miles in length; by reason of the Inhabitants of this Country having (many of them) vast tracts of land, live at least a mile asunder from their next neighbours. This large extent of Parishes obligeth us to keep one, or sometimes two horses to ride on." Virginia minister Alexander Forbes explained to the bishop that the size of his parish impeded his work: the "excessive length of my Parish I have found by long experience to be so incommodious, that I could never perform my pastoral office as I ought, altho' I have spared neither cost nor labor on the attempts." John Boyd, a North Carolina minister, complained that he faced a similarly demoralizing schedule: "The parish I live in is of a vast extent being upwards of 100 miles in length & 50 in breadth[.] I preached in 7 different places, which obliges me to ride every month 260 miles." The risk of having one minister attempt to serve a parish of that size was considerable. Boyd reported general conformity to the Church of England in his own area, but also "a Laodicean lukewarmness and immorality." Farther south of his position, the news was more dire, and he reported the presence of numerous Baptists and Quakers.[13]

But even an overextended minister was better than none at all; some parishes could not even pool sufficient resources to hire and keep a pastor. The southern colonies, and Virginia and North Carolina in particular, had acquired such a poor reputation that English ministers were loath to consider positions there. Many other places in the British Empire, including England, offered better compensation, a more secure tenure, more appreciative parishioners, and greater independence from lay vestries. Many parishes in the Upper South were simply too poor or (according to some ministers) too miserly to compete for the few ministers available. Thus, a general shortage of Anglican ministers plagued the region throughout the colonial era, and parishes often lacked an ordained minister.[14] The limited number of clergy meant even greater difficulties for the ministers who struggled to fill the gaps, like the Reverend Adams, who explained, "For these four years I alone have served, as a Presbyter of the Church of England, the whole County of Somerset, consisting of four parishes, so that six Congregations are supplied by me, which obliges me to travel 200 miles per month."[15] The backcountry, in particular, proved too remote for the struggling establishment: ministers were few and settlers were widely dispersed and often too poor to raise the necessary funds.

As late as the 1760s, conditions had not much improved, especially in North Carolina and the backcountry. In 1765, there were still only five ministers in the colony, and missionaries still reported having to travel vast distances to parish outposts. Governor Tyron reported that his colony's needs were so great that only one church was in "good repair," while the others ranged from "walls only" to "wanting considerable repairs." Moreover, his deceased predecessor had to be interred by a magistrate of the peace because no minister was within 100 miles when he died.[16]

With such uneven coverage, ministers reported back to England a disparate picture of eager residents hungry for preachers and the gospel and dissolute parishioners indifferent to church and religion. With clergy in short supply, some ministers found that upon their arrival to the region, the residents yearned for their ministries and welcomed them and the opportunity for Anglican services. One Anglican minister seemed quite pleased with his parishioners, saying that "the people here [are] generally very Zealous for our Holy Church," though he acknowledged that they lacked instruction in Anglican fundamentals. A newcomer to North Carolina found his parishioners quite receptive to Anglican preaching: "At my first arrival in the countrey, I had such kind invitations from the sev'ral Inhabitants that gave me reason to believe that nothing but the Good I expected wou'd result from such a well dispos'd people as I experimentally found 'em to be. Wherever I preach'd, I had great numbers of hearers." Even ministers who found a great deal to complain about in the colonial South were pleased by the eagerness of southerners for ministerial work. The Reverend Nicholas Moreau was disappointed by much of what he saw in Virginia, finding the other clergy generally immoral, poorly educated, and altogether too Scottish for his liking, and declared shortly after his arrival, "I don't like this Country at all"; he was nonetheless quite pleased by the people in his new parish, writing to the bishop, "I must tell you that I find abundance of good people who are very willing to serve God, but they want good Ministers." Ministers like Moreau found a people earnestly seeking religious guidance and ready to obey the precepts of the Church of England.[17]

Not every minister found the southern colonists so pious, nor did they find their welcome so warm. Throughout the eighteenth century, many clergymen complained that they found southerners backward in religious matters and unwilling to financially support a minister of the Church of England. The residents of their parishes, they reported, refused to attend services, take communion, or have their children baptized. Southerners even seemed indifferent about honoring the Sabbath, according to one Virginia tutor, who found that "all the lower class of People, & the Servants, & the Slaves, consider [the Sabbath] as a Day of Pleasure & amusement, & spend it in such Diversions as they severally choose[.] The Gentlemen go to Church to be sure, but they make that itself a matter of convenience, & account the Church a useful weekly resort to do Business." Unable to muster even that level of generosity, one missionary wrote to his superiors in London, lamenting his arrival at "This unhappy Country":

[W]hat difficulties and unheard of hardships I've here struggled with: I could not have fared worse in Malabar. Our confusions have much obstructed my endeavours, which I crave leave to assure y[ou]r Lordship have been very earnest and indefatigable.... I pray Your

Lordship to make the Societie sensible of my misfortune in being sent to such a wretched place and excite them to consider me whilst here, and either provide better for me, *remove me to a Christian country,* or else call me home.

A missionary in the Carolina backcountry complained that the people lacked "the least Rudiments of Religious Manners or Knowledge (save of Vice) among them. Such a pack, I never met with." The news was as bad in Annapolis, Maryland, where the Reverend Skippon found that "there seems to be an universal disregard (a few only excepted) of holy things." Perhaps the most abject report from the colonies came in 1767, when minister James Barnett lamented that part of his parish was "so unacquainted with the Liturgy that [he] was obliged to make every response [him]self." By the time he wrote his will, the Reverend John Alexander felt the cause of true religion had been lost in the region and moaned, "The manly, mas[c]uline voice of Orthodoxy is no longer heard in our land. Far, therefore, from my grave be the senseless Rant of whining Fanaticism, her hated and successful Rival." Whether or not that disregard was as universal in the late colonial era as Skippon and Alexander feared, it is clear that many Anglican ministers found themselves struggling in this region as they labored to church a people whose values seemed alien and to create parishes in a geography that sought to make itinerants of them.[18]

The Anglican Church's difficulties in reaching the southern population, particularly as it spread into western regions, provided an opportunity for competing sects to convert neglected settlers. Quakers, Presbyterians, Baptists, and Moravians all sought to establish a presence in the colonial Upper South and capitalized whenever possible on the absence of an effective Anglican church structure. This too proved to be a considerable obstacle to the Church of England as it was difficult to subsequently create stable Anglican Church communities in areas with many dissenters. The Virginia Piedmont, for instance, became home to large numbers of Presbyterians and other dissenters, and among North Carolina's ethnically diverse population, the presence of small sects allowed settlers to sample the many faiths of their neighbors. Within these colonies, a number of dissenting sects, then, competed with the established church, often welcomed by a population that rarely saw ministers or preachers. People reported a great variety of sects by many (often unflattering) names: Covenanters, Seceders, Ranting Anabaptists, Dippers, New Lights, Papists, Quakers, Gifted Brethren, Methodists, Presbyterians—all mixed among a healthy number of "Heathen and Infidels." "Religious heterogeneity," according to historian Carl Bridenbaugh, "was a fact in the [southern] interior, whatever the theory of the law."[19]

The Virginia and North Carolina Piedmont had a significant population of Presbyterians, who came to enjoy a comfortable coexistence with the established church. Many Scots-Irish had migrated from Pennsylvania into this region, bringing this faith with them. In the 1740s, the Presbyterian presence in this region increased with a series of revivals that some historians have identified as the southern component of the Great Awakening. Lay groups, unaffiliated with any church, began to inspire enthusiastic religious practices. With the help and leadership of some Presbyterian ministers, this small revival fed into the Presbyterian Church. While Anglican authorities initially responded with hostility, much of that antipathy dissipated by 1760. When more "unruly" dissenting sects began to grow in numbers in the midcentury, the Presbyterian Church benefited by appearing to be an orderly presence and by its relative doctrinal similarity to the Anglican Church. The differences between these two churches appeared less dramatic, for instance, when compared to the growing presence of enthusiastic Baptist churches. The Presbyterians, unlike many Quakers or the Baptists, conformed to the church laws set by the Anglican lawmakers. They applied for licenses to establish places of worship, and their ministers applied for licenses to preach. In short, they conformed to their official status as a dissenting body under the Toleration Act.[20]

The Society of Friends, who also had a notable population of adherents, did not enjoy such a quiet truce with the Anglican authorities. Settling predominately in the northeastern region of North Carolina, the Friends had begun forming monthly meetings in the second half of the seventeenth century. Some Friends gained prominent positions in the North Carolina government and used those positions effectively to block early efforts by Anglicans to establish the Church of England. If devout Anglicans objected to the Quakers' religious beliefs and practices, the hostility became widespread when Quakers refused to bear arms in defense of the colony, even after an Indian attack on the white population in 1711. Quakers continued to thrive even after their exclusion from the North Carolina government, and they established a number of monthly meetings in the Piedmont, where they often benefited from the lack of Anglican clergy.

There were also in the early eighteenth century some scattered Baptist congregations unrelated to the Separates. Most of these had originated as General Baptists, an Arminian group that was often lax in its discipline and organization, even accepting individuals for membership without a conversion experience. In the early 1750s, the Philadelphia Association, the strongest confederation of Baptist churches in the colonies, sent ministers to assist these churches. The Philadelphia Association was a voluntary organization of churches that were doctrinally quite differently from the General Baptists. Known as Particular Baptists, they were Calvinist and insisted on a conversion experience for full membership. A committee of ministers from this association traveled to a number of churches in the Upper South and assisted in reorganizing them along "regular" lines. By 1756, then, there was a newly reorganized (though still very small) Baptist population scattered through North Carolina and Virginia.

West and Central African religions constituted an important but much less visible religious presence in the Upper South. There is little documentation that reveals the nature of African religions among the slave population, particularly for the eighteenth century. Some African American historians and anthropologists have attempted to reconstruct slave beliefs and practices using the models of "survivals" or "Africanisms," suggesting that, while Africans were stripped of the institutional frameworks of their religions, some of their beliefs and rituals nonetheless survived and shaped their world view and faith in North and South America. Drawing upon folklore, recollections, and documented nineteenth-century practices and beliefs, these scholars have sought to uncover cultural cords that may have sustained enslaved Africans and African Americans in the New World. They have found similarities in death rites, naming, ancestral spirits, dancing, and musical rhythms in religious rites which indicate some cultural continuities. Of course, as scholars have been careful to qualify, religious practices and beliefs varied a great deal in Africa, and eighteenth-century slaves lived in a heterogeneous mix of cultures, ethnicities, and languages. With the loss of the context, landscape, and structure of individual African religions, many specific practices or beliefs surely shifted in meaning in the nascent slave cultures of North America. That is to say, slaves themselves had to construct whatever African-based religious systems existed in the colonies.[21]

The European sects engaged in little if any missionary work to convert the slave population, primarily because slave owners would not permit it. In the seventeenth century, many slave owners refused to allow their slaves to be Christianized because they feared that those slaves could then be set free. The Virginia assembly took steps to allay these concerns in 1667 and declared that Christian baptism would not change the status of slaves; it hoped that "diverse masters, freed from this doubt, may more carefully endeavour the propagation of Christianity" by permitting their slaves to be baptized. However, this law did little, if anything, to change white southerners' minds, and slave baptism continued to be very rare. The first institutional effort to Christianize slaves came in 1701 with the creation of the SPG, but Anglican missionaries who instructed slaves continued to meet much resistance and achieve little success. Most missionaries reported back to London that few blacks in their parishes had been catechized and baptized into the faith. They usually blamed the refusal of the slave owners, saying, "Masters cannot be persuaded to instruct them." When asked by the SPG what efforts they took to convert black "Infidels," the majority of Anglican ministers revealed that on this religious matter they deferred to the wishes of the slave-owning class, explaining that their primary effort was to "exhort their Masters to bring them to Church."[22] Even through the late colonial era, the vast majority of Africans and African Americans remained outside of the European sects.

Thus, even as the Anglican Church solidified its position with the colonial governments and worked to increase its ministers and churches, it still faced the challenge of competing dissenting sects. Its relative wealth and relationship to the colonial elite and government provided power but not necessarily popularity. It was gaining strength in the Upper South through the work of the SPG and greater legislative support, but it by no means dominated the whole region. The Presbyterian Church successfully spread through much of the Piedmont, and Quaker communities in North Carolina remained cohesive, while smaller scatterings of Baptists, Moravians, and other groups also created stable religious communities. All of these sects existed—not necessarily harmoniously—under the framework of the established church.

In the 1750s, a new sect joined the southern mix of religions. In 1754, a small group of evangelical Separate Baptists journeyed from New England to the northwestern tip of Virginia. Their arrival created controversy almost immediately, for these Baptists appeared to be quite different from either of the Baptist sects that had been long settled in the region. The Separate Baptists had developed out of the dynamic New England revivals of the 1730s and 1740s—revivals that energized and deeply divided churches, congregations, and communities. Splitting over such controversial issues as styles of worship and preaching, Calvinist doctrine, and baptism, New Englanders reconfigured their church bodies around their new beliefs and a freshly committed membership.[23] Some of these revivalist, or "New Light," groups splitting from their old churches took on the simple designation of "Separates," or Separate Congregationalists, a name that described their actions rather than their beliefs. Since their belief in adult baptism by immersion distinguished them from their infant-sprinkling colleagues, the Separates took on the name Baptists, though they had no formal connection to the other groups of Baptists already present in the British Atlantic world. Having recently organized their membership around specific beliefs during the heightened intensity of revivalism and religious conflicts, the Separate Baptists were an energized, committed sect. Combining religious enthusiasm, Calvinism, and a commitment to evangelize the population, they were a formidable group. When a few individuals decided to migrate south, this small sect proved to be a remarkable missionary force.

It was this small group of New Light enthusiasts who traveled southward into Virginia and North Carolina to engage in missionary work. At the core of this group were Shubal Stearns, his sister Martha Marshall, and her husband, Daniel Marshall. They stopped in northwestern Virginia, briefly joining a Baptist congregation there. More evangelical and enthusiastic than the Baptists they encountered, the new arrivals met with both suspicion and wonder. They soon moved on, hoping for better triumphs, traveling through western Virginia and settling in northwestern North Carolina.[24]

Although they were a small group of only fifteen (mostly husbands and wives), the Separates' missionary work soon produced dramatic results. One minister calculated in 1772 that "in three years time they had increased to three churches, consisting of upwards of 900 communicants.... All the separate baptists sprang hence: not only eastward towards the sea, but westwards towards the great river Mississippi, but northward to Virginia and southward to South Carolina and Georgia."[25] They itinerated well beyond their original churches, traveling throughout Virginia and North Carolina, with remarkable success. Throughout the region, they preached, converted, baptized, and ordained. In 1760, just five years after the Separates arrived in the Upper South, there were approximately eight Separate Baptist churches and 1,032 communicants. Ten years later, there were twenty-five churches and 2,890 communicants.

Many observers remarked on the Separates' unusual behavior in appealing to southern colonists. The preachers' itinerance and the emotion and outcries at these early meetings amazed the local population. Daniel Marshall was reported to have traveled "from place to place, instructing, exhorting, and praying for individuals, families, and congregations, whether at a muster, a race, a public market, the open field, an army or a house of worship; wherever he was able to command attention." The behavior of the listeners was no less remarkable to the vast majority of southerners: listeners often responded to the preachers' messages with "tears, trembling, screams, and acclamations of grief and joy." One observer commented that "it is hardly credible what tremblings, outcries, down-falls and ecstasies of joy have attended the ministry of [Dan River] church." Even those outside the faith marveled at their efforts. A North Carolina Moravian noted in 1766 that "at this time the Baptists are the only ones in the country who go far and wide preaching and caring for souls." Of course, not all who watched this wave of religious fervor saw it as the hand of providence. The intensity of the converts, the zeal of the ministers, the emotional displays in their meetings, and the sheer numbers of those pledging allegiance to this sect inspired suspicion, fear, and hostility. One Anglican missionary in North Carolina complained that the Baptists had "bewildered & I may almost say bewitched the minds" of his parishioners. Their success in the backcountry among poor farming families made some fear their "great influence over the weak part of the world." The Anglican elite's fear increased when the Separates began to Christianize slaves and include them in their religious meetings. When slaveholders had resisted efforts by Anglican ministers and missionaries to Christianize their slaves, for the most part, the Anglican clergy had complied. Thus when this enthusiastic, potentially disorderly sect began to draw in slaves, slaveholders were more than apprehensive: they were angry. Baptist meetings were often interrupted by boisterous or even violent nonbelievers who attempted to disperse the assembled congregation.[26]

Despite southern authorities' hostility, the Separate Baptists were able to grow rapidly, largely by disregarding Anglican notions of "church" and "parish," concepts that were structural and therefore expensive. Because few resources (human or financial) were needed to create a Baptist church, sparsely populated regions did not hinder their efforts to win converts and create churches. Whereas the physical structure was a major part of how the Anglicans conceived of their religious services and worship, Baptist churches, in contrast, referred simply to the membership, those who have been baptized according to the Baptist faith and then joined together as a body. A church then might mean five or six baptized believers who covenanted together to worship as a group and to watch over one another in Christian fellowship. Even after a church was "gathered," Baptist worship in the eighteenth century did not require many financial resources. They did not need a special building for meetings, but could and did meet in homes, barns, and fields. They did not even require an ordained minister. Many churches, particularly in these early years, lacked a minister and instead authorized a few lay members to act as exhorters. Thus, while Anglicans struggled to raise funds for the building of churches and chapels and for ministers' salaries, Baptists could avoid these costs until the membership agreed to take them on.[27]

The Separates also encountered some hostility, or at least suspicion, on the part of the Particular Baptists already settled in the South. One southern minister vowed he would not assist with the ordination of Daniel Marshall because he "believed [the Separates] to be a disorderly set: suffering women to pray in public, and permitting every ignorant man to preach that chose: that they encouraged noise and confusion in their meetings." This suspicion continued as the Separates increased and spread from northern North Carolina through the backcountry of Virginia. One educated Particular Baptist minister, for instance, complained that Separates allowed "weak and illiterate persons" to preach. Particulars were so concerned that they would be tainted by association that they titled themselves the "Regular" Baptists. With such implicit and explicit censures, it was no wonder that some Separates were equally suspicious of the Particulars and resented their criticism of the Separates' practices and preachers.[28]

Much of the early suspicion of the Separates grew out of their practice of allowing many individuals to speak in their meetings. Separate worship was marked by various types of vocal participation by the congregation; listeners commonly cried out, wept, and reportedly even "barked," behavior unheard of in Anglican churches. Indeed, the familiar line between minister and congregants did not exist in these churches. Separate preachers usually had the same education (or lack thereof) as their listeners, and, certainly, meetings held in homes and barns lacked the pulpit that separated religious authorities from churchgoers. Many church members had the opportunity to speak in formal and public ways, usually as exhorters. White men often served as exhorters even when uneducated and illiterate, allowing a great diversity of white men to assume positions of prominence in Separate Baptist churches. It is unclear whether African Americans spoke in these early church meetings, though later in the eighteenth century, when black membership grew, black men clearly acted as exhorters. White women, too, appear to have served as exhorters in early Separate churches, and this phenomenon in particular caused some tension with the Particular Baptists. Martha Marshall was very active in the early Separate ministry. Her work was "unwearied, and zealous" and her speaking marked by "surprising elocution, [which had] in countless instances melted a whole concourse into tears, by her prayers and exhortations!"[29] The Particulars considered this practice disorderly, and it became an important distinction between the two strains of Baptists.

The early conflicts and differences between the Particular and the Separate Baptists, however, can be overstated. In distinguishing between these two groups, some historians have identified the religious expansion of the Baptists specifically with the Separates. Rhys Isaac, for instance, drawing a sharp line between these two strains of Baptists, identified the Separate Baptists alone as the evangelical group that dramatically challenged the Anglican gentry.[30] Overall, however, these two strains of Baptists worked together, directly and indirectly, to build an evangelical missionary movement. As early as 1755, when the Stearns and Marshall party distressed their new Virginia church with their enthusiastic practices, a minister from the Philadelphia Association recommended that the church welcome such ardor and support these members in the practice of their gifts. Likewise, in the 1760s, both Particular and Separate ministers cooperated in a series of outdoor meetings. Itinerant ministers from these two strains also worked together indirectly. One minister who moved through a region might "awaken" residents to their sins, and another might convert them. Particulars and Separates, in fact, both increased dramatically in the decades before the American Revolution. According to Robert Gardner, while there was at most one Particular church (and no Separate churches) in Virginia and North Carolina in 1750, by 1770 the region had twenty-five Separate churches and twenty-seven Particular churches. Membership in both increased rapidly, rising between 1760 and 1770 by almost 375 percent in Particular churches and 180 percent in Separate churches. Overall, the number of Baptists in these colonies conservatively increased from just over 700 in 1750 to nearly 5,500 baptized members in 1770. Since these numbers only represent baptized members whose conversion experiences had been accepted by the church, the actual sizes of the congregations were much larger, ranging from approximately three to five times greater than the membership. For the Particulars and Separates, these gains presaged much greater success after the War for Independence.[31]

Far from evangelism being the particular province of the Separates, the Particulars were also engaged in a missionary enterprise. They too successfully created new churches and spread evangelical zeal to new areas. Minister David Thomas and his church, Broad Run, reveal the evangelizing work of the Particulars and the extensive growth of this sect. Thomas, originally from Pennsylvania, moved to Virginia and became the minister of Broad Run Church in Fauquier County in 1762. Interested individuals, hearing of the unusual work of a few churches, traveled—sometimes fifty or sixty miles—to hear Thomas and then invited him to preach in their neighborhoods. He traveled extensively throughout Virginia, preaching in Berkeley, Culpeper, Orange, Richmond, Westmoreland, and Lancaster counties. His work was centered in northeastern Virginia, but his reach extended much farther. He converted many Virginians and was said to be the "spiritual father" of many other ministers. One of his converts, William Fristoe, became a preacher and traveled to Frederick, Stafford, Fauquier, Loudon, and Shenandoah counties, among other places. His work was centered in western Virginia and the Piedmont.[32] The relative ease of "creating" a preacher and the itinerant nature of this sect created a network of missionary work, converts, and preachers that allowed the rapid growth of this group.

Broad Run Church also demonstrates the Particular Baptists' remarkable growth in the 1760s, well before the Separates gained a substantial foothold in Virginia. It grew so quickly in its early years after its constitution that it formed satellite congregations, or "arms." These branch churches were allowed to meet separately but remained officially under the direction of the "mother" church until they were ready for an independent constitution. By 1770, at least five arms of Broad Run had requested an independent constitution. One of these new churches, Chappawamsick, which formed out of Broad Run in 1766, also grew at a remarkable rate. In the decade after its constitution, its arms also formed independent churches, including Potomac in 1771, Brent Town in 1773, and Occoquon in 1776.[33]

While they came from separate historical origins, the different groups of Baptists soon recognized that they shared a central endeavor as well as many core beliefs. Above all, Baptists sought to make God's kingdom on earth, a kingdom which was to be less a physical space of a planned and closed neighborhood than a human and spiritual community of true believers. Baptists' intentions were deeply spiritual: to honor God, be faithful to his laws, and spread his holy word. Theirs was no small undertaking. They intended to build a community that sought not just to keep God's commandments, but to *live* his commandments. To do so, they sought to live as God's kingdom in the mundane and momentous moments of their lives. They sought to erase the artificial line between sacred and profane time and space: to have spiritual rules direct them outside of the church walls, and to make every day a holy day. Building a local and material version of God's kingdom was a task that they undertook with the utmost gravity and dedication to ensure its purity. Prospective members had to have a conversion experience, be currently living an upright and moral life, and not have any unreconciled conflicts with others in the fellowship. After their admission to the membership, Baptists' expectations and scrutiny of their brethren increased. It was not enough to avoid sin; Baptists had to employ religious edicts in their daily lives, including in their language, dress, lifestyle, economic activity, and family.

If Baptist practices made them seem unusual to their neighbors, their own view of themselves did not contradict this. Baptists believed they were uniquely able to practice and spread God's kingdom, and this belief in their singularity was central to their world view and identity. They saw around them versions of religion that coddled the worldly, the self-indulgent, the sinful. They saw human inventions in theology and church practice observed alongside biblical commands, weighing them down, diluting them, and, perhaps worst of all, intermingling with them until one was indistinguishable from the other. The Baptists, though, sought to return to a biblical purity, to strip away the inventions of priests and the superstitions of people until only the pure biblical commands remained. The modern world too easily incorporated human invention in the name of improvement, advancement, and ease. To withstand that temptation and undo 1,500 years of distortion, the Baptists wanted to model their churches and fellowship on the earliest of Christians. To do so, they articulated a vision of the original church's nature, practices, and values and wrote themselves into that history as the keepers of God's holy truth in the eighteenth century. This "primitivist" urge came not from a longing for the past, but from a longing for the pure. Baptists accepted the possibility of social or technological progress, rejecting only the effort to improve that which could not be improved. Their efforts, they believed, uniquely positioned them as true Christians, heirs to the apostles and first Christian martyrs. They proudly claimed the mantle of God's true remnant for themselves and their churches.[34]

The Baptists employed a strictly bifurcated world view, dividing issues, people, and behavior into the "worldly" and the "godly." They did not have a great deal of tolerance for the gray areas that dilemmas generally produce. They expected to find resolutions. To be sure, they did not anticipate finding them easily—they prayed, discussed, and debated issues for months and even for years—but they nonetheless expected to uncover the "right" answer. With great faith in the Bible as a guide, Baptists felt they could discern and make plain God's truth. Within this bifurcated choice, compromise, for unity's sake, was not valued. There was, after all, a righteous answer to be sought. These beliefs allowed them to stake a claim of having certainty within the marketplace of ideas, a powerful and even enticing claim in an unstable world.

This sense of their chosen and glorious place guided Baptists' decisions and fueled the evident joy in their early evangelism. It was the lens through which they interpreted their experiences in the Upper South. They built churches that consisted only of those who had exhibited the physical and material evidence of salvation and hoped, and even expected, to nurture a previously lost and holy vision of a godly community. To accomplish this task, they happily ignored conventions about educated clergy, dignified church buildings, and erudite sermons. In so doing, Baptists were able to negotiate the substantial challenges of the eighteenth-century social and geographic landscape by building churches that were easy and inexpensive to create, since they required only a handful of believers with a strong commitment. These would not be the last of the conventions that the Baptists rejected. While they did not face many structural obstacles as they sought to Christianize and evangelize the southern population, they did come face to face with the laws governing dissenters' proselytizing activities. Their rejection of the state's authority over their mission encouraged them to try to alter a host of social, legal, and political structures, beginning with one of the most personal, familiar, and deep-rooted: gender norms.

2

We, the Male and Female

In the spring of 1779, twenty-five-year-old Baptist minister John Leland traveled through Virginia on an extensive preaching tour. Like most southern Baptists of the time, he was a newcomer to the faith, having been ordained two and a half years earlier and baptized only three years previous to that. And, like many of his peers, he was a committed and fervent minister, eager to convert the multitudes. While preaching in North Garden, he was approached by a Mrs. Bailey who said that she wished to be baptized, "but her husband had told her, if she was ever baptized he would whip her within an inch of her life, and kill the man that should baptize her." She hoped that, since her husband liked the young itinerant, he might not follow through on his threat, but she bravely declared that even " 'if I am whipped, my Saviour had long furrows ploughed upon his back.' " Leland responded in kind: "if you will venture your back, I will venture my head," and he subsequently baptized her. The itinerant then moved on, safe from the husband's wrath, bragging that "the head of John the Baptist is not taken off yet." Mrs. Bailey, of course, remained to face the consequences, and Leland later heard that she was, in fact, whipped by her husband.[1]

In the late colonial era, evangelical ministers like John Leland and converts to the faith like Mrs. Bailey found the South a hostile and often dangerous place. Leland described confrontations with an Anglican vestryman, a member of the General Assembly, a military captain, and angry spouses, fathers, and sons. Colonial authorities attacked and imprisoned preachers. Anglican ministers denounced Baptists from their pulpits. Mobs disrupted Baptist services and dragged ministers from their congregations. Family members ostracized and assaulted children, siblings, and even parents for attending Baptist meetings. The bitter conflicts marked a new era in the religious landscape as the Anglican establishment faced grave challenges and provided its fiercest defense in the 1760s and 1770s. While there had long been practicing dissenters in Virginia and North Carolina, the Baptists' growing numbers and their willful indifference to the laws and social norms of the colonies coincided with a number of other developments that challenged the church establishment and the existing relationship between church and state. Enlightenment thinking challenged traditional links between religious authority and political authority. Likewise, the developing Whig movement expressed concern about, and eventually opposition to, the reach of English authority and structures. Support for a church establishment had never been more endangered, as individuals from various quarters began to question old ideas about church and state. At the same time, the defense of the state establishment and hostility toward dissenters had never been more virulent. Defenders, who believed that they stood for the true faith and civic order, sought to shore up Anglican authority and quash fanatical sectarians.

These clashes over church and state, though, occurred neither in statehouses nor courthouses but in the fields and homes that served as the locations of Baptist meetings. They were fought as much by minister John Leland resisting civil restrictions on dissenting preachers as by Mrs. Bailey challenging her husband's right to control her spiritual life and behavior. This era of conflict acted as a defining moment for the Baptists and helped them to construct an identity for themselves as a heroic and martyred people. It allowed them to connect themselves to the first generation of Christians and their persecution at the hands of the Romans. With Anglican authorities standing in place of the Romans, persecution was an accolade, and Baptists triumphantly recounted stories of the faithful's struggles against unjust secular authority. Baptist ministers began to write and collect firsthand accounts of persecution and new conversions in the 1770s, an endeavor that continued in subsequent decades. These narratives detailed the people, places, and conflicts at the heart of the evangelical Baptist efforts, and they also served as a type of Baptist "creation" story that marked who these people were and how they came to populate the region.[2] Significantly, while these conflicts occurred over the right to worship undisturbed, the stories that Baptists told about the disputes centered on gender, and gender became an integral part of the conflicts between dissenting sects and the established church. In particular, embracing new gender norms became a chief strategy for countering opposition and spreading the faith. Time after time, women and men were praised for discarding conventional gender roles and assuming new behaviors to serve the evangelical cause. Not only did the Baptists explore distinctly evangelical visions of manhood and womanhood, but they structured them into church membership.[3] By valuing membership over "earthly" distinctions of gender, race, and status, Baptists diffused the power of the churches among the members and offered laywomen as well as laymen opportunities to shape church policy and religious life. This was particularly dramatic for white women, who had new opportunities to craft religious identities that made them integral to the development and maintenance of the religious community, something that was not only recognized but promoted by the male leadership. In contrast to the scholarship that characterizes religious authority as rooted in domesticity and defined as peculiarly "feminine," these women found an identity that was communal and had some important parity with men's.[4] Ultimately, the Baptists constructed an intense spiritual community that combined egalitarian practices and hierarchical norms, creating a religious society with contradictory values, democratized practices, and the demand of total obedience to church authority—a disturbing prospect to outsiders, but an exciting possibility to some groups in the region.

As the Baptists—both Separate and Particular—embarked on their missionary enterprise in the 1750s and 1760s, they focused their greatest energy in the southern backcountry. During this period, the backcountry consisted primarily of the Piedmont, the region between the Fall Line and the Appalachian Mountains, and some white settlements west of the Blue Ridge Mountains. Settlers from the Virginia Tidewater and Pennsylvania had been moving into the Piedmont for more than three decades, but the region continued to be sparsely settled with few roads, ferries, or governmental services. Dispersed settlements were the norm throughout the Upper South, but western settlers had even fewer opportunities for social interaction with their nearest neighbors due to the difficulties of travel and the distances to traditional meeting places, such as parish churches and county courts.

Almost immediately upon their arrival in this region, the Separate Baptists ran afoul of local authorities when they refused to conform to the colonial statutes governing dissenting worship. Although the English Toleration Act of 1689 guaranteed the right of dissenters to worship according to their consciences, southern colonial authorities had established a series of requirements for dissenting sects, insisting that these constituted *regulations* rather than restrictions. Both the Virginia and North Carolina colonial governments required that dissenting ministers be examined and licensed by civil authorities and that all places of worship be similarly licensed. Licensed ministers were then required to be affiliated with a specific meetinghouse and to confine their preaching to that church; itinerant ministers roaming in and out of communities were not permitted. North Carolina authorities had some difficulty imposing their vision of "regulated" worship, even before the multiplication of the Separate Baptists. Since the persistent scarcity of Anglican ministers made them virtual itinerants, dissenters often found themselves free to worship in the absence of a permanent Anglican congregation. Virginia authorities too faced the presence of a number of dissenting sects and a shortage of Anglican ministers, but they proved determined to limit the worship of dissenters. The Presbyterians first felt the repercussions of this determination in the 1740s after their numbers increased due to migration and a series of enthusiastic revivals. Virginia officials attempted to limit this growth with restrictions and fines, arguing, at least initially, that the Toleration Act did not apply to Virginia. While their efforts to press the claim proved unsuccessful, Virginia authorities did enact regulations on dissenters' worship and established procedures to enforce them.

In the late colonial South, while Presbyterians, Quakers, and even many Particular Baptists complied with the statutes concerning dissenting sects and obtained a degree of toleration, the Separate Baptists refused to have their worship "regulated."[5] To this enthusiastic sect, colonial authorities' claim that they could regulate ministers and churches was tantamount to claiming the right (and ability) to regulate the workings of God—proof enough of the authorities' unfitness to govern religious matters. The Separate Baptists insisted that God retained sole authority over ministers and religious worship and that to allow civil government any degree of power in the matter compromised God's supremacy; God, and God alone, could rule their consciences, and human law held no relevance. In that spirit of fervent defiance, they not only refused to limit their worship to specified buildings, they refused to confine it indoors, and they held religious services outside. Moreover, the Separates not only rejected licenses for their preachers, they also allowed unordained (and uneducated) men and women to speak publicly at their assemblies. Some Separate Baptists so embraced their sect's position outside of the law that they deliberated censuring those preachers who conformed to the civil statute by seeking licenses.[6]

The Separate Baptists' disregard for the civil requirements for dissenting sects provided the authorities with the opportunity to attack the sect in the hope of limiting its growth, quieting its worship, and dispersing the "rabble" that appeared drawn to it. In the late 1760s and early 1770s, southern colonial authorities—particularly those in Virginia, who proved to be better equipped to face the dissenters' challenge than those in North Carolina—began arresting Baptist ministers for itinerant preaching, preaching without the proper licenses, and disturbing the peace. The meetings themselves became centers for these conflicts as magistrates and sheriffs disrupted gatherings to serve warrants and forcibly remove the preachers. In 1771, a Baptist meeting was interrupted by the Anglican minister of the parish, his clerk, the local sheriff, and some other men. The Baptist preacher, Brother Waller, was violently hauled off the stage and whipped by the sheriff.[7] A club-carrying Middlesex magistrate burst into a meeting and, "backed by two sheriffs, the parson and a posse," seized four preachers. One minister recounted being dragged from where he was preaching to the local jail: " 'Preaching being over, and, concluding with prayer, I heard a rustling noise in the woods, and before I opened my eyes to see what it was, I was seized by the collar by two men." The magistrates demanded proof of his license to preach, and when he did not produce it, they hauled him off to jail. There were arrests in the Tidewater and Piedmont regions, including in the counties of Orange, Spotsylvania, Culpeper, Middlesex, Chesterfield, Carolina, and King and Queen; one minister estimated that about thirty preachers were arrested in Virginia as a whole. North Carolina Baptist ministers fared better because of that colony's weaker church establishment and the long-standing (though not necessarily welcome) presence of dissenters, although there, too, Baptist preachers faced arrest. Once before the local magistrates, most ministers were offered a choice: post bond for their good behavior and agree not to preach within the county for a year or go to jail. Time after time, the Baptist ministers chose jail.[8]

Far from checking the growth of the Baptists, the jailings seemed to encourage southerners' interest in the sect. Crowds lingered outside the jails to listen to the imprisoned preachers exhort through the windows. Moved by the imprisonment of a Christian minister, crowds gathered outside of James Greenwood's jail and "as the sound of salvation was heard from the grated windows of his cell the multitudes without wept, and many believed unto eternal life."[9] Even those uninterested in or derisive of the Baptists came to the jails to watch the spectacle of imprisoned men exhorting to growing crowds. What began as a spectacle sometimes became a spiritual awakening. Whatever they may have heard about this "enthusiastic rabble" from their Anglican pulpit or their neighbors, southerners were often unprepared for Baptists' powerful and intoxicating belief that the spirit of God dwelled among them. To sympathetic observers, the scene of the imprisoned ministers resolute in their mission to preach the gospel resembled the persecution of the early Christians and their courage in Roman hands. That vision proved increasingly powerful as the crowds swelled, people wept, and listeners called out in the throes of conversion. To some, it seemed that the primitive (and therefore pure) Christian church had been reborn, and its biblical past was unfolding in living color in the Upper South.

The crowds gathering at local jails infuriated colonial authorities and anti-Baptist southerners, and authorities took steps to limit the interaction between the people and the impassioned preachers, filling in with physical force where state regulations fell short. In the county of Chesterfield, officials stopped John Weatherford from preaching from the door of his jail cell. Undeterred, Weatherford preached from his window. His equally determined jailers then built a wall outside of the jail to block his view of the crowd, but even this proved to be ineffective: "A handkerchief, by the congregation, was to be raised on a pole, above the wall, as a signal that the people were ready to hear," and Weatherford would call out to those assembled. In Middlesex County, some hostile individuals tried beating a drum to drown out imprisoned preachers' words; another persistent group "did every thing in their power to drive the people away, singing obscene songs, breeding riots, beating drums, pelting the minister thro' the bars, etc." In Culpeper, hostile forces proved more dangerous, burning brimstone at the door and window of the prison and attempting to blow it up with gunpowder while it housed minister James Ireland. According to minister Robert Semple, the power of these scenes of ministers proceeding with their work despite imprisonment and violence led Middlesex authorities to release a group of jailed preachers, having found that "the preaching seemed to have double weight when coming from the jail; many viewed it with superstitious reverence, so that their enemies [the authorities] became desirous to be rid of them."[10]

The violence against the early Baptists extended beyond the jailhouses and into Baptist meetings and religious communities. Much of the hostility came not from civil or religious authorities but from the converts' own neighbors. Although the Particular Baptists—who had viewed the Separates with some disdain and suspicion in the 1750s and early 1760s—grew somewhat accustomed to the Separates' fervor and novel practices within a few years, many people in the Upper South became increasingly disturbed by this sect as its numbers multiplied in the 1760s. Southerners, from the gentry to struggling yeomen, went on the offensive. There were verbal assaults in newspapers and from the colonial pulpits, warning the populace of these water-dunking "Anabaptists." One Virginia parson instructed his congregation that Baptist beliefs were "only Whimsical Fancies or at most Religion grown to Wildness & Enthusiasm!" Boisterous merry-makers attended Baptist baptisms to jeer at the converts, or rode their horses into the water during the rite. Ministers were often physically assaulted while preaching. The experience of

Samuel Harris was not uncommon: a man dragged the preacher "down from the place where he was preaching and hauled him about, sometimes by the hand, sometimes by the leg, sometimes by the hair." One "mob" broke into the church at Carter's Run and "split to pieces the pulpit and [communion] table." In fact, violence against the Separates was so pervasive that Baptist observer Morgan Edwards felt compelled to explain the lack of local violence against a Goochland church, suggesting that the church was spared because some of the local gentry did not actively oppose it while other elites had even joined it.[11]

Opponents did not limit their hostility to the Separate Baptists but also leveled attacks against the Particular Baptists, who had largely complied with the legal requirements and had previously lived and worshiped in the South mostly undisturbed. Perhaps their reorganization from loosely organized, doctrinally lax churches into disciplined, Calvinist bodies in the early 1750s made these Baptists appear more threatening, particularly since the reorganization was followed by increasing membership. Or perhaps the inevitable association of these two sects, both calling themselves Baptists, made the Particulars appear more suspect. Whatever the reason, Particular congregations also faced violence from southern mobs in the 1760s and early 1770s. Chappawamsic Church, which grew dramatically in the late 1760s, faced great opposition from its non-Baptist neighbors: mobs repeatedly interrupted its meetings, at one time armed to disperse the congregants, another time throwing a live snake into their midst, and at another time throwing in a hornets' nest. As with the Separates, preachers took the brunt of the fury. Minister David Thomas, for instance, was dragged from a meetinghouse "in a barbarous manner" and threatened with a gun. In 1778, a mob dragged ministers David Barrow and Edward Mintz from a meeting to some nearby water. Mocking the baptismal ritual, the members of the hostile crowd repeatedly held the ministers under water, "asking them if they believed."[12]

As victims of public jeering and frequent assaults, Baptist ministers found their very manhood at issue. Suffering insults and abuse positioned them outside of the most common constructions of manhood of the time. What emerged out of that cultural dislocation was a competing, specifically evangelical, version of manliness. Gender ideologies, to be sure, are never stable entities to be defined and measured; they are malleable, contradictory, and can be individualized. This was no less true in the mid-eighteenth century as masculinity blended new paternal ideals with older patriarchal ideas and norms, making patriarchy more palatable at the same time that it undermined a father's absolute authority. But one thing is clear: victimhood and public humiliation were anathema to southern understandings of manhood in this era.[13]

In the mid- and late eighteenth-century South, white manhood was commonly measured through a number of attributes, including independence, reputation, and unabashed prowess. Far from simply reflecting elite values, this vision of manhood extended to all ranks of white men and would as likely be evinced in a tavern as in a courthouse. Southern men displayed these somewhat abstract attributes through quite concrete markers, such as owning (or renting) land, owning a gun, and heading a household. In the eighteenth century, gentry and yeomen alike publicly demonstrated their largesse by "treating" at the local tavern; and, rich or poor, in the face of an insult, they would likely partially strip, a sign that they intended to physically challenge their opponent. While part of a shared culture, some of these expressions of manhood were class specific, as different ranks of men engaged in their own contests particular to their resources and social arenas. In the growing literature on southern manhood, historians have often described this construction of manliness as centered on a concept of "honor," taking a term southern men themselves used to convey a broader system of values that influenced language and behavior. Significantly, however, the markers of manhood were reserved for whites only. Slave men could not own land nor head their households, and even free blacks were restricted from owning guns. Thus, as men obtained these markers, they claimed for themselves not only the mantle of adulthood and manliness but also of whiteness. Rhys Isaac notes that "self-assertive style, and values centering on manly prowess pervaded the interaction of men as equals in this society." The pervasive public displays of these values "stemmed from the importance of demonstrating before all the world that one was not a socially immobilized, apparently humbled slave." Demonstrating one's assertiveness or independence, then, confirmed the gendered and racial privileges of white masculinity; to be passive—particularly in the face of an insult or assault—meant a loss of honor and was a challenge to manhood.[14]

For southern white men, obtaining the mantle of manliness was a constant process or, more accurately, a constant competition. It was a condition or status in need of vigilant defense. White men frequently challenged each other in displays of assertiveness, aggression, and bravado. In ways that were generally class specific, different groups of white men engaged in often public exhibitions of their prowess against other men in competitions of small stakes (such as dice, cards, and cock fighting) or large stakes (such as horse racing and eye gouging). "Gander pulling," a common competition among southern white men, exemplifies these contests. Men would grease the neck of a live gander and tie the bird to the branch of a tree. Then, before an assemblage of men and women, men would ride their horses to the unfortunate bird and attempt to rip its head off. The contest displayed the prowess of the competitors not simply through the evident violence but also by the strength needed to tear off the head of the bird while astride a horse. The event was a public one that would usually be announced in advance so that people would gather to watch the competition. Whiskey was available for purchase, and spectators would bet on the winners. The competitors themselves might vie for the favor of various women present.[15] The southern culture of gaming provided constant opportunities to assert one's manhood—particularly through conflict with other men—in a public arena. Honor, then, was an aggressive and public attribute, constantly sought and publicly displayed.

Despite these powerful cultural attributes, Baptist ministers reconfigured masculinity by embracing an ideal completely their own. Rather than assaulting their honor, the violence leveled against ministers—and their passive acceptance of it—became new and distinctly evangelical sources of honor. Evangelical ministers rejected the use of violence to defend oneself or one's reputation and, when confronted with verbal or physical assaults, responded with words and prayers. Ministers' manhood was not affronted by a nonaggressive response; instead, they found glory in being the recipients of violence while serving the cause of God, and they accepted the assaults levied against them as badges of honor. Thus, they compared their own experiences with the biblical stories of Moses, Paul, the apostles, and even Christ. Indeed, the clergy's passivity in the face of violence became an attribute as ministers were said to have "meekly" borne the abuse heaped upon them. Even a slanderous accusation would not be met with lawsuits or violence. One minister "accidentally heard a man lay to his charge one of the most abominable crimes. At first he felt irritated; but, recollecting his previous reflections [that '*woe be unto you when all men speak well of you*'], he was soon reconciled." In one assault, an armed man broke into a Baptist meeting, drew his sword, and attempted to attack the preacher. But the preacher was saved when his wife, "like a female angel, sprang like the lightning of heaven, clasped her arms within his elbow, around his body, locked her hands together, and held him like a vice," enabling some of the men present to disarm the attacker. Neither the threatened attack nor the fact that a woman defended him appeared to have challenged the preacher's manliness.[16] The man here displayed no discomfort with his passivity nor even the reliance on a woman to shield him from attack. Instead, he, like the other men in these stories, used his passive response to showcase his piety and the power of his convictions. Gentry might claim the power associated with wealth and lineage. Competitors at a gaming table or other contest might claim the power associated with winning, strength, or speed. But these Baptist men claimed a power that was divine in origin, invincible in the cosmic realm, and transhistorical in marking them as heirs to the apostles. In this sense, evangelical manhood included some traditional hallmarks of manhood, such as strength and honor, but the path to that designation was so different as to alter the experience of manhood.

A subtle undercurrent of this model of evangelical manhood was the display of self-control against a backdrop of brutishness. The ministers acted as models of restraint whereas their opponents were portrayed as jeering, obscene thugs. Time after time, the ministers ignored verbal and physical attacks and went about their business, in extreme examples, returning to the pulpit bloodied and bruised. This claim of public self-control provided a nascent link between evangelical versions of manly behavior and emerging gentry notions of masculinity, since gentry culture at midcentury embraced self-control as an essential part of rational, enlightened, and genteel behavior, an ideal that became increasingly resonant in southern culture. Baptists, though, did not see themselves as sharing this value with the gentry; indeed, they often portrayed the gentry as brutish and uncontrolled. It was a claim then not to portray themselves as members of a shared refined culture, but to mark themselves as different from sinful men. Hence, they could quip about some "Virginia bucks" who lacked the "wit enough to sin in a genteel manner."[17]

In these early stories about the Baptists, ministers did not need to seek personal retribution; they were ultimately vindicated without having to physically engage their opponents. The attackers in these narratives met with one of two fates: they were overcome by the godliness of the Baptists and converted to the faith, or they met with a gruesome end. Minister Dutton Lane, for instance, was threatened by his own father, who "pursued him with an instrument of death." His father was unsuccessful in his attempt to kill his son, but instead "was himself slain by the sword of the Spirit," converted to the Baptist faith, and was baptized by the son he had threatened.[18] Other assailants were similarly overpowered by the words of the preachers. The Davis brothers of Virginia, having earned the nickname of "the giants," set out to disrupt a Baptist meeting but, upon hearing the minister preach, became entranced and threatened to silence any who would interrupt him.[19]

Many attackers met a more grisly end. Robert Ashby repeatedly harassed a church in Stafford County, Virginia, leading a gang of forty to interrupt the meetings and torment the worshipers. The minister who recorded the abuse noted, "[T]his Ashby soon after cut his knee which festered and at last oppened the joint that the leg hung by the hame-strings; he would not be touched in his bed till at last he died in his own ex[c]rement, and tho' he desired preaching he began to stop his ears and desired the preacher to desist, for he could not hear it." Another individual who led an attack "was shortly after, in a hunting excursion, and while asleep in the woods, bitten by a mad wolf, of which wound he died in the most excruciating pain." Two other men shocked the gathered faithful by joining a preacher on stage and offering him a drink. They then pulled out a deck of cards and began a game, daring the minister to respond. They too met a tragic fate: "both died soon after, ravingly distracted, each accusing the other of leading him into so detestable a crime."[20] Indeed, dying in a "distracted" manner appeared an all-too-common fate for the men—and they were virtually always men—who troubled the Baptists.

The stories of persecution against the early Baptists were a constructed historical memory, retold and preserved in the 1790s and early 1800s as the first generation of Baptist itinerants began to pass away. The stories served not simply as representations of historical experiences, but were the past told as morality tales. They were emblems of the values that the early Baptists wished to praise and inculcate. As stories of the first heroes (and heroines, as we shall see) who faced down the oppression and built a network of churches, they represented for the Baptists the quintessential values of Christ's kingdom. These stories not only described ministers as meek, they glorified them and compared them to New Testament martyrs. The stories further asserted that meekness would be successful against even the most aggressive opponents: those attackers not felled by the power of true gospel preaching would soon face eternal judgment. Justice, the Baptists insisted in these anecdotes, came not at the hands of a combative minister but at the hands of a just and almighty God. Godly men did not respond with aggression, but meekly and unwaveringly pursued their mission.

For Baptist women, the ideal of the genderless believer functioned differently than it did for their male peers. For women, the requisite meekness proved no great departure from eighteenth-century ideals of white womanhood. If white men during this era were commonly praised for displays of prowess and honor, women were praised for submissiveness and modesty.[21] These virtues were specifically associated with being a wife. In the eighteenth-century South, wifedom—and its submissive, dependent character—was heralded even more than motherhood as the true measure of womanhood. Treatises and articles addressed to women commonly instructed them on how to be good wives, emphasizing submission to their husbands. One *Virginia Gazette* article on the "Good Wife" declared that women should be "submissive from Choice, and obedient from Inclination." Another letter of advice to wives counseled, "Study his Temper, regulate your own.... Read often the Matrimonial Service, and overlook not the Important Word OBEY." In these treatises, wives' obedience to their husbands was identified as a central component of the domestic hierarchy, one which also subjugated slaves to masters and children to parents, and which served as the very foundation of an orderly society. Wives' submission, then, was intricately linked to the subordination of other dependents. To disturb one relation of dependence threatened to unhinge the larger structure of southern society, ensuring that women's obedience and meekness were powerful and fiercely held tenets of southern society.[22]

But Christian meekness was only one component of the true believer; the faithful were also required to be steadfast, a characteristic that demanded that individuals resist worldly authority, if necessary, for the sake of their beliefs. For women, this expectation drew notice most frequently when it brought them into conflict with their unconverted husbands and fathers. One woman's struggle with her family began in 1778, when she converted to the Baptist faith. Although "her father [was] one of the greatest opposers in all the parts," she was baptized. After her baptism, she "never dared to put her foot in her father's house. He cursed and swore and wished her in hell." Minister William Hickman later baptized her brother, and their father "drew his cane on him" but did not strike him nor bar him from the house. The children may have escaped unharmed, but the man's wife feared far greater consequences. She approached Hickman about being baptized but told the minister, "my husband must not know it, if he does I know he will kill me." Hickman reassured her that this would not happen, but "she replied, 'I know him better than you.'" For four years, she kept her baptism a secret, attending meetings and sitting "in some by-corner covered with a large handkerchief."[23] Women, particularly wives, may have been particularly vulnerable to this violence since, as in this case, a son or daughter might escape a father's home, but wives had fewer options and usually bore the brunt of their husbands' fury.

The Baptists themselves certainly perceived conversion as dividing families, husbands from wives, and parents from children. When they told of these family conflicts, however, they usually spoke of valiant wives and angry husbands. Minister John Leland described multiple situations where wives wanted to join the evangelicals, but their husbands objected. One "gentlewoman" decided to be baptized, apparently without informing her husband; when she told him of her baptism, he vowed to neither sleep nor eat with her. Another woman in Windsor, North Carolina, wished to be baptized, but "her husband, who was violently opposed to it, and a great persecutor, had threatened that if any man baptized his wife, he would shoot him." In June 1777, the husband followed through on his threat, tracking the minister to another location and wounding him. Whereas Mrs. Bailey, whose experience opened this chapter, was the object of her husband's wrath, Captain Robert York's wife proved more fortunate; her husband directed his fury toward

Leland, vowing to "lash [him] out of the county." Time after time in these stories, the wives refused to submit to their husbands' wishes. Instead they defied them, often choosing to suffer violent repercussions rather than conform to their husbands' beliefs.[24]

Although many, or perhaps all, of these stories of husbands and wives engaged in a violent struggle over baptism may have been true, their repetition and consistency suggest that this construction may have been a literary trope in Baptist writings. The violence against ministers and against wives formed the two primary templates in stories concerning the persecution of the Baptists; there were no comparable stories of violence against the male laity. In the typical story, a wife intended to be baptized by a Baptist minister against the wishes of her husband, who then threatened one or both of them. The minister and wife proceeded with the baptism, usually with violent consequences. The stories often concluded with the triumph of the minister, wife, and cause of God as the vigilante husband was noted to have later converted. Minister Richard Major's experience was typical: "a certain man," whose wife he baptized, "determined to kill him on sight, and went to meeting for that purpose," but the husband was moved by what he heard and instead converted to the faith.[25] Versions of this story can be found repeatedly in the early evangelical literature with different locales, ministers, and marriages.

In pitting the husband against the wife and minister, these narratives depicted a triangle with decidedly sexual undertones. Indeed, the husband often responded to the minister as he might to a wife's lover, threatening him with violence or death. Perhaps because ministers led wives into an experience known to involve passion, even frenzy, husbands reacted with fury. Of course, the mere act of defiance could likewise act as a trigger, given the weighty expectation of wives' submission. And here, wives' acts of disobedience and independence were inspired by men who were often young and charismatic. One angry husband waited for the minister who baptized his wife and shot him in the "thigh," a term that could have an implicit sexual meaning during this era.[26] Thus, women's betrayals of their husbands, even in the Baptists' own stories, had powerfully threatening elements. Nonetheless, women's behavior in these stories was heralded since they were portrayed as the valiant upholders of the faith. Far from a damning character flaw, their willful disobedience signaled a godliness that could not be constrained by earthly duties, and they were often ultimately vindicated in their defiance by the conversion of their husbands.

A woman's baptism, a central component of these stories, marked and symbolized her separation from her unregenerate husband, a separation all the more threatening because of its perceived sexual connotations. Often the moment when a husband confronted the minister and wife was at her baptism, when the minister was to lead the woman into the water and submerge her, welcoming her into his community while spiritually dividing her from a reprobate spouse. Perhaps equally humiliating to the husband, her declaration of commitment was public, occurring in front of neighbors and gathered crowds, sometimes numbering in the hundreds. The very act of leading a woman into water and immersing her may have appeared to be a sexual, or at least an intimate and immodest, act. To Anglican itinerant Charles Woodmason, it was downright "offensive." To him, the Baptists' ritual of baptism was one in which "Lasciv[i]ous Persons of both Sexes resort, as to a Public Bath." He proceeded to describe the ritual in vivid language: "I know not whether it would not be less offensive to Modesty for them to strip wholly into [the] Buff at once, than to be dipp'd with those very thin Linen Drawers they are equipp'd in—Which when wet, so closely adheres to the Limbs, as exposes the Nudities equally as if none at All." To Woodmason, the publicness in which a "gaping Multitude" viewed "the poor wet half naked Creature" belied the Baptist claim that this was a sacred moment; it could only be an obscene spectacle.[27] Even Baptists were forced to acknowledge this interpretation of their ritual. Minister John Leland tried to counter the criticism, acknowledging, "it is said by some, that baptism, by immersion, before a large congregation, especially of the female sex, is very indecent."[28] It is no wonder, then, that in these early years the baptism of a woman often became the catalyst that sparked a husband's fury.

With the repetition of these stories, women converts became the heroes of the early evangelical era along with the first generation of ministers. Women may have been the earliest (and easiest) converts since they were frequently portrayed as converting before their husbands. Depicted as steadfast and devout, they willingly suffered for their beliefs and often proved to be inspirations for their husbands. A number of ministers, including William Hickman, Jeremiah Moore, Henry Toler, and John Poindexter, recalled that their wives' devotion to the evangelicals created anxiety about their own spiritual state, ultimately inspiring their conviction and conversion. Significantly, membership numbers do not wholly bear out this pattern since men generally outnumbered women as baptized members when churches were founded in the 1750s, 1760s, and 1770s. This makes it all the more remarkable that early Baptist writers emphasized this narrative of ministers converting wives and then wives converting their husbands.[29]

In addition to being heralded for being courageous and fervent converts, women were praised for their participation in disseminating Baptist beliefs and building the evangelical movement in the 1760s and 1770s. Women frequently invited traveling ministers to preach in their neighborhoods and hosted Baptist meetings in their homes, even when meetings were provoking hostility and violence. Early Baptist writers also credited women with assisting their minister husbands. When James Read "entered the ministry, he could neither read nor write. Under the tuition of his wife, he was soon able to peruse the pages of unerring truth," and he became a successful itinerant throughout Virginia and North Carolina. Minister John King "married a woman of education, [and] he received much valuable information under her tuition. She appropriated much of her time in affording such assistance as he needed. A great improvement in his manner of preaching was perceptible." Martha Marshall, perhaps the most prominent woman in the early Baptist evangelical movement, was one of the original Separate Baptists who brought the evangelical Baptist message into the South, journeying from New England with her husband, preacher Daniel Marshall, and her brother, preacher Shubal Stearns. As the wife and sister of itinerant preachers, it is not surprising that she was integral to their work. Wives of itinerants either remained at home, running a farm and household alone, often for months or years at a time (ministers received no pay for their work), or they traveled with their husbands, performing "domestic" labor such as laundry, sewing, and food preparation without a domicile. Martha Marshall, though, was called "a Priscilla, a helper in the gospel. In fact, it should not be concealed, that [her husband's] extraordinary success in the ministry, is ascribable, in no small degree, to Mrs. Marshall's unwearied, and zealous cooperation." In and of themselves, many of these women's acts were unremarkable, even commonplace. Yet recounting women's participation became a common motif, structuring these stories into narratives of men and women together suffering for the holy cause and together laboring (albeit in different ways) to build a legion of God's faithful.[30]

The egalitarian sentiments displayed in the narratives that emerged out of the early evangelical movement were reflected in some of the actual practices of Baptist churches. The daily practices of membership, like the stories of the evangelical movement, reveal a sect willing to rethink southern social norms. Baptists emphasized *membership* over worldly status, a distinction that allowed them to downplay, and even ignore, contemporary gender norms and embrace their own vision of godly behavior for men and women. Laywomen had remarkable opportunities to participate in their churches, as did the male laity. The relative egalitarianism of these churches laid the foundation for African Americans to choose to join in large numbers in the decades following the Revolution. For disparate groups of southerners, the call of fellowship and this vision of godliness proved to be very powerful. New Baptists built churches that demanded a total commitment and a willingness to identify with a community that consciously positioned itself as apart from society.

As the Baptists began to draw in converts and create new churches in the southern backcountry, they organized dispersed settlers into cohesive, disciplined communities. Throughout the colonial South, communal organization and identity on a local level was elusive, even absent. The dispersed farms, frequent migrations, and scarcity of social institutions hindered the development of visible communities, or at least communities that mimicked northern patterns of densely settled towns.[31] Thus historians have turned to individual counties to study southern communities, arguing that counties served not only as political units but also provided the social institutions, such as the county court and parish church, which bound residents together. Both the county court and the Anglican Church served needs beyond their immediate legal and religious functions, as southerners used these sites for a wide variety of activities. Court days at the county seat contained so many activities—from cock fights to slave auctions to social drinking on the green—that they had a fair-like atmosphere. Likewise, Anglicans used Sunday services as an opportunity to post notices of runaway slaves, court prospective spouses, transact business, and plan social events.[32] The county court and parish church, however, could serve these social functions only for those who lived a reasonable distance from them. Western settlers had even greater difficulties building the social networks and local institutions that constitute community. Since western counties often were quite large in order to amass enough tithables to pay for the county government, many residents of these counties lived a considerable distance from county seats and parish churches, making those traditional gathering places less effective as communal centers. Moreover, frontier territories were marked by recent settlements, frequent migrations, and short-term residents, which left people even more unfamiliar with their "neighbors."

A Baptist church, though, could spring up virtually overnight, even in sparsely settled neighborhoods, following the visit of an itinerant or the gathering of some devout individuals. It required almost no material resources, but demanded a solemn and profound commitment. Once a group of believers assembled together, their first task was to create a "church," a body they envisioned as an imitation of the early Christian church: a group of baptized believers meeting together to pray and to instruct each other about the gospel. By claiming the mantle of the primitive church, they created a connection between themselves and the early Christians that could at times be more powerful than their ties to their non-Baptist contemporaries. To form a church, the converts wrote a church covenant to articulate their promises to God and to each other. Creating a covenant was both a solemn and a public endeavor as new churches believed that they acted "in the prescence of the great and everlasting God... and in the presence of angels and man."[33] God, they hoped, would sanctify their church bodies, and "men" would recognize them as set apart from worldly society. As a religious statement, covenants usually included both a statement of beliefs and a list of the members' responsibilities to God and to their fellow members. As a public document, the members openly declared their beliefs and intentions and affixed their names to the covenant as if it were a civil contract.

They intended to create intense, insular communities, separate from the world, in which they could live out their mission. In their covenants, Baptists constructed profoundly communal documents, relinquishing individual autonomy and pledging mutual responsibility. Members covenanted with both God and each other, vowing to love and watch over one another. In creating a church, they pledged to join together as one body, often stating that they acted "unitedly" or "unanimously" in this endeavor. Matrimony Church, for instance, vowed, "We do by the assistance of divine grace unitedly give up ourselves to God and one another in covenant promising... to act towards one another as Brethren"; another church promised to "stand fast in one spirit with One mind." The language of the covenant often evoked a familial commitment, such as Mill Creek's "promise to bare one anothers burdens, to cleave to one another." At High Hills, Virginia, the members "unanimously" pledged

> to give ourselves to one another by the will of God.... We will as God shall enable us "walk together in brotherly love,["] exercise Christian Care and watchfulness over each other, and faithfully admonish, or entreat one another, as occasion may require[.]
>
> That so far as it may be in our power, we will visit the sick, [and] relieve the distressed.... That we will endeavour to bring up Such as may be, at any time under our Care, in the nurture and admonition of the Lord, and by a pure and lovely example, to win our kindred and acquaintance's to the Saviour, to holiness and eternal life. That we will participate in each other's joys, and endeavor, with tenderness and Sympathy to bear each others burdens and Sorrows.

Not surprisingly, some of these pledges—such as watchfulness and entreating each other—concerned the spiritual well-being of the congregants. Church members also vowed, though, to care for each other's physical and emotional welfare, promising to assist the sick and needy, and to share each other's joys and burdens.[34]

The act of creating and signing a covenant served as a ritual in the creation of a community, one that was separate from the world but linked to a network of other Baptist communities. Each group of believers followed the same procedure: they agreed among themselves that they wished to form a church, sent out a request for "helps" (leaders of other Baptist churches able to assist them), and, finally, if found "ripe for constitution" by the Baptist leaders, wrote their covenant, articles of faith, and church rules. The "helps" served to validate the new church body and mark its inclusion into the network of churches. Affixing names to the covenant delineated the boundaries of the community, providing a public and visible statement of belonging unlike anything most southerners had experienced. The initial group forming the church (men and women, whites and blacks alike) signed the covenant (or had their names recorded), and subsequent members were considered parties to and bound by the covenant when their names were added to the membership list.

Inasmuch as the covenant served to mark the creation of a community, it also set this body apart from the non-Baptist world, exemplifying a sense of separateness from members' neighbors who were outside of the faith. Baptists explicitly rejected what they termed "worldly" society, positioning the church and the world as opposing realms with mutually exclusive allegiances. Separating themselves, they hoped, would preserve them from the polluting elements in the larger society. To that end, members could be expelled for mixing too much with the world or embracing its values. Church rules sought to preserve such boundaries, so churches prohibited members from taking other members to court and distinguished between accusations and testimony from non-Baptists and those of baptized members. Constructing these strict boundaries, Baptists believed, protected the cause of God and true religion from the corrupting influence of secular society. One church vowed to always take a member's word over "any of the World, (whose Business it generally is, to revile the Professors of Godliness)." These divisions became visible markers of church members as Baptists displayed their separateness physically in their demeanor, dress, ornaments, and hair. Enlisting what Leigh Eric Schmidt has called communication "aimed at the eyes instead of the ears," they chose simple, even austere, dress and assumed a solemn demeanor. One minister recalled that early Baptists "were very strict in their dress. Men cut off their hair... and women cast away all their superfluities; so that they were distinguished from others, merely by their decoration." These choices conveyed— even to a mere observer—a variety of messages: a rejection of hierarchy, an ethic of simplicity, and an identity as a distinct community. Like their river baptisms, men's distinctive hair and women's plain dress became a visual spectacle that demanded that the most casual observer "hear" their testimony and conveyed Baptists' sense of belonging to a distinct family of believers.[35]

Language also served to mark member from nonmember while also creating tightly knit, insular communities. In and out of the church, members referred to each other as "brother" or "sister" and rejected the use of any worldly title, a move that sought to overlap familial ties—specifically, fraternal and sororal ties—with the ties of membership. Colonel William Gaskins, owner of a considerable estate in upper King and Queen, Virginia, was known simply as Brother Gaskins, placing him (in name at least) on the same level as humbler congregants. Slave members were also known as brother and sister, though being identified by their given name (Brother Will, Sister Betty) distinguished them from their white brethren. Even the leaders of the church (ministers, deacons, and clerks) used these designations. At the same time that these titles distinguished the spiritual community from the world, they also diminished differences among the brethren. Within the ideal church fellowship, there was to be no distinction by wealth, slave status, sex, or education; the only divisions were to be between brethren and nonmembers. These familial designations were not simply markers of membership. The Baptists understood that the church body—the members—were to form a spiritual family. Particularly in the early decades of harsh repression, the churches did create powerful ties among members. One minister fondly remembered this early period, saying that "the church was composed of children of one family—no rents nor party spirits: we tried to look to the Lord for direction and protection." Another minister recalled of the 1770s that "Baptists in those days could be told in any company—they loved one another."[36]

As some scholars have noted, the Baptist construction of fellowship corresponds with anthropologist Victor Turner's model of "communitas." According to Turner, communitas is a "modality of social relationship" marked by intense personal relationships within a group, less-structured social categories of rank and sex, and suspension of normative social relationships such as kinship, and it emerges in liminal spaces or times. The Baptists certainly embraced many of these elements in their churches. They worked to construct communities based not on locale but on membership, groups that claimed the language and intimacy of family and demanded obedience and total commitment.[37]

Membership in these churches provided remarkable opportunities for all congregants to participate actively. Baptists believed that whatever hierarchies existed on earth, all souls were nonetheless equal. They peppered their writings with a variety of phrases and biblical verses that undermined social hierarchies and stressed the spiritual equality within God's kingdom. One district association reminded its member churches that they were all "children of the same Grand Parent," and another drew on Romans 2:11 when it admonished its members to remember, "[n]*either is there respect of persons with God.*" Before God, all people were humble and unworthy, and only the saved were wholly exalted. God's grace would not be bound by earthly categories of race, sex, rank, or status. A true conversion experience was the only meaningful division between people, and it was to be a gateway to this alternative type of community. Conversion was an intuitive, emotional moment, unrelated to education, doctrinal sophistication, or even the ability to read the Bible. The conversion experience, they believed, altered the meaning of earthly rankings before God and his people. Just as this theology inspired Baptist preachers to spread the word to African Americans, so too did it influence church practices and policies. After their baptism, slaves were to be full members: they were to be welcomed as brothers and sisters in the Lord and were "entitled to the free priviledges of church members." Membership was intended to ignore (but not erase) earthly status and make each believer equal before God and the church.[38]

While still influenced, and even to some degree structured, by social hierarchies, Baptist churches implemented the belief in the equality of all souls into church membership, albeit incompletely. Equality of membership was an ethic many early churches took quite seriously in the 1760s and 1770s. Early covenants identified white women and African-American men and women as church founders. The founding members who affixed their names to one Virginia church covenant, for example, included three females and four males. Sandy Run Church in North Carolina began its articles of faith with "We, the members of the both Male & Female, Do [illegible] unto the Lord..." During his travels through the colonies, Morgan Edwards recorded the founding members of churches and consistently listed white women and African Americans among them.[39] Not only were African Americans and white women recorded as church founders, but early membership rolls also paid little attention to race or sex. Most early rolls mixed the sexes and races, recording all members together in a single list; if they separated members' names at all, they did so by sex, listing all men, black and white, and then all women. Hartwood Church, for instance, constituted in 1771, intermingled all 157 of its members in one membership roll. Seating in eighteenth-century Baptist churches followed a similar pattern: in most, there was no effort to segregate the members, though if a church did separate the members, they did so by sex, not race.[40]

Despite the ideal of equality of membership, churches did contain hierarchies that privileged some members over others. These hierarchies were visible even in the recording of new members' names. Because Baptists wanted to mark themselves off from worldly society, they went to great efforts to register members in their churchbooks, and church clerks were remarkably faithful in recording names. White and free black men's names were rarely omitted from membership lists. The admission of free women, white and black, was conscientiously recorded, though if their husbands were members, their given names might be omitted, hidden under the words "...and his wife." Single women and women married to nonmembers consistently had their names recorded, even when their fathers or sons were members. But clerks were less consistent about recording slave members by name. Slave men's names were occasionally omitted from membership lists and business in the churchbooks; instead, they were identified by their owners' names and their sex, for instance, "Mr. Harris' male servant." Slave women, because of their sex, race, and status as chattel, most often remained unnamed in the churchbooks, as their names could be hidden by their relationships to masters or husbands, such as "Brother Bob's wife," or "Mr. Green's servant woman."

In spite of these omissions, participation in these churches proved increasingly appealing to slaves after the 1770s. While only a small fraction of the colonial Baptist population, slaves began to join churches in large numbers after the conclusion of the War for Independence.[41] As early as the 1780s, some churches were evenly divided between black and white, and some Baptist churches (primarily in Virginia) had black majorities by the 1790s. One historian calculated that in Virginia Baptist churches, African Americans made up 4.5 percent of the total membership in 1770; by 1780 that percentage had more than doubled to 11.6 percent, and by 1790, African Americans were nearly one-third of all Virginia Baptists (30.35 percent).[42] Only the Methodists sustained a similar effort to church slaves. The Methodists, like the Baptists, believed in the equality of all souls, and they began their missionary work within a few decades of the Baptists and by 1790 had also created many biracial churches. The evangelicals' creation of biracial organizations was a phenomenon of the late eighteenth century and unique within the South.[43]

Prospective black converts commonly faced more obstacles than did their white counterparts. To bring in slave members, evangelicals had to do more than church them (bring them into a specific denomination and congregation): since the vast majority of slaves in the late colonial and revolutionary eras were not Christian, they had to *convert* them. Moreover, since their families and fellow slaves were often not Christian, they faced alienation from their existing communities. White slave owners also threw up impediments, particularly during the 1750s, 1760s, and 1770s. Slaveholders loathed evangelical efforts to preach to slaves, fearing not only the message of spiritual equality, but any gathering that brought slaves together. Thus they often did not permit their slaves to attend and participate in evangelical meetings. Trouble too came in the meetings themselves, where anti-evangelicals sometimes targeted slaves who attended these meetings. Even after the early decades of hostility passed from the southern landscape, African Americans still had difficulty participating as members, given work duties that prohibited attending meetings and the necessity of obtaining permission to travel to services.

Nonetheless, slaves were increasingly drawn to Baptist preaching, and many converted and joined churches, making African Americans the fastest growing proportion of Baptists in the late eighteenth century. Perhaps drawn by the egalitarian ethos, or curious about the group that prompted so much fury on the part of the gentry, slaves attended the large outdoor meetings. One minister on a preaching tour even noted that "the Number of Blacks by far exceeded that of the whites," though most meetings drew only a very small number, if any, before the 1780s. Eighteenth-century and early nineteenth-century black Baptists, who were mostly illiterate, left precious few written accounts of their response to evangelicals or their evaluations of church membership, but their actions indicate that membership was something they wanted and were willing to fight for. Because membership was not a right that could be secured through simple attendance, parental membership, or an owner's membership, these numbers represent conscious choices by slaves. African Americans, like all other prospective members, had to request membership from the church body, publicly expressing their desire to join, describing their personal conviction of salvation, and reconciling any grievance with any member before they could be extended the "right hand of fellowship." Once they became church members, African Americans' actions within their churches indicate that membership was indeed valuable to them. Even in the 1780s and 1790s, observers noted that slaves were among the most enthusiastic participants in evangelical meetings. One minister noted, "when [slaves] engage in the service of God, they spare no pains. It is nothing strange for them to walk 20 miles on Sunday morning to meeting, and back again at night.... When religion is lively, they are remarkabl[y] fond of meeting together, to sing, pray and exhort, and sometimes preach, and seem to be unwearied in the procession." Like white members, African Americans used the churches to raise and mediate their grievances with other members. When accused of disorderly behavior, they defended themselves, and when excommunicated, many slaves sought readmission, renouncing their offending behavior and asking for forgiveness.[44]

Egalitarian impulses that encouraged ministers to seek slave audiences and demanded that churches welcome slaves as members were also broadly reflected in church structures and policies. Baptist churches offered all laypeople, including non-elite white men, white women, and slaves, the opportunity to participate publicly in the church and even some opportunities for leadership and authority. They eschewed the hierarchy between the laity and clergy of the Anglican Church, believing that the authority of a church resided in the congregation, not in the minister or church officers. New churches usually wrote their covenants and rules first and then chose ministers to guide them. Ministers were often called from among the members forming the church; education, wealth, and even literacy were not required, only a gift for preaching. Most churches also chose deacons (usually two or three, depending on the size of the church), and a few churches appointed elders. These officers collected and distributed donations to assist struggling congregants, obtained the necessary items for communion, and assisted the minister; they also watched over the congregation, initiating disciplinary actions when necessary. Finally, churches appointed clerks and entrusted the church minutebooks to their care. Although given positions of authority, men in these positions were first and foremost members of the church. Some churches explicitly limited ministers' power within the church, insisting that "the Minister shall not... Lord over the Church; nor act [in] any Matter belonging to the Church, without their Consent."[45] Church officers continued to be addressed as "brother" and could lose their position (and their membership) if found guilty in a disciplinary matter or simply by a vote of the church.

Some churches also provided official roles for white women, including positions as deaconesses and ruling eldresses. Minister Morgan Edwards identified nine Virginia and three North Carolina churches as having deaconesses and two North Carolina churches as having eldresses, listing these offices perfunctorily within an enumeration of positions and rites each church allowed, suggesting that he saw nothing remarkable about these offices. Although he did not describe the nature and responsibilities of these positions, it is likely that they corresponded to their English counterparts in having primarily charitable duties. English Baptist churches allowed deaconesses and specified that their "cheef office is to visite and relieve the widow, fatherless, sick lame, blind, impotent, weomen with child, and diseased members of the church"; only widows over the age of sixty were eligible.[46] Southern churchbooks themselves made virtually no references to these positions, either the electing or appointing of women or women acting in these official roles, whereas references to (male) deacons occurred frequently. Perhaps this omission was incidental, since elders too were rarely mentioned in churchbooks. Some historians have speculated that these female positions were part of the early "radical" decades of Baptist growth, in which the Separates experimented with unusual rites and practices, and have suggested that this radicalness died out after the Separates grew into a substantial and stable church body and combined with the more "staid" Particular-Regulars.[47] While the Baptist minister-historians of the early nineteenth century did not mention the continued existence of deaconesses and eldresses, these positions may have continued into the nineteenth century. In 1812, the church at Flatty Creek, North Carolina, "order'd that the Church Appoint or Set Apart four Sisters To act as Deaconesses Which was accordingly Carried Into Effect And Sisters Elizabeth Pendleton, Ann Markham, Polly Gankins and Ann McDonald was Chosen by private Ballot." That the clerk of the church recorded this proceeding so casually suggests such appointments may not have been altogether uncommon even in the early nineteenth century.[48]

Women also served as informal exhorters, particularly in the early decades of evangelicalism, occupying a position that was both prominent and controversial, a lightning rod for early opponents. Individuals who undertook this role were entrusted with the weighty responsibility of conveying God's work in their life and assumed a public persona before both supporters and opponents of these sects. Baptists saw exhorting as having great spiritual authority. Indeed, early southern evangelical communities recognized the spoken word as enormously important. Not only was the Upper South a predominately oral society with relatively low literacy rates and less access to printed materials than many other British colonies, but the Reformed Protestant tradition also invested speech with great importance. Unfettered words, so Protestant theology indicated, could be the tool of God to reach the hearts of listeners. Baptists, therefore, not only allowed but encouraged a variety of believers to speak or exhort at their meetings and refused to confine speaking to the ordained or to the literate. Unordained white men, white women, and slaves all had opportunities to deliver public prayers and personal reflections should they wish to do so.

In the 1750s and 1760s, women exhorters played a key role in the spread of the Baptist message, at a time when there was only a handful of ordained evangelical preachers. Martha Marshall, who journeyed from New England to the South in the 1750s with her husband and her brother, both of whom were preachers, was one of the best known female exhorters. She, unlike her male relatives, was not and could not be ordained as a preacher but she was praised nonetheless as a powerful exhorter, a woman of "surprising elocution, [who] ha[d], in countless instances melted a whole concourse into tears, by her prayers and exhortations!" Another woman was praised for "great aptitude to converse on things of religion," an aptitude so powerful that she was compared to "Deborah the prophetes[s], risen from the dead." One woman's "zeal in the cause of religion [wa]s such, in her own circle, she preach[ed] away in whatever company she [wa]s in." The opportunity to exhort continued in the following decades, though it appears to have been uncommon. In 1787, the North Carolina church at Flat Rock agreed that "a Woman should not undertake as a publick speaker to unfold Doctrine [or] Advance Doctrine. But might from an Immediate Impression of the spirit speak in Publick." By 1827, a minister could talk of women "prophecying" in the church as something of the past. But when praising one godly woman, he took the time to ask if such women should again be invited to exhort in the church. He answered, "nothing but the pride or folly of man would object to it.... [I]n some churches the greatest strength of intellect and counsel is the females."[49] Even after women's formal opportunities to exhort declined, women still did so under a different guise since their conversion relations required them to talk about God's holy work. These too were noted as stirring events that awakened other individuals. Minister John Taylor encouraged a young woman to describe her hope in the Lord. She agreed but was overcome and was subsequently dismissed by her father for shedding tears. Yet Taylor noted, "[W]hen she began to talk, his strongest philosophy could not bare him up, big as he was he retired from the room, though not out of hearing, that he might give vent to the tender emotions of his own heart." One slave woman's conversion relation was similarly powerful, being, so Taylor affirmed, "more striking to the assembly present, than the loudest preaching." A relation before a church was a singular moment in some ways, not to be repeated. In other ways, as the moment of true awakening that brings the convert into the presence of God, it was an event to be repeated and relived. By requiring a conversion experience, these churches ensured that women would continue to talk about their experiences of the divine and remain active participants in the religious culture.[50]

Female exhorters became increasingly rare in the late eighteenth century, but women continued to be heard in official capacities within their churches. Female members participated vocally in the business of their congregations by such actions as voting, helping to select a minister, bringing disciplinary charges, and delivering reports to the church. Due to the congregational structure of the Baptists, each church was empowered to create its own rules without concern for a higher church authority, and a number of churches gave women broad authority to speak and vote in their churches. Providence Church of Kentucky asked in 1787 "whether all members of the Church Male & Female have a privilege to speak to any Subject that comes before the Church, petition for Releaf of any Grievance or [D]ifficulty." And it quickly answered, "they have." In 1787, when Waterlick Church was constituted, the members of the new church wondered "[w]hether a sister in the church is at liberty to have a vote." To decide the issue, they referred the question "to the Serious consideration of all the members of both sexes." The men and women then elected to give women the liberty to vote. In 1808, the church reaffirmed that "[t]he Sisters are to be invited to attend church meetings and are to be considered to enjoy all the privileges in voting etc in the church, as male members."[51]

For other churches, the scriptural prohibitions against women speaking in church outweighed any egalitarian ethos. Some congregations cited the Pauline injunctions in 1 Corinthians 13:34–35 and 1 Timothy 2:11–12 as the foundation of their policy. Even these churches, though, generally focused on limiting women's participation in church policy and government, rather than issuing sweeping restrictions on women speaking. High Hills Church of Virginia, for instance, limited the degree to which women could be heard on certain church matters. In 1787, the church covenant declared, "Females shall have a voice in the Church in certain cases, such as chooseing officers, Deligates, in giving information, receiving to fellowship, or rejecting any who are unworthy, but shall not have the government in their power." Female members then could be heard when choosing ministers and deacons and when discussing members, but would not be allowed to seize control of the government of the church. Roanoke Baptist Association came to a similar conclusion when debating the duties and privileges of female members. It agreed that women could serve as witnesses, vote on the admission of applicants or the expulsion of members, and bring grievances before the church. But the association also noted the scriptural prohibitions on women speaking in churches and delegated "all Matters of Debate in [church] government" to male members.[52] It chose to limit women's speech to specific topics, but did not silence them; the question in these cases was when female members should be heard, not if.

Most churches authorized both female and male members to perform the regular duties of ordering the church body through their participation in the discipline. Churches were often careful to specify women's right to participate in disciplinary cases: to accuse an individual, give testimony, and speak on their own behalf. Even churches that did not permit women to be heard on questions of church policy did allow women to participate fully in all questions of membership, including discussions about applicants to the church and matters of discipline. All members—whether male or female, slave or free—were expected to protect the purity of the church community and were charged with monitoring others' behavior and reporting any offenses to the church when necessary. Church discipline provided a powerful means by which members could influence their congregation and their fellow congregants' behavior. Any Baptist could accuse someone or be accused of a wrongdoing. In fact, church rules often explicitly *required* all members to watch over each other's conduct and initiate disciplinary proceedings when necessary. Although each individual church retained the right to establish its own rules and practices, disciplinary procedures, like most Baptist practices, remained quite consistent from church to church. They based their proceedings on their understanding of the Gospel of Matthew 18:15–18 and believed that this text provided the scriptural blueprint for discipline in a gospel church: an offended member was to confront or "deal with" the accused privately, and, if reconciliation were not possible, bring the charge to the church.[53] Once an accusation had been laid before the congregation, the church agreed which members should "cite," or summon, the accused to appear before the church. Both the accused and the accuser made their cases to the congregation; the sitting church could then vote for acquittal, admonishment (a warning to avoid the offending conduct), censure (a loss of church privileges until satisfaction was gained), or excommunication (expulsion from the church). All members had the right to participate in these church proceedings. Women frequently appeared in all phases of the disciplinary process as accusers, accused, and witnesses. Women, like men, performed this work of ordering evangelical communities, whether the complaint concerned intimate relations within a household, disputes among neighbors, or business disagreements. Sister Hudspeat of Flat Rock Church brought charges against David Harwell for drinking too much and riding about at "an unseasonable hour." Sister Esteop of Cove Creek brought an accusation to her church against William Esteop of misbehavior with a young woman. Slave women were also at liberty to bring charges of misconduct to their churches. In May 1777, Albemarle Church of Virginia noted that "an accusation [was] Brought [in] by a black Sister, Dinah against York for attempting her chastity (or something of that kind)." The church heard the evidence from all parties, and York was excommunicated.[54]

In addition to initiating disciplinary proceedings, women also served on disciplinary committees charged to interview the accused, examine witnesses, and deliver their report to the whole church for a decision. When a sister was accused of drinking too much, Mount Tabor Church appointed three female members of the church to investigate. The committee made its report at the following meeting, explaining that while the charge was true, "she appear[e]d to be humble, and very sorry for what she had done." The church followed the committee's recommendation and forgave her sin. When investigating allegations of sexual misconduct by women, churches were much more likely to assign women to look into the charges and report back to the church. In 1805, for instance, Mill Creek received information that Phebe Robinson gave birth to a "base born," or illegitimate, child. It then assigned two women, Mary

Buckles and Mary Ingle, to investigate the report. Buckles and Ingle visited Robinson and spoke with relevant witnesses. Two months later, the two women appeared before their church and delivered their report, which declared that Robinson was innocent. Based on their report, the congregation of Mill Creek agreed to keep Robinson as a member. Abbott's Baptist Church of North Carolina heard disturbing allegations about two of its members when it was reported that Tabitha Gefford and Elizabeth Montgomery were "Each in a State of pregnancy." "To find the truth," the church assigned two women to investigate the accusations and report back to the church with their findings.[55]

While churches empowered a diverse array of individuals, social hierarchies did act as a significant factor in facilitating or limiting women's and men's official responsibilities in church discipline. White men were most often called upon to investigate charges and give testimony, and their right to vote in these cases was unquestioned. White women too quite frequently participated in the disciplinary process, though they were assigned official responsibilities less consistently. Black women and men were not excluded from disciplinary committees by any formal rule, but were appointed infrequently and then only in discipline cases involving other African Americans. Some black men were accorded positions of authority, receiving the right to exhort and to be ordained as ministers and deacons. These men were frequently entrusted with overseeing the black congregants and initiating disciplinary proceedings. For African-American women, the opportunity to serve their church in official and unofficial ways was severely limited, and black women rarely were appointed to participate in investigations, even when they involved charges against other black women. Fellowship was allowed to challenge some social hierarchies, but it would not dissolve them.

In the early years of the Baptist evangelical movement, religious enthusiasm and the difficulties of evangelism in a hostile climate combined to allow some experimentation with social hierarchies and gender norms in particular. The evangelical Baptists firmly believed in the equality of all souls, and, in the course of their missionary and church-building efforts, they came to value all participants' contributions. Thus, godly manhood became less about public displays of physical prowess and more about Christian forbearance and patience, and godly womanhood came to include strength and independence, as well as modesty and submission. These ideals were manifested in the activities and structures of the early missionary efforts. Women as well as men actively and publicly participated in the building of this religious movement, and the churches themselves translated their belief in the equality of souls into church policies that empowered members. This had particularly important ramifications for laywomen. Baptists publicly recognized women as crucial to the development of the sect and as instruments of God's holy work, beliefs that were structured in church policies. Despite New Testament admonitions against women speaking in churches, some women in the early evangelical movement acted as exhorters and deaconesses, and women had a variety of other official roles that allowed them to assist in the pursuit of holiness. For many Baptist women, being empowered to pursue this spiritual goal was the greatest reward. This participation—and the public acknowledgment of it— reveal a model of evangelical womanhood that was active, vocal, and outside of the domestic realm. These women shared the duties of the male laity, though they performed them less frequently and in more circumscribed ways. Baptist womanhood was, in sum, a communal identity and one that had a rough parity with the roles of laymen. At the same time, the ethos of the equality of all souls remained unfulfilled in many ways. As Baptists' theology intersected with social norms and the hierarchies of southern society, contradictions about the meaning of church membership developed. With church discipline, the contradictions became plain as Baptists attempted to implement their vision of a Christian society through controlling church members' behavior, efforts that directly inserted church authority into marriages and families as the Baptists turned their attention to ordering the southern household.

3

Our Domestic Peace

In September 1775, five months after the outbreak of the War for Independence, British commander Lord Dunmore raided the Virginia coast, and rumors raged that the British soon intended to land their fleet and level their military might on the nearby towns and farms. In Lunenburg County, neighbors erupted in their own affray. It began when John Hawkins went to his Baptist church and accused Old Sister Rivers of making shocking accusations about another elderly sister in the church. The investigation into that charge embroiled much of the congregation in conflict. According to Hawkins, Old Sister Rivers had said that Old Sister Haley had "pulled up her clothes before some people in a most Scandalous ridiculous manner." Surely, no one in the church wanted to believe such a charge against an aged member of the church. They may then have been relieved when Haley's adult son, also a member of the church, declared it had not happened, though, regrettably, "his evidence [was] weakened on acc[oun]t of his being charged with drinking too much."

The matter did not end there. If Sister Haley had in fact kept her clothes arranged as demurely as God intended, then Sister Rivers had slandered her in suggesting otherwise. And that charge of slander provoked other brethren to bring their grievances against Rivers. One member accused her of not properly resolving a grievance between them; another accused her of slighting one of her daughters. Brother Walton accused her of slandering or "Scandalizing him concerning a Mulatto Girl." Out of these (and other) conflicting stories, accusations, and counter-accusations, the church at Meherrin had to tease out each allegation, investigate its veracity, and render a judgment. Some of the members believed Old Sister Haley to be guilty, and she was briefly censured for lifting her dress. The charges against Sister Rivers had to be numbered to better keep track of them and ultimately led to her censure.

Determining the veracity of the accusation against Brother Walton proved to be quite complicated. Rivers (apparently voicing the suspicions of many of the brethren) had accused him of fornication with his female slave. The slave herself had consistently insisted that her pregnancy was a result of a sexual encounter with her master, Walton, and maintained this allegation through brutal punishments and also under the questioning of midwives during the particularly difficult childbirth. When the baby was born, however, it appeared to be "a remarkable black child, a Negro without any doubt." Nevertheless, each member—male and female—was polled about Walton's guilt or innocence. Only a small minority believed him to be guilty, but the church was determined to have unanimity and talked with every member until each agreed with the majority that he was innocent of the charge.[1]

In these investigations, the church acted quite quickly (every charge was ruled on within a month), but also thoroughly, taking evidence from members, neighbors who were not members of the church, and the midwives. Even in wartime Virginia, investigating slander, the slighting of a daughter, and sexual misconduct provoked the involvement of the entire Baptist community. One did not need to excite such a neighborhood-wide conflict to attract the attention of the brethren—having a "disorderly corn shuck" or neglecting worship at home would do as well. Baptist churches quite deliberately set out to eliminate any "disorder" in their midst, directing a great deal of attention and energy toward that end. As one Kentucky church declared, "Disorder Can't Be Countenanced."[2]

Far from simply being concerned with matters of theology, churches consistently involved themselves in the intimate matters of their members' lives and claimed an expansive influence over their members' familial relations. As intrusive and difficult as this sometimes was, they believed their efforts were necessary to their ongoing endeavor to fulfill their covenant with God and protect the purity of the church from sin and sinners. In so doing, Baptists proved one of the most determined voices seeking to define marriage in the late colonial and early national South. In this, they joined southern governments (mostly at the state level), which likewise desired a stable and orderly family unit. Marriage, after all, was a capacious institution that structured gender, labor roles, economic exchange, and individuals' relationship to the state. In her sweeping study of American marriage, Nancy Cott argues that government efforts to regulate marriage increased substantially over the course of the nineteenth century and that it maintained an interest in ensuring monogamous, lifelong marriage subject to the authority of the state.[3] Yet state governments were ill equipped to manage even the most basic of regulations in the early republic. (Before 1800, southern states had difficulty even providing enough officials to officiate at wedding ceremonies.) Baptist churches stepped into this breach, taking a free hand in regulating the marriages of their members. They followed principles that suited the needs of their sect, inserted church structures and religious authority into white and black family life, and created practices that diverged from civil norms, at times quite dramatically.

In claiming authority over marriage and family relations, churches intruded on matters that were being increasingly defined as under the sole purview of the white, male householder and proved a countervailing influence against the trend toward household privacy and autonomy then under way in the late eighteenth- and early nineteenth-century South. This broad trend encompassed a series of architectural, legal, and cultural changes that worked to transform the physical space of the household and the social understandings of the household unit. Spatially, southern homes themselves included more private space as new architectural designs separated family rooms from receiving spaces. During the eighteenth century, more houses came to be designed with a separate entryway or hallway, instead of an outside door opening into the family common room. For the gentry in particular, the home increasingly became separate from many other kinds of social behavior. Stranger hospitality, once a hallmark of higher status, became rarer, as gentry homes primarily welcomed kin and acquaintances, excluding strangers and travelers. Even farming families with only two rooms tended to define one for social uses and the other for the family only.[4]

Greater attention to a spatial redefinition of private and public extended to land ownership as well. In her study of the South Carolina Low Country, Stephanie McCurry found that in the early decades of the nineteenth century, many land owners moved to fence off their property, even land that had been used by the public for generations. Southern courts supported this trend, granting land owners broad authority over any activity within the bounds of their enclosed land. These spatial and legal changes enabled southern white men to gain greater control over their households and secure for themselves a status of "patriarch" that was increasingly unconnected to wealth and land.[5] The rise of evangelicalism, though, acted as a countercurrent to this trend: as church bodies effectively claimed a right to supervise and judge behaviors within families and homes, they impeded notions of the household as a private arena.

Baptist churches engaged in extensive efforts to supervise all aspects of their members' lives to ensure the purity of their spiritual mission. Since each church had formed a covenant with God, each had a divine charge to nurture its members in fellowship, ensure the holiness of the church, and ferret out sinful behavior. To outsiders, church discipline may have appeared intrusive, officious, and perhaps demeaning, but Baptists wanted it to be a watchful and loving curative for all sinners, reminding them of their duty and restoring them to the path of righteousness. As Gregory A. Wills has argued, they "placed discipline at the center of their church life.... Not even preaching the gospel was more important to them than the exercise of discipline."[6] It was the guardian of each member's salvation and a shibboleth for the church itself. No wonder, then, that they enforced church discipline fervently and vigilantly, and the majority of the business of the churches worked to this end. Baptists' understanding of sin or "disorder" was quite broad, encompassing everything from the most public to the most private behavior. Charges within an individual church could easily number into the hundreds, covering a wide range of sexual, religious, leisure, and business conduct. Churches prosecuted charges of sexual misconduct, such as fornication, adultery, bigamy, and whoring. Religious offenses included heresy, disobeying the church, working on the Sabbath, criticizing the church or minister, and baptizing an infant. Misconduct concerning leisure activities included drinking to excess, keeping bad company, dancing, attending a horse race, and singing worldly songs. Members were also charged with such offenses as fraud, breaking a contract, defrauding creditors, hard trading practices, and price gouging. Churches prosecuted individuals for disorderly speech, including gossiping, backbiting, bad language, swearing, and slander. This dizzying array of sins guaranteed that church meetings were filled with charges, investigations, evidence, witnesses, and even countercharges which might spin the proceedings into a different direction. It is no wonder then that one Baptist was moved to compare his church to a "Bull Ring"; it is equally unsurprising that his ungenerous observation got him promptly suspended.[7]

The prosecution of misconduct ensured that order and disorder became the dominant language of the churchbooks, which recorded the "business" of churches, a category that included everything except the worship itself, such as the reception of new members, doctrinal questions and answers, discipline of members, information on expenses, and collection of moneys. Throughout discussions of church business, the words "order" and "disorder" appear frequently. Church discipline often stemmed from charges of disorder, such as disorderly conduct, disorder at home, and disorderly speech; and questions for debate generally began with the words, "Is it orderly..." The repeated use of this language suggests a near-obsessive concern with the maintenance of order. As Rhys Isaac notes, "the recurrent use of the words 'order,' 'orderly,' and 'disorderly,' in the Baptist records reveals a preoccupation with establishing a tighter regulation of everyday life."[8] Whether a Baptist attended a frolic, drank to excess, or committed adultery, the procedure for discipline remained the same, following the method outlined in the Gospel of Matthew (what they called "gospel dealing" or "gospel steps"). Individuals themselves, in a fit of remorse, could report some offending behavior to the church, which would begin an inquiry. More commonly, another member who had observed or heard a report of disorderly behavior initiated disciplinary procedures, first by discussing the matter with the accused, and, if it could not be satisfactorily resolved, bringing it to the attention of the church. Once the allegation was before the church, the entire congregation became involved. All testimony, including the defense, was heard by the whole church, and church members voted on a judgment that was expected to be binding in all Baptist churches. The accused could be acquitted either through proof of innocence or because of insufficient evidence of guilt. If found guilty, the accused could "give satisfaction" by expressing suitable remorse and be retained in the church without penalty, could be censured (which included a suspension of church privileges), or could be excommunicated. Usually, these penalties were decided by a majority vote, but churches often worked toward unanimity, particularly in excommunications. Because those in communion with one another were to be in harmony with one another, restorations to church membership (like admissions) were usually expected to be unanimous. These disciplinary proceedings were a constant process: most meetings of business, which usually met monthly, involved some formal disciplinary proceedings and, at any one time, church members would likely be engaged in a number of informal disciplinary actions that had not yet reached the church.

The whole church body—which is to say, the individual baptized members—participated in defining its own rules and practices and determined its own disciplinary standards. Churches further determined what consequences to level against offenders. A church might, for instance, choose to deal informally with someone who drank to excess, or it might promptly excommunicate such a person. Or, if church members felt that some misbehavior was rampant within their community, they might compose a declaration attacking the behavior and then attempt to purge offending members. For every disciplinary matter brought to the church (and thus recorded in a churchbook), there might be several matters that were successfully resolved and thus, barring an overly zealous clerk, not recorded in the minutes of the church. Taken together, these disciplinary proceedings formed a locally defined code of conduct. In defining their code of behavior, the Baptists deliberately constructed one that was all encompassing and explicitly intrusive in intent and practice, believing it was part of their mission to regulate the day-to-day activities of their fellow members.

Monitoring the household was a primary area of focus. Baptists saw marriage as a divine institution and an orderly family as a fundamental part of good Christian life, and evangelicals sought to supervise relationships from their beginning. Scrutinizing courtship provided an early opportunity for churches to assert authority over members' personal relationships and discourage any belief that marriage and family life could be defined as private, protected from the scrutiny of the brethren. In the late eighteenth century, decisions about choosing a spouse involved not only traditional concerns about the economics of a match and compatibility but also newer ideals of romantic love, increasingly defined as a crucial part of a good marriage. The rise of new values in marriage did not reduce concerns about courtship; in fact, it likely had the opposite effect, raising additional questions, such as which factors were to take precedence in choosing a spouse, who would make decisions about courtships, and what was appropriate behavior during courtship now that love was expected to be a prerequisite for, rather than a result of, marriage. Rather than deferring these questions to families, Baptist churches composed de facto codes to guide relations between the sexes.[9]

Baptists did not object to familiar interactions between men and women, but they did insist that young people conform to certain behaviors, thus creating limits on social spaces and activities. Church events, supervised domestic spaces, and controlled communal events served as acceptable places for unmarried people to meet and chastely socialize. Attending dances, barbecues, or events that degraded into "frolicks" was unacceptable, as was indecorous or frivolous behavior at social occasions. These limits may have served to encourage Baptists to court only those of their own faith (perhaps including other evangelicals, who faced similar prohibitions), but Baptists of this era did not go to great lengths to promote endogamous marriages, and churches often had members whose spouses had not joined.[10] They did, though, fastidiously monitor their young members' behavior and expected them to carry themselves in a solemn fashion, even while young and single. Both men and women were regularly chastised by their congregations for indelicate behavior, with churches generally using the same types of language for men's and women's misbehavior (such as "getting too great" with a member of the opposite sex or behaving "lightly") and dispensing the same sort of consequences (most commonly a censure and a chance to repent). Lovesick behavior could not be tolerated. Susanna Rogers was called before her church "for forging a letter of love from Mr. R. McCullock's name to her, which sin she lived in the best part of a year, unrepented of & undiscovered," and when she refused to repent, she was excommunicated. Polly Plemons also found her conduct scrutinized when, against the advice of her friends and family, she married a stranger after knowing him only eight days. Her church took sides, with one side objecting strenuously and refusing to use her married name, and the other (including her relatives) agreeing to fellowship her. Only after an extended conflict and her withdrawal from the church were the two sides able to come together.[11]

Sex outside of marriage, of course, was never acceptable to Baptists, and it almost always resulted in the excommunication of the accused, whether male or female, slave or free. Justice could be swift for such a heinous charge, as Joseph Odell discovered when he confessed to his church that he had fornicated and was promptly excommunicated.[12] Some historians have argued that women during this era were disproportionately accused of sexual misconduct because women were assumed to be more responsible for sexual sins than were men, which ensured their conduct would be scrutinized more than men's.[13] While women (both black and white) were accused more often than men, the discrepancies were not as great as might be expected and indeed were in keeping with their higher membership numbers. To be sure, women's pregnancies could offer physical evidence of fornication that might otherwise be lacking. However, when there was no pregnancy (or at least none mentioned), Baptists accused men and women of sexual misconduct in numbers proportionate to their membership. They also punished them in similar ways (excommunication being the standard), particularly in light of the physical evidence of guilt that pregnancy provided. (See Table 3.1.) Even when sex was a prelude to a legal marriage, Baptists maintained their condemnation of premarital fornication, summoning individuals and couples who had a baby in less than nine months after marriage. In 1778, Charles Bell was accused of a "Clandestine & Unlawful Connection with his Present Wife before Marriage as apears by her haveing a Child before the time of Women" and was promptly excommunicated. A Kentucky woman escaped this fate when she voluntarily confessed to her church and "Shewed So much tokens of Repentance both to the Church and to the World" that the church agreed to only suspend her for a few months.[14]

Race, though, proved a significant determinant in Baptist responses to sexual misdeeds. While slaves were accused at rates that were not very different from their membership numbers, the response to accusations against slaves was more harsh. Ninety percent of slave women who were accused of

TABLE 3.1. Accusations of Fornication and the Excommunication Rate

Charge	Total	White Men	White Women	Slave Men	Slave Women	Other or Unknown
Fornication without pregnancy	78	18 (23.1%)	31 (39.7%)	12 (15.4%)	16 (20.5%)	1 (1.3%)
Fornication with pregnancy	55	5 (9.1%)	44 (80%)	0	6 (10.9%)	0
Fornication (All)	133	23 (17.3%)	75 (56.4%)	12 (9.0%)	22 (16.5%)	1 (0.8%)
Excommunicated	113 (85%)	17 (73.9%)	63 (84%)	12 (100%)	20 (90.9%)	1 (100%)

Sources: Based on the records of 78 churches in Virginia (25 churches), North Carolina (18 churches), Kentucky (18 churches), and Tennessee (19 churches) between 1765 and 1815. For a complete list, see Table A.3.

fornication were found guilty and excommunicated, compared to 84 percent of white women, and 100 percent of slave men compared to 74 percent of white men. This indicates that churches were less willing to hear or believe slaves' defense against such accusations. Baptists saved their greatest condemnations for interracial sex. Most cases of fornication simply announced the member's exclusion or excommunication. But Susanah Leftrage received a much more vehement denouncement when Hartwood Church declared she had "now swerved intirely from the line of truth and brought publick scandal on our holy professions by Commiting fornication by Cohabiting with a negro for which cause it is Resolved to Excommunicate her and put such an Evil person from amongst us." There were similar denunciations of others who violated interracial sexual prohibitions, including a slave woman for "keeping a white man, as husband unlawfully" and a white preacher whose sexual misdeeds so scandalized his church that the clerk devoted several pages to detailing his misbehavior.[15]

When working on ordering members' household relationships, churches most often focused on marriages. Because membership was generally extended only to adults, churches' attention focused on adult responsibilities and behavior. In the late eighteenth century, Baptists constructed a vision of marriage with mutual, though largely distinct, duties for husbands and wives that defined spouses as harmoniously interdependent. This vision designated wives as having a shared responsibility for the workings of the household, and it limited some of the rights of husbands. By claiming the right to interfere in the most intimate marital disputes, Baptists located power over the household not exclusively in the male heads of the family, but also in the church body itself. The church membership—in secular terms, neighbors, relatives, business associates, masters, mistresses, and slaves—claimed and exercised the right to supervise domestic and marital relations.

While eighteenth-century southern Baptists rarely published essays or sermons on marriage, after 1810, Baptist leaders began to articulate their vision of the ideal marriage and family more frequently.[16] In their discussions of the family, Baptists usually identified separate responsibilities for husbands and wives, but they nonetheless emphasized parity in the marital relationship. Husbands were often identified as heads and guides of the family, but wives were often also described as heads of the family. The Stockton Valley Association, considering the "godly household" in 1810, placed the matrimonial relationship at its center. God had destined marriage, the association explained, to be the happiness of the family. It advised husbands and wives to maintain a harmonious relationship: "Saint Paul says husbands love your wives and be not bitter against them—wives Reverence your husband as *co-partners* of domestic enjoyment." Emphasizing partnership was a rather tame interpretation of Paul's admonitions to wives in Ephesians 5:22–24—"Wives, submit yourselves unto your own husbands as unto the Lord. . . . [A]s the church is subject unto Christ, so let the wives be to their own husbands in every thing"—but it was a typical Baptist exegesis. This shift from giving submission to reverence, and from being a subject to a copartner, was a substantial rhetorical transformation that made possible a significant reevaluation of authority in marriage and the family. Given that women outnumbered men in most churches after 1780, if only one spouse was a member of a church, it was more likely to be the wife. Churches, then, were wise to buttress women's authority in the household as they tried to maintain an active presence in the domestic arena and influence family behaviors. This repositioning of the marital hierarchy was broadly in keeping with changes in the ideals of marriage in the early republic. The new emphasis on romantic love as a crucial element to a marriage and mutual responsibilities between spouses shifted the rhetoric about the function of marriage and how a good marriage should operate. In step with these larger trends, the Concord Association insisted that love was the first responsibility of a husband to his wife. Love, to be sure, did not unmake a husband's authority (indeed the Concord Association used biblical citations to identify the husband as related to her as the "Lord" and the wife as a "weaker vessel"), but it could temper or even reshape it, requiring a mutuality between spouses and privileging the emotional content of the marital relationship.[17]

The duties of husbands and wives were at times discussed separately, but even then Baptists tended to emphasize parity in marital roles. The Stockton Valley Association stressed a partnership between husbands and wives by identifying them as "heads of households" with responsibility for maintaining religion within the family and household. A husband's duties were primarily twofold: to love and care for his wife and to provide for the temporal good of his wife and family. The Concord Association detailed the respective duties of a husband and wife in 1812. The duties of a husband, it declared, were to give a "love superior to any shewn to any other person, a love of complacency and delight... Provision for the temporal good of the wife and family—1st Tim. V, 8. Protection from abuse and injuries, 1st Sam. XXX, 5, 18. Doing every thing that may contribute to the pleasure, peace and comfort of the wife..." The responsibilities of a wife were easier to enumerate: "reverence, subjection, obedience, assistance, sympathy; assuming no injudicious authority, and continuance with him, Tit. II, 5." This list of duties may have required less explanation and less scriptural support because it may have been a familiar litany of the ideal wife's characteristics in the late eighteenth century. In a world where adulthood was virtually synonymous with the matrimonial state, marriage acted as a primary vehicle for defining the gender roles of men and women. As Nancy Cott explains, "The whole system of attribution and meaning that we call *gender* relies on and to a great extent derives from the structuring provided by marriage."[18] For the Baptists, men's marital responsibilities were heavily weighted toward the financial whereas women's were predominately emotional and supportive. Much of what women were to *give* was actually a negative; that is, women were required to suppress their will and *not* contribute what a husband gave, namely, financial and domestic leadership. Concord's litany told women three different ways to be obedient, a veritable thesaurus for obedience. Submissive to God and husband, the dutiful wife was to provide what vague "assistance" she could without assuming undo authority.

While Baptist treatises on marriage remained infrequent through much of the early national era, church discipline provided an ongoing and immediate lesson in marital expectations. In particular, churches insisted that spouses maintain some degree of harmony and frequently disciplined members for marital discord. Most often, husbands and wives were brought before the church together to answer for any conflicts within their marriage. The Tennessee church of Dandridge summoned John and Naomy Johnston to answer for their conduct in 1803. John was censured for abusing his wife, and Naomy was excommunicated for "burning a house upon her own premises" and telling contradictory stories. A marital conflict need not involve arson or assault to prompt a church to intervene. Even smaller conflicts between husbands and wives drew Baptists' attention. Brother and Sister Bungaman found themselves called before their church to answer for quarreling and swearing and were quickly expelled. The Dasses of Virginia also found themselves explaining their marital troubles to their congregation, the Goose Creek Baptist Church. The church had been involved in the Dasses' troubled family life previously, when Molley Dass left her husband and was subsequently suspended. Perhaps then it was no surprise when, one year later, domestic difficulties again brought Brother and Sister Dass before the church. They both blamed the other for their difficulties: Brother Dass complained "that his wife Treats him ill and not as a wife should do," while Sister Dass made a similar complaint, insisting that "he does not use her as a Husband ought to do." The church agreed to suspend both husband and wife in the hope that it would facilitate a reconciliation between them, but gave up within a few months, excommunicating both "for not living as becomes the gospel." The tangible result of Baptist policies was that churches came to be an arena for arbitrating marital disputes, where disagreements could be heard and, when possible, resolved. The church at Bryan's Station in Kentucky was able to provide such a service when Joseph Rogers fought with his wife, rashly accusing her of "Embezzling" his property and sending it to her children; fellow Baptist Leonard Young brought the matter before the church, and members met with Rogers until he became convinced that his accusations were false and expressed regret. Through these interventions, churches offered a type of marital counseling and functioned as a family court.[19]

Extending their reach even further, churches came to be a literal presence within the household. Family and neighbors, of course, might often know of conflicts within particular households, but as members of Baptist churches, they would have the right and responsibility to investigate, mediate, and judge those disputes, acts that brought members into houses to question the accused and witnesses. Baptist investigators then brought their observations back to the church congregation, which might supply other observations or request more information. These frequent investigations marked marriage as a public, not private, institution. Beginning in the 1770s and continuing through the early decades of the nineteenth century, people found their family disputes—whether irrational, embarrassing, or devastating—laid open for scrutiny, and their words and actions judged. Through the sheer volume of cases, as well as the breadth of issues undertaken, church discipline embedded religious authority and, more specifically, the church structure in the architecture of the evangelical family. There was no expectation of privacy. On the contrary, those who refused to submit to questioning or attempted to limit church access were excommunicated, as a North Carolina woman found out in 1799 when she refused to explain why she had left her husband.[20]

Far from shrinking from the scrutiny of their brethren, some individuals themselves brought their marital disputes to the churches, authorizing the members to mediate in "private" disputes. The Warrens of North Carolina used their church in such a manner when "Brother Warren la[id] in a matter against his wife," an act which began an investigation. His wife denied his accusation, and the church sided with her, clearing her of her husband's charge. The church of Well's Chapel served a similar role for Brother and Sister Newton. The church first intervened in the Newton marriage in 1799 when they fought "to such a highth that they came to Blows in anger." In 1814, Sister Newton sought the judgment of the church and accused her husband "of keeping Company with Lewd Women and being guilty of the Act of Adultery with them." Her motives in bringing this to the church remain unclear. Perhaps she again wanted the members' help in bringing about a matrimonial truce or at least to shame her husband, a former deacon, into better behavior. Or perhaps she brought these accusations forward simply to use the church to punish her husband.[21] That such accusations—and the involvement of his neighbors in his sexual life—did shame Newton seems likely given that he refused to meet with the committee, a decision that he knew from his days as a deacon would surely lead to presumptions of his guilt and excommunication.

Baptists like Sister Newton (and even Brother Newton before it hit too close to home) brought the church polity into the most intimate domestic matters. The North Carolina church at Sandy Run had claimed the Carliles as members for some years. It recorded the birth dates of their ten daughters and one son. It also recorded the breakdown of their marriage in April 1777 when "Edward Carlile [was] excommunicated for the Sin of uncleanness whith his negro wench." Edward's wife, Sary (or Sarah), faced the church that same day as she was "excommunicated for the Sin of drunkenness." No matter was too delicate or private to come under the scrutiny of the church in a public hearing. Elizabeth Mullin was hauled before her church "for Leaving her Husbands Bed," though the minutebook is silent as to how such information became available to the church. She then had to meet with members of the church to explain her reasons for doing so, namely, "that her husband is connected with another Woman," in order to gain their approval and thereby retain her membership. Showing no concern for privacy or public reputation, churches claimed a purview over even the most fundamental elements of family life, a claim that competed with white men's authority over their households.[22]

Evangelical men could be no more secure of their absolute dominion over their children than they could of their authority over their wives. Discussions of children and child rearing occupied church communities less than marital relations, because churches focused on members, and membership was generally limited to adults. While children were certainly part of the larger congregations attending services, they usually would not attempt to join a church until adolescence or later and thus did not play prominent roles in church matters. Child-rearing decisions, though, did at times occupy a church's attention, and churches insisted that members raise their children according to Baptist principles. Many church covenants declared that members were required to bring their children up "in the nurture and admonition of the Lord" as required in Ephesians 6:4. Parents were required to maintain some worship within their households, which churches usually defined as prayers or scriptural readings in the morning and evening. Churches expected that members would compel their children to participate in these sessions, and some churches also wanted (though rarely required) slaves to be included. The Virginia Portsmouth Association stressed this responsibility to both children and slaves:

> Both children and servants are naturally ignorant of God's word, and who can be considered more proper to instruct them in the knowledge thereof than their parents and masters? For as parents, we are the means or instruments by which our children were introduced into existence; and what parent can be unconcerned whether that existence is to them an eternal blessing, or an eternal curse.[23]

In this statement, the Virginia Portsmouth Association repeated the language common to other Baptists, in focusing on the duties of parents rather than fathers. When Benjamin Million allowed a male slave "two much liberty amongst his family" he failed, his church complained, to exercise "that Authority that was incumbant on him as a parent," a failure that Million had to repent to keep his membership. As this church indicated, this responsibility to restrain children fell to parents not fathers, and churches generally designated both mothers and fathers as sharing this responsibility (though not necessarily equally). Thus at the same time that Baptist men found their decisions questioned, churches generally designated men and women as jointly responsible for decisions over the household, in keeping with Baptist prescriptive literature. Women as well as men, then, were called to answer charges of a disorderly house. In 1785, for instance, John Adkins and his wife were both called before their church to answer for "Rioting" in their home. She accepted the judgment of the church and was admonished and kept in fellowship, but he was suspended after he tried to deny knowledge of the revelry, a claim that may have worked had he not been home at the time of the said riot. Designating wives as heads of household could have been a practical response to the realities of adult membership in a voluntary society. Churches could not expect all of the adults in a household to be members of the church. In fact, it was more likely that a woman would be a member than would her husband,

and she might therefore be the only Baptist (or, what they would have termed the "only Christian") in a family. Thus, all adult members needed to be empowered to enforce religious values and represent the church's standards in their families, and they were held accountable for such.[24]

Churches positioned themselves in these cases as the safety net when parents failed to properly control their children, a fundamental duty of parenting. The actions of unbaptized children reflected not only on the parents but on their churches as well. Thus, in addition to requiring members to teach their children religious doctrine, churches intervened when they objected to parental decisions regarding minors' conduct. As nonmembers, children were not subject to the church, but Baptist parents would answer to their church for their decisions. Parents who allowed their children to go to parties, or who sent their children to dancing school, would often be called before their church to answer for their conduct. Forks of Elkhorn Church in Kentucky wanted to make clear how serious it believed this issue to be. In 1807, the church asked and answered the question: "Is it not a matter worthy of Exclusion for parents to suffer their Children (that are under their Jurisdiction) to attend Barbacues, Balls &c[?]" The following month, the church agreed on its answer, declaring it a "duty of parents to prohibit their Children from all licentious practices as far as possible," and when parents sanctioned this behavior they should be disciplined by the church and excommunicated if necessary. Salt River Church created a similar if more decisive rule, declaring simply that any member who allowed his or her children to go to dancing school should be excluded.[25] Parents who violated these rules often found themselves explaining their and their children's conduct to the brethren, as did Elizabeth Smith when her congregation received a report that she allowed her children to attend dancing school. Smith though explained that she had attempted to prevent it, and the church allowed her to remain a member. Brother Tolbert of Tate's Creek Church had no such excuse and was excommunicated when his church discovered his sin. Through these decisions, churches extended their reach from members to nonmembers and from the adult population to the younger generation, and marked territories of responsibility to the church: members were responsible for not only their own actions but also the actions of those minors under their control. But more than that, churches secured their authority over their members in ways that were concrete as well as powerful, as church bodies asserted themselves as the rightful judges of all behavior and relationships within the household.[26]

Clearly, the involvement of the church community in domestic issues, such as marital disputes and child rearing, could be not only uninvited but also unwelcome. Families—nuclear and extended—often joined the same churches, and church discipline, then, at times, raised complicated issues of familial allegiance versus the rulings of the church body. Family members repeatedly objected to church rulings when the judgment went against a family member. When Lucy Haggard stopped attending her Tennessee church, the members began an inquiry into her absence. She explained she was grieved with the church members because they had been too hasty, she felt, in excommunicating her husband for fighting; her concerns about the church's actions were so grave as to make her doubt her own Christianity. Perhaps her husband, who had a long history of a bad temper, encouraged her dissatisfaction with the church, because she continued to oppose the decision of the church and soon asked the church to excommunicate her as well. Membership in such a case could be a source of friction within a family, as one person was declared unworthy of that status; there would be constant reminders of that difference as excommunicants could no longer be called "brother" or "sister," receive communion, or vote on church matters. Fellowship demanded that spouses and other family members side with the church body in any disciplinary matters, a requirement that was sometimes too much to bear. Elizabeth and William French explained how the scrutiny of the church threatened their "Domistec peace." Elizabeth found in 1796 that some portion of the church membership was hostile to her and believed they were plotting to get her expelled; the antagonistic atmosphere of the church, she declared, was "Trying to inger the Happiness of our Domistec peace." Her husband concurred, writing that "my wife is to me as my Self and its my Opinion that the whole of the Buisiniss was aimed at Sapping the peace and happiness of my Family. . . . I stand and fall with my wife and do Consider my Self know more of your body." The church had become too powerful of a player in the Frenches' domestic life, and they chose to leave it. For other southerners, the presence of the church within their households was a necessary, even welcome, component of the broader effort to bring an evangelical order to southern society, something about which the Frenches also remind us: still powerfully drawn to the intrusive church experience, they publicly repented and requested readmission to the church five years later.[27]

Churches' intervention in domestic matters could and often did serve to lessen men's authority over their households. Simply by insisting on their right to mediate and judge such disputes, churches challenged male householders' autonomy, positing the local church's power to oversee the domestic realm. Moreover, men's actions within their own households were subject to scrutiny, as William Embry learned in 1772 when he allowed "Riotous doings" in his house and was censured by his Virginia church. Likewise, in 1800, when Jacob Coalman allowed dancing in his house, he had to admit he was wrong and ask for the forgiveness of the church to keep his membership. Persuading men to accept this level of intrusion into their domestic authority proved no easy task. Some men loathed church interference and preferred to give up their membership rather than submit to the humbling experience of explaining their family decisions to the church. One Kentucky man, for instance, withdrew his membership shortly after being asked to explain why he allowed revelry in his home. But others welcomed it and exposed their actions to their congregations, including Brother Hughs, who reported his own misconduct of getting drunk and abusing his family. This insistence that white men take a position rarely required of them and subject themselves to the authority of the church may explain, in part, why they found church membership less appealing in the nineteenth century than did white women or African Americans, who would have found subjection a more familiar experience.[28]

With the church polity watching over them, men encountered real limits to what they could do to govern their own households. Churches asked men to answer for swearing at their families, becoming unreasonably angry, mistreating elderly parents, and abusing children. Churches also brought charges against husbands for beating their wives. In most such cases, charges were not raised by the wives even when they were members, but by other church members, an indication that women may have feared retribution from violent spouses for asking for their brethren's intervention. While men would rarely be expelled outright for such a charge (unlike, for instance, charges of adultery), churches often took these accusations quite seriously. The Virginia church of Broad Run issued a declaration against wife beating, unusual for its length rather than its sentiment, when it declared:

> Joseph Drury was deeply censured for whipping his wife: An action in our esteem, not a little scandalous[.] For a husband to beat his wife we judge to be a practice contrary both to Scripture & Reason, to the law & the Gospel—And as such, not to be once named among Christians[,] Not to be tollerated in the Church of Christ, on any pretense whatever.[29]

While the church appealed to the law, southern law contained some ambiguity about wife beating. Common law allowed husbands to physically chastise their wives to a "moderate" degree. Abuse, though, could be grounds for the rarely granted legal separation (bed and board) and the exceptionally rare divorce. The line between moderate chastisement and abuse was murky at best—and left women at the mercy of individual jurists and with few options. Women who could prove excessive physical cruelty might try to persuade the court to require a bond for good behavior or perhaps authorize a separate maintenance that would enable the wife to leave the home (but still left her legally bound by coverture). Traditionally, battered women would also have had the informal protections of kin and neighbors, who might provide other services, including temporary shelter, intervention, and mediation. Late eighteenth-century southern society, though, was not conducive to this type of protection, as migration removed women from kin networks, and rural settlement patterns left them fairly isolated. An attentive local church, then, could be very valuable to women with violent husbands.

In many of these cases, the churches gave the accused men an opportunity to renounce their behavior. As in any case undertaken by a church, however, the ability to punish and eliminate antisocial behavior depended entirely on the importance of church membership to the individual. In one Kentucky slave family, the mediation of the church seemed to be effective, if temporary. Brother Charles was accused of whipping his wife. An investigating member found Charles unrepentant and reported to the church that Charles "thinks himself justifyed in said act." The following month, however, Charles proved more pliable; he "came forward & gave satisfactory Acknowledgements to the church for abusing his wife." Beaver Creek Church was less successful in appealing to Palmer Hall, who was also charged with whipping his wife. The church found him "guilty of the crime charged, and neglecting to hear the Church" and therefore excluded him. Exclusion may not have been a significant act to Hall, nor would it protect his wife, but these proceedings identified this sect's understanding of the limits of men's power in the household and gave battered women a possible arena for appeal. It also reminds us of the limits of church influence: once the church excluded Hall, it had no sway over his conduct.[30]

Church discipline could also reinforce husbands' authority over their wives. Some women were called before their church to answer for disobedience to their husbands. In 1797, for instance, a North Carolina church excommunicated a woman when she refused to be subject to her husband. Likewise, in some spousal abuse cases, the wives were also brought before the church for provoking or fighting with their husbands. In more subtle ways, too, churches worked to bolster traditional gender roles, disproportionately disciplining women for jealousy, backbiting, and being quarrelsome. Churches did not intend to dismantle patriarchal power; instead they intended to establish a twin authority, ideally working with heads of household, to sustain an orderly family, a charge that demanded controlling women as well as men.[31]

Yet, churches did grant wives some types of power in their marital negotiations. This was particularly true in regard to women's access to marital property. If churches shared an interest with the state in regulating marriage, they diverged greatly over fundamental questions about the relationship between women and marital property, a key issue in the civil function of marriage itself. Ensuring the straightforward transfer of property guided much of the government's regulation of marriage as the state sought to be sure of monogamous marriage with clearly identified heirs. Under the legal construct of feme covert from English common law, a married woman could not own property; ownership of any property she possessed prior to her marriage or received during the marriage transferred directly and absolutely to her husband. This structured a married woman's status as a dependent, a subordinate whose need for financial support and protection provided a husband with the necessary claim of being a superior, in essence, a *petit* governor, earning his place in the body politic. Married women's financial impoverishment and dependent status ensured their legal and political penury, erasing their presence from the civil world just as matrimony had erased their names. They had no legal authority to sign contracts, own property or their wages, or execute a deed. Through the law of feme covert, the state consolidated the financial and political rights of a married couple into a single identity subsumed under the personhood and name of the husband. Early Americans believed that coverture ensured the right workings of government and the stability of society with property firmly under the control of the male head of household.[32] Churches, though, displayed vastly different values when they dealt with specific cases, at times empowering wives to claim marital property and sanctioning their actions against their husbands' wishes and material interests. A North Carolina church considered the case of Sary Spoolman leaving her husband and "taking away property and Disposeing of it Contrary to his will," and the church chose the relatively mild response of suspending her membership until it investigated further. Such a course indicated that the members believed there might be a reasonable explanation for these actions, and, in fact, when Spoolman appeared before the church and gave her "Relation," the church removed the suspension and restored her membership. That same church adjudicated a similar case some fifteen years later and again responded mildly. In 1812, Rachel Teague resorted to deceit by "perswading her husband to Leave home on a certain Night to Stay at his fathers In order to get an oppertunity to Elope from him and having gone away and Took part of his property away with her." The church censured her and suspended her membership. But within only three months, Teague was restored to full membership. The church membership found her crimes of leaving her husband and taking property to be objectionable, but their response was relatively lenient, a brief suspension.[33]

Providence Church in Kentucky faced similar questions in its dealings with member Nancy Martin. The church had long been aware of the difficulties in Martin's marriage. The members had considered charges against her regarding conflicts with her husband and, after investigating the case, agreed to retain her as a member with an admonishment. In 1817, a member again brought a series of charges against Nancy Martin. According to the charges, Martin had recently left her husband and arranged a lease with her brother that included a condition that if she ever returned to her husband the lease would be void and she would lose her improvement in the property. Adding to this offense, she intended to use her maiden name when signing the lease. Finally, Nancy Martin bound her children out and admitted that she had done so "for the purpose of keeping them from under the Controle of theire Father." Martin's actions were a veritable laundry list of challenges to her feme covert status, having laid claim to her name, marital property, a legal identity, and her children. They were also a more personal challenge to her husband, who retained a series of overlapping legal rights: as a husband to determine Martin's residence and name; as a head of household to control the property decisions of his domestic dependents; and as a father to maintain supreme power over his children. While the church felt these actions were sufficiently serious to merit calling another meeting to investigate them further, it quickly concluded its investigation and, remarkably, agreed not to level any disciplinary action against Nancy Martin; she retained full membership in the church and the right to significant independent action. While the actions of Nancy Martin were exceptional, the decisions by the members of Providence Church were not. They insisted on their prerogative to judge Martin's conduct and summoned her before the church to justify her conduct. And agreeing to tolerate, even accept, a wife's challenge to her husband was in keeping with a broader pattern of activity.[34]

In the early evangelical movement, Baptist leaders praised women for such actions when they occurred in the name of piety and the "true" church. Likewise, in keeping with the emphasis on "co-partners" in marriage, Baptists offered wives authority within the marriage and the household and expected women to be accountable *to the church* in those roles. We would be wrong to interpret church interference as an unmitigated blessing for wives. Yet the broad pattern of church actions did two things. First, it ensured that there were possibilities present in the local church that were not possible (or less possible) in the civil realm. More broadly, it meant that the church maintained an active and powerful presence in the home, with oversight of all domestic relations and behaviors. While Baptist churches were never entirely comfortable with such independent actions by women, they were also willing to intrude in domestic relations and shape behavior in households in ways that often benefited women.

If Baptist churches occasionally departed from civil norms regarding marriage, nowhere was this more apparent than their policies toward slave unions. In the pre–Civil War South, the institution of slave marriage did not legally exist, yet evangelical churches recognized and sanctified slave marriages. Baptist churches were among the first in the South to perform and recognize slave marriages. These were not legal ceremonies, of course, but then no marriages performed by Baptist clergy before the 1780s were legal unions since, according to colonial law in this region, only licensed clergy could legally perform a marriage rite. However, early Baptist ministers ignored these restrictions and sanctified marriages, white and black, within their congregations. Having acknowledged slave unions as permanent and sacred, churches ultimately created practices that were at odds with both the legal system and owners' economic interests. Here too, the evangelical code—rather than what was allowable under the civil code—was expected to guide members' behavior.[35]

Slave marriage raised new issues for churches, issues that forced congregations to examine their beliefs about what constituted adultery or bigamy, the effects of slavery on marriage, and their white members' actions toward their human property. Forced separations were a fact of life for slave families. One historian estimated that one in three first marriages ended with the sale of a spouse. And the realities of this were made plain to Baptist communities as their slave members formed new unions when previous ones were shattered. Churches then created special rules that allowed their slave members to remarry in the event of a forced separation from their spouses. That is to say, slaves reconstructed family life, and Baptist churches created rules to support it. While Baptists permitted white members to remarry only if their spouse had died or in a few cases of long desertions, they made new policies when faced with slave members' needs.

Church after church found it had to rethink its policies about marriage and remarriage given the circumstances of their enslaved members' lives. One Virginia church asked its association, "What shall be done with a negro sister who was parted from her husband against her will, and has taken another?" The association published its response for this and its other churches: "Answered by a majority. When they part voluntarily it is adultery. [O]therwise not." In 1814, a Kentucky congregation at Beaver Creek wondered whether "there [was] any case that could occur, which would justify blacks to marry again, while their companions are alive," and agreed that there was. That same church soon had an opportunity to consider the practical meaning of that decision when a slave woman named Ferrby requested the advice of the church through her owner, a Brother Ferguson. She intended to marry again "having been once before married and her husband yet living in the state of Virginia, [and] alledg[ed] an involentary separation having parted them beyond the hope of reunion." The church members then agreed to "set her at liberty to act as at discretion and advise accordingly," permitting Ferrby to remarry if she wished. At that same meeting, the church disciplined a white woman for fornication; new sexual rules for slaves did not alter the rules for free members.[36]

The involuntary separation of slave couples forced the Baptists not only to rethink their beliefs about bigamy and remarriage but also to face their white members' complicity in the disruption of marriages. And some Baptist churches and associations took steps to eliminate that practice. At the urging of the church at Bent Creek, the Holston Association in Tennessee recommended that its member churches "consider the premises of the prenitious practice of being active in parting Married Negroes" and report back to the association the following year. The seventeen churches that reported back could not agree, but the association did "advise the Respective Churches to avoid parting Married Negroes." Not all evangelicals were willing to take the extra step to condemn white members' conduct in separating slave spouses. In 1810, a Tennessee association debated "*is the marriage of slaves Binding for life*, yea or nay?" When the question had originally been raised two years earlier, the church representatives could not come to a consensus and referred the debate to subsequent meetings. Even after two years of debate, they could not agree on an answer and explained in their minutes: "*as we are not able to answer the the [sic] same as a body, we unanimously agree to dismiss the query at the request of the Church* from which it came." But they included this addendum: "with this advice to the *respective Churches, to be careful to have no hand in parting married negroes, where it may be avoided.*"[37]

The phrasing of the original question reveals the great quandary that slave unions presented. Marriage, as eighteenth-century Baptists understood it, was by definition binding for life (though some churches allowed for the dissolution of a marriage after adultery), but the deliberating ministers were unwilling to take a strong stand against selling slaves to enable lifelong unions. Instead they settled for a weaker statement that individuals should avoid the offending behavior, and even that they weakened by adding "where it may be avoided." Some churches and associations were willing to take a bolder stand against this practice and bring disciplinary action against members who sold slave spouses away from each other. Upper King and Queen Baptist Church considered whether "it [is] agreeable to Scripture for any member to part Man

& Wife," and the members answered with an unequivocal no, ruling that "any member who shall be guilty of such crimes shall be dealt with by the Church for such misconduct."[38] Even those rules that offered less protection than Upper King and Queen's recognized slave marriage and brought it a legitimacy that it lacked in civil society.

If Baptists redefined marital rules for their slave members regarding remarriage, in other ways churches demanded that slave unions conform to the norms that they tried to enforce on white members. Slaves too were called before the church for fornication, marital discord, spousal abuse, voluntary separation, and adultery. Accusations against slaves for adultery and bigamy were disproportionately high. Many slaves shared the experience of Charles and Gilly, two Kentucky slaves, who were excommunicated from their church for having too frequently "part[ed] from being man and wife."[39] Despite provisions for forced separation, white members may not have understood the tremendous challenges within slave marriages. They may have had different expectations of what distance was bearable, or what proximity was bearable when someone could not protect a family member from violence. As always, Baptists who did not submit to the intrusive authority of the church could expect excommunication. For slave members, though, interference in their family life was not as great a departure as it was for white Baptists, particularly white men. Slave families, under constant attack by the practices of slavery, experienced the late eighteenth century as an era of expanding white interference as owners' indifference to slave culture gave way to a new interest in controlling slaves' nonwork hours. This is not to say that all evangelical slaves experienced church discipline as benign. But these cases were premised on the conviction that slave unions were marriages and therefore sacred and to be protected.

Baptist churches' intrusion into the relationships of the household was a consistent practice of late eighteenth- and early nineteenth-century churches. By intruding into household affairs, Baptist churches challenged the autonomy of the household and designated churches (bodies that included white women and slaves as full, though not necessarily equal, members) as authorities within that realm. Their mediation of the power and authority of the head of household did not always work to the advantage of white women or slaves, but it did provide the opportunity for outsiders to negotiate within the marital and owner-slave relationships. Far from being a private sphere, the household—and the relationships within it—was very much considered subject to the authority of the church community. Evangelicalism created its own space within the internal dynamics of the southern household and effectively tied itself to domestic order. Significantly, marital and family discipline was part of the larger efforts to root out sin and, when possible, reclaim the sinner. Just as the churches supplemented the work of the state in regulating marriage and families, so too did they supplement or replicate the work of the government in other types of church discipline and policies. Their intentions were narrowly directed at their congregants and spiritual in nature as they sought to protect the purity of their churches. And yet, through their church discipline, Baptist churches broadly acted to create order in southern communities by monitoring the behavior of their congregants. Their dogged efforts and disciplinary strategies allowed Baptists' efforts to rout disorder to take on larger significance in the highly migratory society of the revolutionary and early national South in which traditional restraints on behavior were weakened or even nonexistent. By firmly entrenching themselves in the new western communities as well as the eastern settlements, churches' authority would become part of the foundation of southern communities.

4

On a Scale of Justice

In the summer of 1803, Virginian James Yancy fought with his neighbor and fellow Baptist Leonard Oden over what Yancy considered fraudulent trading practices. Yancy had bought a lamb from Oden, and when the lamb appeared sick, he confronted Oden with charges of shady dealing. Rather than take this dispute to their local county court, however, the two men approached their congregation, which appointed a committee to investigate. The church quickly determined in favor of Brother Oden, declaring the lamb was "well & marketable."[1]

This Baptist church's involvement in a civil dispute was no anomaly in the late eighteenth- and early nineteenth-century Upper South. Just as churches stepped in on behalf of the state to regulate marriages and families for their membership, they also sought to act in the place of local government, assuming a host of responsibilities that were typically associated with county civil offices in the late eighteenth century. County courts acted as the basic unit of local government in the Upper South, but they struggled to meet the needs of a southern population growing numerically and geographically, particularly in large, often western, counties. Baptist churches, though, took on many civil functions, acting as "overseers to the poor," land processioners (securing property boundaries), grand juries, and courts. Most often, they replicated the adjudicating functions of courts, arbitrating disputes over business and debt and prosecuting offenses such as theft, slander, and assault.

Churches also handled matters that had little, if any, place in the southern county court system, such as monitoring individuals' conduct as they migrated to new areas and judging cases of wife beating and abuse of slaves. These civil functions ensured that churches acted to create and sustain order in their communities, often in ways that served the nonevangelical population as well.[2] Ultimately, in acting as a type of local government, Baptist churches helped to shape the local political economy and constructed a version of "citizenship" for their members, including those excluded from definitions of citizenship during the revolutionary and early national periods.

While Baptists performed this work for spiritual reasons, it had valuable uses for Baptists and also for non-Baptists in what was a highly migratory society. In western regions where courts were inaccessible, churches offered alternatives for economic mediation. In new settlements where individuals were unknown, churches offered a type of guarantee of good conduct. Migration alone, though, does not explain why Americans during this era needed courts (at best, it explains why courts might be particularly useful in specific locations). They required them because of issues of everyday economic exchange, since such issues were becoming more salient to people's lives at this time. As Americans increasingly grew foodstuffs and produced goods for the market and for profit, they began to participate in a series of economic shifts that historians have dubbed the market revolution, a revolution as chaotic and ill defined as any political or social revolution. Courts, along with local, state, and federal governments, eased the progress of the market economy; so too did these churches. In keeping with their goal to construct a church community that was thoroughly holy, Baptists insisted that their faith guide their relationships in the marketplace and that their churches serve as clearinghouses for decisions on congregants' economic transactions. The resulting inquiries had implications beyond the boundaries of the church. Through their work tracking individuals' behavior across space and by creating mechanisms for enforcing contracts and the payment of debts, these churches facilitated their members' participation in the market revolution. Church courts provided a safety net in an otherwise risky economy, and they provided a measure of insurance to those who would transact with Baptists. These judicial and economic activities allowed churches to dissolve boundaries between the secular arena and the sacred, to infuse religious rules into the local political economy, and to serve as civil as well as spiritual structures.[3]

When the Separate Baptists began their missionary enterprise to Virginia and North Carolina in the 1750s, it was not a new phenomenon for a church to take up civil functions. The colonial Anglican Church not only had performed civil activities in the Upper South, but throughout the seventeenth and much of the eighteenth century, it acted as an important and official component of local government, identifying misbehavior to secular authorities, confirming property boundaries, and caring for the poor. These roles allowed the Church of England to assist the local government in maintaining order in this society not simply by promoting religion and morality, but also by assisting in law enforcement and providing communal services.

Throughout the second half of the eighteenth century, however, the Anglican Church in both Virginia and North Carolina gradually lost these civil functions, yielding these powers to secular authorities. Although historians have tended to examine the separation of church and government in this region as a legal transformation that developed during and after the American Revolution, this process involved much more than state law and began on a very local level in the 1740s and 1750s as county courts increasingly took over civil duties from the vestries. For instance, rather than Anglican church wardens presenting charges of wrongdoing to the courts, local grand juries increasingly did so. The timing of the transition from vestries to grand juries varied by region and county but generally occurred around midcentury. Likewise, other nonreligious duties passed into secular hands. In 1760, the North Carolina Assembly transferred the responsibility of paying wolf bounties from the vestries to the county courts. In 1762, it also authorized county courts to assume responsibility for orphans and their estates, a task previously assigned to the vestries.[4] Thus, the responsibilities of religious and secular authorities underwent a gradual realignment throughout the mid- and late eighteenth century and, while initiated by colonial authorities, occurred on the local level as parish and county governments shifted jurisdictions.

The disestablishment of the Anglican Church in North Carolina and Virginia (in 1776 and 1786, respectively) further eliminated the church's claim to civil functions. The responsibility of delineating property boundaries fell to the courts. Likewise, caring for the poor gradually began to be delegated to local civil authorities as the Virginia and North Carolina legislatures instructed counties to elect overseers of the poor. In some counties, these bodies continued to be connected with the Anglican-Episcopal Church, as the name was simply applied to the vestrymen who previously had been responsible for care of the poor. In the 1780s and 1790s, however, partly at the insistence of the Baptists and other dissenting sects, the overseers of the poor were gradually separated from the Anglican-Episcopal Church and became distinct, nonsectarian bodies.[5] The ultimate result of these realignments was a new distinction between secular and sectarian activities and jurisdictions, expressed in a more centralized civil authority in county governments (and expanded county courts) and a narrowed, "religious" purview for churches.

This trend of relinquishing civil functions to the emerging state was not followed by the evangelical sect, and Baptist churches claimed for themselves tasks, such as poor relief, that the Anglican-Episcopal Church had gradually yielded to secular bodies. Unlike the colonial Anglican Church, which was responsible for all residents of the parish regardless of their religion, the Baptists contributed materially and financially only to members of their community. Thus, they assisted considerably smaller numbers of people than was typical in an Anglican parish, aiding perhaps one or two families or individuals in each congregation. In this case, however, the numbers mask their remarkable undertaking, as Baptist churches were young, relatively poor, and unsubsidized and unaided by the state. Beginning the practice under the Anglican establishment, Baptists continued to provide for their poor even after nonsectarian bodies took over this function. Indeed, after 1790, churches increasingly confirmed that it was their duty to assist needy brethren. In 1792, Upper King and Queen Church declared that it was a duty of deacons to serve "the Table of the poor Saints in distress by a collection from the other Members for their assistance." In 1803, Tomahawk Church insisted it was the members' duty to contribute to brethren in distress. Wilson Creek Church resolved in its 1804 covenant to relieve the poor. A Virginia man felt so strongly about this duty that when his church failed to assist a needy member, he borrowed the language of excommunication and "unfellowshiped" the church body.[6]

Baptists' aid to their poor and disabled came in a variety of forms, indicating the ad hoc nature of this aid. Each church agreed on its own policy about helping the poor, determined which individuals would receive the assistance, and voted on what kind and how much aid to offer. Churches contributed cash, goods, and even services to struggling individuals and their families, and churches issued directives to the deacons to collect and distribute necessary items to the needy. A North Carolina church, for instance, gave money and corn to Brother Nelson and his family because of his "affliction." Forks of Elkhorn Church provided for brethren to work for Brother Maslin "in his Distress" and three years later provided a wheel for Sister Martin. Recipients of such aid were not necessarily destitute but might merely have suffered a temporary setback, as did Sister Barnett of Bryan Station Church when she "mett with the loss of her Cloathes by fire" and received $4 from her congregation. Occasionally, churches paid for doctors' services for sick congregants or their children, and congregants also agreed to take others into their homes.[7] While this individualized method of handling poor relief required little institutional discussion of Baptist beliefs on poor relief, one Virginia association did consider the issue and divided the poor into four categories: the world's poor, the devil's poor, the covetous poor, and the Lord's poor. It identified the world's poor as those who were able-bodied but lazy, the devil's poor as those who spent their money in sinful practices like gambling or drinking, and the covetous poor as those who lived near a rich man's kitchen or "negro huts." The Lord's poor, however, lived frugally and industriously but still found themselves in want. Only this final group, the association argued, deserved Baptist assistance.[8]

This Virginia association may not have identified the Lord's poor with a particular sex, but in practice white women appear to have made up the bulk of this group. Although most individuals who received aid were not named in churchbooks, those who were identified were predominately white women. With their marital status, as always, hidden under the title "sister," these women tended to be listed as individuals rather than as members of families. It is likely that many were widows, and some were identified as such, like "Sister James a widow" and "Sister Gale widow." Indeed, one church rejected generic nongendered language to refer to the needy and specifically identified widows as the church's concern, declaring it the "Churches Duty to support the Widow, & also the Lord's Table &...a Minister."[9]

In a rather exceptional case, the North Carolina church at Sandy Run went beyond providing poor relief when it took responsibility for two orphaned children who had recently lost their mother. In November 1782, it authorized a member to sell the deceased woman's property for the support of the children and subsequently distributed the money to those members caring for the children. The church apparently retained control over the children because four years later it threatened to remove one of the orphans if the woman caring for her moved away as planned.[10] In performing this work, they resembled Anglican vestries, which had provided some care for the poor, disabled, and orphaned. However, as the civil powers of the established church were dismantled in the late eighteenth century, these tasks were expected to be yielded to the developing state. Even as the Anglican Church began to yield these powers in the 1770s and 1780s, Baptist churches claimed these tasks as their own for their membership.

Some of the churches' actions were less material and tangible than distributing corn and money but were nonetheless valuable. Using a network of churches that spread cheaply and easily into new settlements, churches tracked migrants and monitored their conduct. This proved to be particularly useful with the migrations into the western territories during and after the American Revolution, with territories marked by new, and often temporary, residents who were disconnected from traditional guarantees of good conduct (such as court, family, and reputation), the absence of local civil government, and the promise of ready access to land. By 1770, a handful of brazen surveyors, hunters, traders, and other profit-seekers had journeyed on foot and horseback across the Cumberland Gap, extending the line of white settlement into what would later become Kentucky and Tennessee. In Kentucky, permanent settlements of whites developed as early as the mid-1770s, nurtured by a culture of geographic mobility. For generations, Virginians and North Carolinians had migrated frequently, often establishing homesteads in sparsely settled western regions and returning to eastern communities only when hard times set in. This migratory culture was in part encouraged by the Virginia and North Carolina colonial governments, which had granted land bounties to veterans of the French and Indian War. As these land-seekers trickled west during the 1770s, they immediately clashed with Native Americans. The influx of European Americans increased in 1780 and 1781 and showed no signs of abating, guaranteeing at least a generation of bloody conflict. The years during and after the American Revolution saw an ongoing process of colonization in which lands held by Native Americans were settled and claimed by whites (often in that order).

As numerous as these settlers were, this migration was not a sweeping flood of homesteaders; instead, it created pockets of white settlement in a land that was more Indian than European. Although there were no permanent settlements of Native Americans in the Kentucky region in the late eighteenth century, a number of Indian nations still claimed the land as hunting grounds. The Shawnee, in particular, but also the Cherokee and the Chickasaw, used the area for hunting and as a trading and communications route between the northern and southern tribes. Located north of the Ohio River, the Shawnee proved to be hostile foes to European-American intrusions into the region and, while only numbering around 4,000, they powerfully affected early white settlements. Angered initially by white hunters killing valuable herds for their pelts, the Shawnee soon found their access to the land threatened by white land practices, such as exclusive ownership and enclosure. As the number of white migrants increased, so did the conflicts between the Shawnee and white settlers, which quickly became fierce struggles over control of the land.

When violence erupted, white settlers often abandoned their homesteads and returned to the relative safety of forts or eastern communities, a choice that would ultimately complicate land claims. In spite of the tales told by early Kentuckians of fearless, gun-toting frontiersmen and their sharp-shooting (yet still womanly) wives, Shawnee attacks sent migrants scurrying to the nearest fortified station or to relatives' homes back east. But southerners, intent on wresting the fertile Kentucky land from the Native Americans, always conquered their fear and left the forts as war parties and settlers. Indeed their respites within forts were acceptable only because they were a temporary measure in a larger plan. Settlers repeatedly returned to the rich farmland, often only to be chased back when hostilities renewed. And since white "ownership" of the land often meant no more than occupying and improving it, the traumas of the wars with the Shawnee threw the American land tenure process into chaos. Settlers' rude dwellings and young crops were abandoned and destroyed, perhaps to be reclaimed by former occupants, or new ones, but often with different boundaries and only until the next violent conflict, failed crop, or migratory urge. As successive occupants improved and therefore claimed the land, they set the stage for decades of conflicts over competing rights of "legitimate" ownership.

White intrusions into present-day Tennessee followed a similarly muddled trajectory. The Cherokee had a number of towns in the southeastern corner, but they claimed much of middle Tennessee as hunting grounds and a buffer zone. Their claims clashed with the Chickasaws', who claimed much of western and middle Tennessee as hunting grounds. Even the Shawnee and the Iroquois had laid claim to parts of the region in the eighteenth century. Tennessee, then, similar to Kentucky, was frequently traversed by Native Americans for the purposes of trade, hunting, war, and diplomacy and had far-reaching significance to a variety of nations beyond the permanent settlements. While some early white settlers negotiated directly with the Cherokee for land, European Americans quickly settled beyond areas stipulated by treaties and aroused Cherokee hostility. In the 1780s and early 1790s, the increasingly familiar pattern continued: some efforts at agreements with Native Americans, often complicated by conflicting land claims, contradictory treaties, and bad-faith negotiations; a rush of white settlers (occasionally with their black slaves) moving into areas claimed by Indians; and mutual suspicion, hostility, and ongoing warfare.[11]

Dissatisfaction with colonial and local governments increased some southerners' drive to move westward. Western North Carolina, in particular, was beset by unrest in the 1760s and 1770s, leading to a mass emigration farther west. The eastern and western regions of the colony developed quite separately, having different ethnic and religious make-ups and also different economies. With the large population growth of the Piedmont in the mid-eighteenth century, these differences festered into conflicts over representation in the colonial government. As the western population grew, the legislature created new county governments (and hence representatives), but they also created new eastern counties, allowing the East to retain control of the government. Westerners viewed the endemic corruption of local officials as daily and personal reminders of eastern power, since governor-appointed justices selected most local officials. Western protests began in the early 1760s with circulars and culminated in the organization of the Regulators, who sought to expose and resist abuses by civil authorities, particularly relating to taxation. Minor clashes erupted throughout the late 1760s, though the true showdown came in 1771 when the Regulators met the colonial militia at Great Alamance Creek and were quickly routed. Thousands subsequently moved to the "western country." Once there, some migrants felt beyond the reach of colonial authorities and outside of the bounds of colonial law, free to claim land and even to negotiate independently with Native American nations.[12]

Colonial and revolutionary land law increased the disorder of southwestern settlements. Neither Virginia nor North Carolina officially surveyed their western lands to facilitate and regularize land claims. Instead, they allowed the individual land-seekers to survey the land and stake their own claims. This method led to chaotic and overlapping claims that were often irregularly shaped. Settlers often used natural boundary markers, such as trees or scratched marks on rocks; these provided little long-term protection of property claims, since they could be altered by a storm, deliberately removed, or accidentally missed by another surveyor. The large numbers of squatters further complicated backcountry settlements. All of these elements of land settlement ensured constant boundary disputes and ongoing chaos.

The appearance of disorder in western settlements only increased with the onslaught of migrants after the Revolution. Even in a society characterized by dramatic population movements, the number of migrants traveling west of the Appalachians after the war was remarkable. Prefigured by an early surge from 1779 to 1781, a rush of migrants—some veterans of the late war with soldiers' land grants in hand, some families seeking better land—pushed into Kentucky in 1784. John Floyd remarked in 1780 that "near 300 large boats have arrived this spring at the Falls [of Ohio] with families." Daniel Drake, a Baptist who as a boy moved with his family into Kentucky, recalled:

> When we arrived at Mr. May's deer lick, in the autumn of 1788, there were no inhabitants in that part of the county. But immigration ... was a constant, not a mere wet weather stream. Within the six years that elapsed, the number of settlers had increased to such an extent that one could not wander a mile in any direction, without meeting with a clearing of two to ten acres, ... and designated as a human residence by a one story unhewed log cabin.[13]

The rapid increase in settlers in the 1780s provoked an increase in hostility from the Native Americans, who continued to challenge white intrusions west of the Appalachians, resulting in nearly a decade of alarms, scares, guerrilla warfare, skirmishes, and organized military campaigns. The violence accompanying American colonization efforts did not deter white land-seekers, and by 1790, Kentucky and Tennessee, though still officially part of Virginia and North Carolina, had populations of over 73,000 and 35,000, respectively.

Because so many Baptists populated the southwest, they not only had front-row seats from which to observe the drama of westward expansion, but they also made up a significant portion of the participants. Indeed, some Virginia and North Carolina churches experienced so much migration that their churches were virtually deserted. One traveler observed that a North Carolina church declined from 606 to 14 members, probably as part of the large migration out of western North Carolina after the defeat of the Regulators. The tremendous movement of people during the revolutionary era visibly affected many congregations. More than half of the people who joined Broad Run Church before 1780, for example, left that church. Some found that the increasing number of Baptists in northwestern Virginia allowed them to create and join new churches closer to their homes, and many others left the church to move south or west.[14]

Some migrating Baptists may have attempted to settle near members of their particular congregation given that some churchbooks identify migrants as moving to the same location month after month. A few congregations even moved together into the western country, settling together and creating a close tie between church and neighborhood. Members of one Virginia church journeyed en masse with their children, cattle, and packhorses from Fredericksburg across the Blue Ridge Mountains and through the Cumberland Gap to Gilberts Creek, Kentucky, where they reestablished their congregation. Another Virginia congregation was caught in the turmoil of the migratory culture of the 1780s and agreed to dissolve their church and reconstitute it in Kentucky: having found "a principal part of the members with their Minister being about to Move to Kentucky, it was agreed they should Carry the [church] Constitution with them." The clerk noted in the churchbook that they successfully "arrive[d] in Kentucky and settl[ed] on the South Side of the K[en-tuck]y River near Craggs Station." Because of some unnamed "Turn of Gods providence," the church members collectively moved again to the other side of the river. The churchbook gave no hint as to why the congregants decided to migrate together, but they clearly expected to reconstitute themselves as formerly and noted that they must temporarily appoint a new clerk, "the former Clerk not yet having moved to the North Side."[15]

Located, as many Baptists were, in the western region and being frequent participants in migrations, the Baptists directed their attention to this chaotic process to make migration more "orderly." Churches passed rules seeking to monitor their members' behavior before, during, and after a relocation. Indeed, concerns about orderly migrations were so pervasive and commonplace that churches commonly created such rules in their founding constitutions, requiring members to move in an "orderly" fashion. Members of the church of North Fork, for instance, vowed "not to remove our residence or abode to any distant part of the world without informing the Church and advising with our brethren and taking a regular letter of Dismission." Likewise, members of the church at Cherokee Creek in Tennessee agreed "not to remove our abode out of the Bounds of this Church without informing and Consulting the Church."[16]

Churches monitored each step of migration, from settling obligations in the old neighborhood to moving into a new community and joining the local church. First, churches required members to alert the church of their intention to move and to request "letters of dismission" from the church. This public announcement provided the opportunity for community members to collect unsettled debts and to insist on the completion of contracts. It also allowed the church to establish that no unseemly behavior had prompted the move (such as an illicit pregnancy, or a desire to escape charges of fraud). Members' former churches remained responsible for their behavior until they presented their dismission letters to a Baptist church in their new community and were received as members. The letters of dismission, which notified the new church of individuals' previous congregation and their standing in the church, were carefully dated, marking the last time the individuals' behavior was observed. In a society where whole communities appeared transitory and individuals rootless, letters of dismission provided a kind of introduction and a guarantor of past good conduct.

In theory at least, no Baptist was ever rootless. Churches proved to be remarkably diligent in monitoring members' behavior during the period in which they were not connected to a particular community. Every Baptist had to turn in the letter to a new congregation upon arriving in a new location. If the new congregation found the letter and the potential member "in order," the church then accepted the individual into the church and assumed responsibility for his or her behavior. Churches checked the dates on which the letters were issued, and when an extended period of time had passed—indicating a period of unmonitored behavior—they inquired into the individuals' activities during that time, writing to people or churches if necessary to verify good conduct. Likewise, when a church issued a letter but did not hear of the dismissed member joining a new church, it inquired after the person and his or her behavior and then instructed the individual to join a nearby church immediately. When necessary, the church of origin demanded the return of the letter, in effect withdrawing the person's membership. In all of these ways, Baptist churches deliberately served as a network of local institutions to supervise people during migrations and to provide a framework for the construction of orderly new communities.

More broadly, churches interposed themselves between members and the market economy. Seeking to define and delineate their members' appropriate place in the market, churches debated the very economic structures of the early republic and inserted their authority over many economic transactions. In so doing, they sought to define a specifically Baptist political economy. This is not to say that capitalism and evangelicalism were incompatible nor that Baptists rejected the values of a market economy, such as profit seeking and competitiveness. Quite the contrary, churches expected members to be engaged in their worldly professions and to pursue financial success. Indeed, many of the behaviors that churches worked to inculcate (for instance, temperance, accountability, industry, self-control, simplicity, and staidness) could facilitate economic success. But, at the same time, Baptists also displayed a lingering unease about what a market economy meant. Mill Swamp Church, for instance, debated in 1778 whether it was "agreable to the spirit of Christianity to buy and sell principally with a view of getting gain," a question that raised the possibility that Baptists could not participate in the market economy because of their belief system. The church agreed that members could do so, provided that "no unlawfull means be taken." For other Baptists, the issue was how much profit was godly and when profit seeking became extortion. To discern that line, churches and associations sought to define extortion, arriving at a variety of conclusions: "any undue advantage," "unjust gain by oppress[io]n," "taking Advantage of Another's necessity in Selling any kind of Property," or taking "advantage of any ones Ignorance, or necessity in the act of selling." In defining what was an immoral (and unacceptable) profit, churches sanctioned other profits as moral and just and authorized members' participation in commerce.[17]

Permission to participate, however, was not to be construed as a blanket endorsement of all economic transactions. Having designated some economic behaviors as immoral, churches guaranteed the ongoing need to judge members' transactions. Whereas government regulated the economy using common law and legal statutes to guide judicial opinion, churches sought to define their own policies to guide their membership. If churches were willing to depart from state law in favor of their own practices regarding the licensing of ministers and marriages, they did not propose economic regulations that conflicted with state practice. They did, though, set up additional restrictions on members to ensure a political economy that conformed to their readings of republicanism and Christianity. Some kinds of employment, such as tavern keeping, land speculation, slave trading, and even such low-profit enterprises as oyster selling came under particular scrutiny, as some churches debated whether good Christians could engage in these trades. More often, though, churches worried about the question of profit. One association asked whether the "market price in commerce [was] the privilege of Church members"; it concluded that it was "not in [their] power, to regulate commerce" but that members should use their consciences and not allow their prices to exceed the common market price.[18] In 1805, the Strawberry Association debated whether it was extortion to sell corn at $3 per barrel *to brethren*; it decided that the price was not excessive, but the question itself suggested that faith and membership might require pricing that distinguished members from nonmembers. Troubled by accusations of extortion, a Kentucky church decided to set prices for some commodities: the price of corn could not exceed 3 shillings per bushel and hemp and flax seed could not exceed $1 per bushel. Likewise, "distress" about extortion prompted a North Carolina church to set prices for corn, wheat, flax seed, oats, rye, and potato seed. Members who ignored these rules or the complaints of their brethren risked the censure of the church, as Thomas Hopper found when he was excommunicated from his church for extortion.[19] Through their debates, rules, and discipline, churches indicated that they expected to steer members' participation in the market; in so doing, they posited a model of the political economy in which both church and state were guiding forces.

In other ways, Baptist churches replicated, and in some cases replaced, the work of government to regulate economic transactions. For Baptists, this was biblical imperative. Following biblical directions regarding separation from nonbelievers (2 Corinthians 6:17) and Christian conflict resolution (Matthew 18:15–18), they used their churches as quasi courts for their members and insisted on exclusive jurisdiction in adjudicating conflicts between members. Thus they heard, mediated, and ruled on a variety of disputes concerning debt, trade, property, and business. In performing these semi-judicial proceedings, which overlapped with and sometimes replaced the county court, churches acted as a type of local government for their members.

County courts served as the basic units of local government in colonial Virginia and North Carolina, performing a broad range of administrative and judicial duties. The courts' administrative duties included collecting taxes, appointing surveyors to open and maintain roads, licensing ferry operators and tavern keepers, and regulating and inspecting tobacco and other products. As judicial bodies, they heard a wide variety of cases, except those that involved loss of life or limb and those that involved large amounts of money or tobacco. Allegations of offenses—whether made by vestries or, more typically after 1750, by grand juries—typically concerned drunkenness, assault, selling liquor without a license, profane swearing, and the failure of road surveyors to perform their jobs. Courts also commonly heard cases of debt, probate of wills, and transfers of property. With these varied responsibilities and wide jurisdiction, and with few other institutions in place, courts functioned as the primary body of local government. Courts also served a cultural function, acting as locations to define the local community and manifest its values. Court days, which were part judicial business, part business transactions, and part social gathering, also allowed the elite to display their status. Their prominence at court—one of the few places of large public gatherings—solidified their status as gentry men and local leaders.[20]

Despite its centrality to local government and southern communities, the court system did not always effectively provide either the appearance of order or a local system of legal adjudication. Instead, county courts, particularly in the backcountry, faced a number of difficulties that made them inaccessible and also appear undependable or untrustworthy. Additionally, the continual migrations westward, which increased dramatically after 1775, made for large counties with dispersed populations. No sooner might a western county court establish rudimentary services than white settlers would move to its outermost fringes and demand court services there. Petitioners from western counties frequently complained to the Virginia and North Carolina legislatures that their county was too large and the county seat too far away to be of use to them. The continuing migrations, then, ensured that the structures of local government could not extend far enough or fast enough to meet the demands of the growing population of the backcountry. Other difficulties arose for the county court system because of the "astonishing mobility" that characterized the late eighteenth-century southern population.[21] Whole communities frequently underwent a process of dispersal. Settlements then—both new and old—commonly included recent arrivals, short-term residents soon to move further on, and old residents preparing to migrate. Faced with significant populations of migrants, some local officials faced difficulties in maintaining order.

As courts in the southern backcountry struggled to meet the needs of dispersed and recent settlements, they often focused less on prosecuting small or moral offenses than on providing the necessary services to a developing region. Richard Beeman found in his study of frontier Lunenburg that the court primarily attempted to establish basic services and facilities, such as establishing and maintaining roads and licensing ordinaries. Moreover, as

A. Roger Ekirch has documented for North Carolina, many southerners were suspicious of local authorities, particularly in the West. In the backcountry, many local officials often had little or no experience in government. Having recently gained their wealth, they were often highly acquisitive and used their positions to further their gains. Corruption was widespread. Western local officials' claims to authority were also weakened by settlers' unfamiliarity with their officials and the absence of deferential relationships, which bolstered authority in eastern counties.[22]

Given the complicated relationship between southerners and the court system, it is perhaps no surprise that Baptist churches had a similarly uneasy relationship with judicial authority as they both discouraged its use and imitated it. Again following the code of gospel dealings from the Gospel of Matthew, Baptists required that all disputes come under the mediation of the church if they could not be resolved privately. Baptists understood these scriptural directions to apply to every transgression, whether sexual or financial, public or private. To violate this code by using the court to recoup financial losses or to enforce a contract incurred church discipline. The restriction against court action applied only to disputes between members; Baptists could and did take non-Baptists to court. Churches and associations repeatedly issued declarations against "going to law" or "warranting" other Baptists. Wheeley's Church in North Carolina, for instance, considered "whether should members go to law with each other for debts. Answered No." Likewise, a Tennessee church listed this restriction as a church rule when it was constituted in 1802: "All controversies either of debt or trespass should be brought to the church and referred to judges that may be appointed to settle such matters for brother should not go to law with brother." Violating the rules against "going to law" with another member prompted disciplinary procedures in the churches. When individuals were accused of going to law with another person, churches usually attempted to use their own mediation to settle the dispute. In May 1801, Waller's Church of Virginia began to investigate a dispute between Sister Cason and her son, Edward. The church believed that Sister Cason had cause to be grieved by her son; however, it declared "that Sister Cason ought first to dismiss the suit in court against her son, before the church can adhere to her Grievance." Sister Cason, apparently unmoved by either church policy or parental affection, was determined to bring her son to court and ignored the requests of the church to dismiss her suit. A member reported that "he waited on Sister Cason & conversed with her conserning dismissing the suit she had Instituted against her son, Bro. Edwd Cason, she pointedly refused, in consequence of which she is Excommunicated from the fellowship of this church."[23] Like the resolute Sister

Cason, a handful of members preferred legal remedies to church mediation even at the cost of their membership. In the churches in this study, twenty-six people were accused of taking another member to court; of these, six refused to hear the church and were subsequently excommunicated.

Clearly, Baptists' prohibition against suing fellow Baptists threatened to injure some members' interests, such as creditors with recalcitrant debtors, or trading or business partners when agreements went sour. Concerns such as these may have prompted Meherrin Church to consider "whither civil Suits at Law is not allowable in some cases, against members in fellowship?" The church debated this question in 1793 but came to no resolution and so referred the question to a later meeting. The passage of time, however, brought the church no closer to an agreement on reconciling members' desires to protect their legal rights with the perceived scriptural prohibition against such action: the members continued to leave the question unanswered through four years of meetings. Finally, in 1797, they agreed on a resolution: "That [legal action] is lawful in some extraordinary and particular cases." That it took the church four years of debate to agree on only limited and "extraordinary" exceptions to this rule suggests the importance that Baptists placed on the ethic.[24]

As they limited their members' use of county courts, Baptists recreated a judicial arena within their churches that took on many of the characteristics of civil courts. Much of the churches' language and procedures resembled those of secular courts and reveal that Baptists were quite familiar with the courts. After receiving an accusation, a church would typically cite the accused member to appear and answer the charge, because, as Buck Marsh Church explained in one case, "it is necessary his accusers and himself should be face to face." Baptist churches expected accusations to be sufficiently proved before taking disciplinary action, and some churches noted when they reluctantly dropped a disciplinary matter because of insufficient evidence.[25] Some of their language during these proceedings mimicked that of the courts, including "acquitted," "on trial," "dismissed for lack of evidence," "testified," "called as witnesses," and "no proof so thought innocent."[26] These disputes used the churches' members as juries. The accusation, defense, and testimony were heard by all members attending the meeting; the voting members then rendered their judgment. Voting rights varied by congregation and often remain somewhat of a mystery unless the church explicitly identified its practices. Certainly, all white male members could vote, and some churches explicitly allowed women (without specifying a race) to vote in disciplinary cases. In some churches, black members were allowed to vote, particularly on discipline cases concerning other blacks; however, they probably did so infrequently, since they could not often attend the Saturday business meetings. All members—whether white or black, male or female—could bring charges against other members and give testimony.

As Baptist churches investigated and judged cases similar to those tried in the secular court system, they participated in the creation and maintenance of local order. Some of the more frequent types of cases tried in both county courts and Baptist churches during this period involved debt. Nonpayment of debt became a heightened concern in this highly migratory society in which individuals could move to avoid the demands of creditors and the reach of the law. Because it required dismissal letters, Baptist church policy itself provided some surety against the possibility that debtors might migrate without first settling their obligations. This requirement provided an opportunity for congregations to raise any unresolved issues, including unpaid debts, as in the case of Joseph Ellis of Buck Marsh Church: "B.^{r} Joseph Ellis applied to this Church for a Dismission, But under his present Circumstance the church thinks it duty to suspend his Dismi[ssio]n untill he shall first acquaint his Creditors of his intention." The church also required Ellis to inform it of his creditors' opinion of his removal. That the creditors' opinions were not sought directly suggests that his creditors were not Baptists, but members of the larger geographic community. That their opinions were nonetheless sought attests to the importance Baptists attached to fiscal orderliness. Ellis complied with his congregation's request and was granted a letter of dismissal.[27] This close monitoring of members, even as they prepared to leave a particular congregation, was typical of Baptist churches in this region.

In the event that a recalcitrant member slipped through their fingers, churches used the networks between congregations to discipline disorderly members, including those who contracted debts and left the area before paying them. The Virginia church at Waterlick faced such a problem in 1788 when George McDonald "allowed himself to get into debt as much as he could and then went off into the night with the property of several which he either borrowed or contracted for but never paid." George McDonald was not a member of the church, but his mother-in-law, Amelia Plank, was. The church went to her and requested her assistance in tracking McDonald, but she insisted she had no knowledge of his plans or whereabouts. Much to the church's dismay, Plank herself soon disappeared, also "contracting debts previous to her departure without disclosing any desire to satisfy same.... And it appears likely that she ha[d] connived with the villainous conduct of her son-in-law." Having made numerous inquiries, the church ultimately used a Baptist church near her new residence to track and contact her. It is unclear whether Amelia Plank or her "villainous" son-in-law paid their debts, but the church's ability to locate the two would certainly have made the collection process possible. This ability and commitment to track and monitor congregants, even when out of the immediate vicinity, made the Baptist churches a unique institutional network in the Upper South.[28]

Even when migration was not involved, Baptist churches acted to ensure that members paid their just debts and, in doing so, coordinated processes that were crucial to a market economy. They exercised church discipline to force delinquent debtors to pay their creditors and also mediated payment schedules and interest payments when necessary. Burks Branch Church, for instance, agreed "that Brother McGaughey owe[d] Brother Mullikin a Sum of money and that Brother McGaughey sh[ould] pay Brother Mullikin Twenty Dollars By our next meeting [and] the Balance in the fall." Two years later, the church again became involved in a dispute over a debt and gave one of its members three months to pay his debt of $20 to Brother Johnson of the Fox Run Baptist Church. Likewise, a Virginia church took steps against both the delinquent debtors and the creditor who attempted to sue them: "Bro. James Pendleton was appointed to cite Bro. David Corey to attend the next church meeting to answer for his Conduct in ordering Suits in Law against Several members of the Church[.] Bro. Rice Garnett was appointed to cite the s.^{d} delinquent members to shew cause if any they have why such Debts was not paid."[29]

The monitoring of members' financial accounts protected not only Baptist creditors, but non-Baptists as well. Rules about going to court applied only between members, but other standards of conduct concerning such issues as paying debts, amounts of interest, transfers of property, and fulfilling contracts applied to all transactions. A nonmember was usually unable to bring charges before a church personally, but members hearing of such misconduct were expected to initiate the regular disciplinary procedures. Such rumors could easily reach the ears of the membership. Many individuals attended Baptist services even if they were not members, and congregations tended to be three to five times as large as the membership. Also, sometimes, members brought cases to the church on behalf of family members or neighbors. Thus, some cases of nonpayment of debt came before the church because of "reports prevailing." The Tennessee church of Garrison Fork protected the larger community when it suspended Ransom Pruit until he paid his debts, and it refused to restore him to his former status until he produced receipts from his creditors, which included at least one nonmember. The Tennessee Baptist Association also acted to protect the general public when it considered what to do with members who left the area without paying their debts: it advised churches to warn the person's new community by sending a letter to a local church or even simply to the community itself.[30]

Certainly, not all of the churches' mediation in financial disputes worked. Unlike courts, churches held no power of physical or financial coercion. Their ultimate sanction could only be exclusion from the church and its religious community. Thus, churches' decisions were effective only to the degree that membership and the goodwill of their brethren mattered to the individuals concerned. In some cases, certainly, members facing discipline were willing to sacrifice their membership rather than conform to the voice of the church. In one such case, Brother Killian Creek complained in his Kentucky church against Brother Newell for not paying a debt. The church heard the dispute and ruled that Brother Newell must pay his debt "with the interest from the first day of last Oct[ober] till paid." Newell, though, rejected the church's decision and was accordingly expelled from the church. Having excluded Newell, the church no longer had any power over his conduct and could not force him to pay Creek; however, with Newell's exclusion, Creek was free to pursue the matter through the county courts.[31]

In addition to conflicts over debts, congregations also heard members' disputes concerning property, trade, and business. These types of cases were quite common to the churches of this region, and they ranged from minor sums and small, neighborhood trades to complicated contract or land transactions. Baptists ruled, for example, on what constituted a fair trade for a $4 gun; exchanging a heifer for a steer in a purchase; selling beeswax with tallow in it; killing hogs when the owner did not promptly claim them; selling an unhealthy horse; building rails of dubious quality; selling corn at too high a price; conveying property to defraud creditors; buying notes at a discount to harass a debtor; appropriate compensation for bed and board; "hard" (or aggressive) trading practices; violating a contract; and selling an unhealthy slave as healthy.

Given that churches often considered cases concerning small amounts of money and neighborhood trades, women may have been more likely to bring charges to the church than they would to the court. While white men brought the majority of these cases, white women do regularly appear as parties in them. Most of the cases involving women concerned trading and financial transactions between neighbors. In one such case, Old Sister Shelton complained against Brother Harrelson "for his Board at her house for a Certain time also for keeping of his Child." Brother Harrelson argued that he had compensated her adequately. When the church initially investigated, it found "their Accounts in a Situation So that the Matter Could not be Determined" and postponed ruling on the matter. The committee assigned to reach a settlement announced two months later that an agreement had been reached. This religious arena may have been particularly valuable to white women in the late eighteenth century and early nineteenth century as civil courts became increasingly professionalized. Women were, after all, consistent participants in the market, but were increasingly absent from civil institutions; they could produce, buy, and sell but were much less able to sue or litigate. Historians have documented the increased use of lawyers and English law in colonial courts in the early eighteenth century. In colonial Connecticut, for example, the Anglicization of the court system and the growing complexity of the commercial economy resulted in a decline in white women's participation in legal cases after 1700.[32] Churches acted as an institution that protected and facilitated the participation of individuals like Old Sister Shelton for whom the courts proved less accessible.

While claiming jurisdiction over civil disputes could have potentially brought these churches into conflict with civil authorities, there is no evidence that secular leaders objected to churches' actions. In the years before the Revolution, political authorities opposed the Baptists for a variety of reasons, including evangelicals' disregard for the statutes governing dissenters, their exuberant preaching and worship styles, their willingness to preach to slaves and accept them as members, and their moralistic rejection of many elements of southern elite culture. However, the early attacks on the Baptists did not specifically mention their assumption of civil duties. Of course, the churches' appropriation of these functions was a central part of a philosophy and lifestyle that colonial authorities opposed vehemently. The adjudication of civil matters was part of the Baptist insistence on "separateness"—the belief that they, as the true, pure Christian community, should set themselves apart from worldly society in thought, speech, dress, belief, and behavior—a world view that many in the South found suspicious and disturbing in the 1760s and 1770s. Nonetheless, of the many elements of this philosophy that critics assailed during these years, the assumption of civil duties was not among them. Perhaps the fact that these cases were handled during church meetings hid them from the critical eye of nonevangelicals. More likely, given that almost nothing escaped detractors in these years, the desire for law and order outweighed any concerns that this work was an affront or a challenge to the authority of civil courts.

Nonetheless, the overlapping jurisdictions of church and state could require some difficult negotiations. Evangelicals were part of a civil as well as a religious culture, which could, at certain times, create competing demands. As far as they were able, Baptists insisted that their members place the duties and ethics of the religious community over those of worldly society. The civil arena, though, could propel its way into the churches. For instance, charges pending in courts forced congregations to initiate their own investigations of members' conduct. Other overlaps were embodied in individuals struggling to balance their civil responsibilities with their religious ones. One Virginia church debated whether a sheriff could justly collect his back pay through the legal system. In another case, Brother Fryar of Kentucky found himself in an unenviable position when he, as a magistrate, came into evidence against one of his brethren. The rules of fellowship required that Fryar bring any accusations of bad conduct before the church, so in 1801 Fryar appeared before his church and explained that, as a court official, he had obtained a slanderous letter allegedly written by Brother Broudus. In the course of the church's inquiry, Broudus asked "to see the Letter a few minutes & suddenly Walked off with s[ai]d Letter whereon Br. Fryar followed him & Publickly forewarn'd him not to Destroy it;—but in a short space s[ai]d Broudus Return'd Again & said he had Destroyed it." Destroying court evidence not only ensured his excommunication, but it put the magistrate in a very difficult position, since the justice himself provided the prospective defendant with the opportunity to destroy the evidence as part of the religious meeting. Brother Fryar's difficult situation stemmed from the two claims on his loyalty. Church membership and local government would not necessarily—or even often—conflict, but when they did, Baptists expected the claims of fellowship to take precedence over any other.[33]

Baptists' adjudication of civil cases occurred not only in the backcountry, where there may have been a particular need for a local semi-judicial body, but also in long-settled counties with viable alternative arenas for civil disputes. Some historians have noted churches' involvement in these courtlike disputes, but have identified it as a temporary expedient of a frontier society. In 1933, William W. Sweet examined the wide diversity of discipline in churches and argued that churches acted as "moral courts" in the southern frontier. Richard Beeman's work supports this conclusion, as he briefly notes that Baptist churches in Lunenburg County in frontier Virginia acted as substitutes for or supplements to the struggling local court.[34] These studies, however, specifically focused on backcountry regions and identified these courts with the immediate needs of a new settlement. This model of a frontier phenomenon suggests that the number of civil cases would be considerably lower, or even nonexistent, in the Tidewater areas of North Carolina and Virginia. The number of civil cases in the Piedmont would decline in the 1770s and 1780s as this region became more densely settled and more closely integrated with eastern counties. Likewise, according to the frontier model, the western areas of Virginia and North Carolina should have seen a similar decline around the turn of the century. Churches in eastern counties, however, also adjudicated these cases. Far from being a temporary measure of a frontier society, this was a consistent practice of Baptist churches throughout the Upper South. In 1805, for instance, a church in Spotsylvania County, Virginia, investigated a charge about fraudulent practices in a horse trade. Another church in Stafford County, Virginia, considered a charge in 1803 that a brother had improperly surveyed a parcel of land. In 1805, a church in Chowan County, North Carolina, considered a woman's charge that a man had sold some household furniture that he had agreed to sell to her. Each of these cases, like many others, took place in a long-settled county in which a county court and a local elite offered the more traditional options for dispute resolution.[35]

Dispositions of cases of debt, trade, and property, unlike the more common types of church discipline, did not necessarily attempt to determine moral and immoral behavior but instead focused on mediating a fair settlement between two or more conflicting parties. A Kentucky church attempted to arrange such a settlement in a land dispute between some neighbors. The congregation chose a committee of men to "fix the lines and corners" of four men's property "upon a scale of equaty and Justice which is to be a final decision to the business." Though they ultimately succeeded in settling the matter, resolution did not come easily. The church needed six months of committees, surveys, and haggling before a settlement could be reached. In one particularly heated Kentucky case, three men, all members of the Baptist church, accused and counter-accused each other of trying to increase their land at the others' expense. Brother McDaniel accused Brother Cole of "making unrighteous land marks on brother John Graves land," while Cole had accused McDaniel's sons of destroying corner trees that marked the boundaries of their properties. Someone may have appealed to the religious ties among the men, because Cole also declared that he had no more fellowship with McDaniel than he had with the devil himself. The church ultimately settled the matter: one brother assisted in verifying the boundaries, and the church reproved Cole for his nasty declaration. In this case, and others like it, the church did not simply act as a moral authority, delineating good and bad behavior, but also acted as a civil arbitrator, hearing and examining evidence and arranging a settlement among conflicting parties.[36]

Altercations over broken contracts required a similar kind of mediation by Baptist churches. A 1792 case in Buck Marsh Church, for instance, centered on a contract dispute between Brother Alexander Smith and Brother Shepherd. The two men had agreed to purchase a mill seat together, but Shepherd backed out of the partnership and got a title in his own name. The church decreed: "B.^{r} Shepherd is not Justifiable in destroying the Joint agreement and Taking a right in his own name, & Leaving B^r Smith out[,] and that B^r Smith has a right to hold his Title agreeable to the Joint agreement first Enter'd

Into." The two men apparently agreed to abide by the church's decision since the churchbook records no additional discussion on the matter, and any effort to bring the case to the court would have resulted in further discipline.[37]

As white men of some means, Shepherd and Smith could easily have taken their dispute to the county court. The same is not true of the slaves who shared their churches. Denied the status of a civil being—an individual with rights under the law—slaves were unable to call on the state to mediate disputes between them. They could, however, if they were members, turn to the Baptist church just as their white counterparts did. In August 1799, two slaves, George and Ben, brought their business dispute to Buck Marsh Church, though their altercation concerned considerably less money than the one between their Baptist brethren Shepherd and Smith. Ben had requested that George purchase some seed potatoes for him and gave him a small sum of money to make the purchase. When George returned with the potatoes, Ben refused to accept them and demanded his money back. The two men came to a settlement and shook hands on it in the presence of some other men, an agreement which Ben subsequently denied, calling George a rogue and a cheat. The church again mediated the dispute, and the two men eventually reached a settlement.[38]

The opportunity to bring charges to a church could be particularly valuable for enslaved African Americans who had no redress to the civil court system for any wrongs they suffered. For slaves and free blacks, evangelical churches filled this need and provided opportunities for African Americans to bring charges, give testimony, and have their disputes adjudicated. In one such case, a slave named Arch brought a charge to his Baptist church that "Yellow Daniel" had not paid him a just debt and in addition had falsified his work and had gone into a rage. The church proceeded to investigate the accusation, sending a white male member to ask Daniel to appear before the church, and when Daniel failed to do so, sending five men to meet with him and mediate the conflict. When the committee met with Daniel and all agreed to a settlement of $2.25, the matter was dismissed. Within four months, Arch received at least a measure of the redress he was seeking.[39]

Access to a judicial arena was one part of African Americans' participation in this quasi-governmental body. They consistently participated in this institution which, for its members, controlled marriage, dictated behavioral standards, and mediated disputes over money, land, and property in much the same way as local governments did. Specifically, they participated in forming church covenants, establishing church rules, and disciplining members; in civil terms, then, they signed constitutions, voted on laws, and sat on juries. In essence, they found a form of citizenship that was denied to them in the new nation.

Citizenship, whether in the nation or in the church, however, did not mean equality. Baptist churches were not at any time idyllic republican communities. They had hierarchies and internal contradictions between belief and practice. But in this, too, they resembled the nascent republic. Citizenship in the nation, as in these churches, did not guarantee equal rights or status. Civil citizenship in late eighteenth-century America was a very ambiguous category. The dramatic political transformations—from a colonial system to a confederated union and then to a federated republic—yielded a great deal of debate about citizenship and ultimately privileged some groups of people over others in their access to the political powers of government.[40] In the Upper South, where county governments served as the immediate agent of the state, county courts became the arenas in which people sought, and some secured, the right to the protection and assistance of government. Many white men, for instance, commonly used the courts to settle their disputes, secure their debts, and protect their property. Slaves, in contrast, could do none of these things, nor could they give testimony in civil courts, except to testify against other slaves.[41] Ecclesiastical citizenship in Baptist churches also privileged some members over others. White men, for example, had privileges and access to power that were denied to both white women and blacks.

Nonetheless, this ecclesiastical citizenship was meaningful. It was an inclusive category that encompassed all Baptists regardless of race, sex, or status. It provided all members with some opportunities to define disorder, claim the right of redress, and prosecute offenses, opportunities which many Baptists lacked in the civil sphere. In Baptist "courts," white women, slaves, and free blacks could be more than defendants; they could be, and were, plaintiffs, witnesses, and even jurors, roles which offered them new opportunities to define law and order in their communities. Ultimately, this ecclesiastical citizenship and the civil functions of Baptist churches demonstrate that authority in the Upper South was not exclusively located in civil bodies. Instead, churches worked concurrently with local governments, defining and enforcing standards of order and disorder.

The chance to bring charges and testify provided an added protection for Baptist members if and when civil authorities failed to offer them redress. Churches, for instance, judged a variety of assault cases, some of which would rarely have been heard in a civil court. While the vast majority of assault cases occurred between white men, churches also prosecuted violence against white women, usually committed by their husbands, and violence against slaves, usually committed by their owners. The opportunity to prosecute civil matters that secular courts rarely considered may have been a very appealing prospect to battered wives. Wife beating was to some degree legal in the late eighteenth- and early nineteenth-century Upper South; "moderate chastisement" was not considered extraordinary and fell within the purview of a husband as the head of a household. Wife battery usually precipitated legal proceedings only if it exceeded this vague standard, and thus it appears in the court records only sporadically. Baptist churches, in contrast, did not need to be concerned with legal standards and could consider charges of spousal abuse more easily. Jefferson County, Tennessee, provides an interesting case in point. Two Baptist churches whose records survive indicate three cases of wife beating before 1815, while the court records have none.[42]

While some white women could potentially have sought the protection of the county court, Brother Charles's wife, a slave, certainly could not have. The Baptist churches' consideration of assaults against slaves—whether from spouses, other slaves, or owners—was another way that "citizenship" in these churches benefited their members who were denied citizenship in the civil state. Churches heard cases of assault involving blacks in much the same way that they heard assault cases involving whites. The majority of these concerned men fighting or assaulting other men. A Kentucky church, for example, censured "Moses the property of Mr Chinaults for striking his fellow servant" and also Neal's Reuben for offering to fight some fellow slaves. Some of these assault cases concerned spousal abuse within free black or slave families. For instance, Brother Gabriel was "charged with abuseing a sister and striking his wife" and was suspended by his church until "he [saw] the evil of his conduct." In these cases, church discipline offered protection to black women, a group particularly vulnerable to violence. As we will see, churches also considered cases of violence by whites against blacks. A number of churches declared their belief that members should not physically punish their Baptist slaves before attempting a reconciliation through the gospel steps. And some churches heard charges of white members assaulting slaves. Meherrin Church in Virginia agreed that it was unlawful "for a Bro^r or a Sister to whip or beat one of their servants or children" if members had not taken gospel dealings; they then suspended a member for abusing one of his slaves. As in this case, churches at times attempted to prevent extreme forms of violence against slaves, whether they were members or not.[43]

While these assault cases demonstrate some of the benefits of citizenship in this institution in its role as a civil body, assault cases also reveal the limits of this citizenship and the hierarchy that differentiated members. These cases reveal that even with this access to and involvement in this quasi-civil body, white women and African Americans were not full and equal members. In spousal abuse cases, for instance, it was not uncommon for the husband and wife to be jointly called before the church, he for abusing his wife and she for misconduct to her husband. A Tennessee woman faced this situation when her church investigated a charge against her and her husband: "the said [Brother] Roberts is excluded for abuseing his wife and his wife for her disobedience to her husband."[44]

Slaves proved to have even fewer rights. Brother Duke, a white member, was called before his church for whipping a black sister, Short's Agness. At the following meeting, the church debated "whither any case could arise that would justify a member of this church to correct or chastise a servant or person under their authority which is a member of said church without dealing with them in the church in gospel order." Unlike Meherrin Church's declaration against such physical punishment, this church agreed, "there might such a case or cases arise which they would be justifiable." Following this decision, the church ceased to refer to a whipping, but "acquited" Brother Duke for "correcting" Agness. The church then called on Agness to answer for her conduct to Duke.[45] The scriptural admonition for gospel dealings, which proved so central for ordering relations within the church, did not necessarily apply to slaves.

Although slaves were allowed to bring charges against whites and to testify against them, it is clear that slaves rarely did so, and when they did, their testimony did not carry the same weight. Thus, charges against whites for mistreating slaves were rare and often dismissed. Nancy, a slave woman in Kentucky, tried to bring charges against a white couple. She complained of brutal treatment at the hands of Brother Stephens and his wife, accusing them of whipping her, keeping her in irons, and denying her food and water. These accusations were corroborated by a white man who had previously brought charges to the church that the Stephenses abused Nancy, kept her in irons, and refused to allow her to see her child. The Stephenses were acquitted on all charges. Nancy, however, was not so fortunate. She was excluded from the church for slandering the Stephenses.[46] In some of the cases brought before Baptist churches, the women who were battered by their husbands and the slaves who complained of mistreatment were punished by the churches as harshly, or even more harshly, than those charged with the assaults.

Why, then, would citizenship in this body have mattered to those who were not always well served, as it so dramatically failed people like Agness and Nancy? Certainly, Nancy could not even have brought these charges to a court and could not have testified against any white person. While her testimony was decreed slanderous, she had an unusual opportunity to speak against the white couple who abused her and to be heard by a public gathering, and she did gain the support of at least one white congregant. Despite the considerable limitations of ecclesiastical citizenship, slaves and white women ultimately did have the opportunity for redress in an accessible semi-judicial body and the right to bring charges, give testimony, and, at least at times, vote.

Indeed, the existence of these semi-judicial proceedings and the rights of citizenship in these churches may in part explain the decreasing proportion of white men in Baptist churches by the early nineteenth century. The number of white women and both black men and black women in Baptist congregations increased considerably in the last decades of the eighteenth century, while the number of white men increased at a considerably slower rate.[47] As access to civil courts became easier, access to a semi-judicial body may have had less importance to white men. White men, after all, had more stable and more powerful civil identities as citizens, merchants, creditors, and officials. Thus, the competing claims of civil and religious communities would prove the most difficult for white men to navigate, requiring a difficult, and sometimes costly, negotiation. In fact, churches' semi-judicial work may have been increasingly unwanted, because this "court," for all of its hierarchies and acceptance of social rankings and norms, still offered a unique, if limited, form of citizenship to white women and African Americans—whether slave or free, male or female. Women could publicly charge their husbands with spousal abuse. Slaves could sue and give testimony. As citizenship in the republic was being defined quite narrowly, Baptist churches offered a religious alternative in which a wide array of members participated in the formation and maintenance of civil as well as church order.

5

Unusual Strugglings of Mind

In 1802, Thomas Jefferson wrote his famous letter to the Danbury Baptists in Connecticut, thanking them for their good wishes upon his inauguration. The Danbury Baptists, like other well-wishers throughout the country, had sent Jefferson an address congratulating him on his election, and they expressed their hope that, as Jefferson's influence shone "like the radiant beams of the Sun," the principles of religious liberty would be upheld in their own state. The exchange seemed ordinary enough: after his election, Jefferson received many notes of congratulations and had read many addresses by churches on the topic of religious liberty since he had championed that cause in Virginia dating back to the 1770s. (Indeed, this note of congratulations was a good deal more mundane than the 1,200-pound cheese that another Baptist community felt best expressed their affection for the new president.) Yet this simple correspondence produced one of the most important documents on church-state relations, a letter that would, in its day, expose the great cleavage between Jefferson and his faithful Baptist supporters and, in the days to come, bedevil scholars and jurists. In his letter of thanks, Thomas Jefferson praised the wisdom of the First Amendment in far-reaching terms: "I contemplate with sovereign reverence that act of the whole American people which declared that *their* legislature should 'make no law respecting an establishment of religion, or prohibiting the free exercise thereof,' thus building a wall of separation between Church & State."[1]

This was different language than could be found in the Constitution. The actual words of the First Amendment limited *only* the actions of the government, and indeed how could it do otherwise? How could a statement prohibiting government's interference in religious matters also dictate church activities? Yet, as Jefferson explained to the Danbury Baptists, he envisioned a wall, a barrier that functioned to limit exchange on both sides. Government ought and must stay out of religion; so too, a wall implied, should churches stay out of the realm of government. While Jefferson suggested, with his use of the word "thus," that this two-way barrier was a natural conclusion, scholars and jurists have long debated whether this statement explains the intent and meaning of the First Amendment or whether it misrepresents it. This chapter will not take up this long-debated (and often partisan) issue.[2] Instead, it seeks to restore one missing part of the dialogue implied in this letter; it will explore how Baptists (specifically, the Baptists whom Jefferson knew best: those in Virginia) understood the legal and material relationship between the political and religious realms. Baptists did indeed want government to remove itself from religious and church matters and actively supported Jefferson's efforts; they did not, however, entirely support the reverse. They insisted that religious identity mediate believers' relationship to the political culture and embraced an expansive church authority to monitor their members' participation in the political realm. Baptist churches leveled the same intense scrutiny of members' political behavior (though not, significantly, their voting choices) that they did of other aspects of their members' lives, and here churches' authority directly clashed with the principle of a strict separation between church and state. In short, the early decades of the new republic had made clear that, in matters of church and state, Jefferson and his Baptist supporters were dramatically at odds.

This was not apparent in early political debates about church and state in the Upper South. The Baptists consistently had allied with political leaders such as Jefferson and James Madison, becoming among the most vocal and determined supporters of disestablishment efforts, at times following and at other times leading efforts to limit government's authority over religious belief and practice. Responding to the disruption of their meetings and the imprisonment of their preachers in the late 1760s and early 1770s, Baptists led the agitation against Virginia's laws governing dissenters, mobilizing to challenge legal restrictions on the exercise of their faith. Responding to this public pressure and wartime exigencies, Virginia authorities debated and rethought the place of government in religious matters. Ultimately, they chose to dismantle the colonial church establishment during the revolutionary era, eliminating not just favoritism for a particular church, but state support for religion and religious bodies of any kind. The extended public debate not only fundamentally restructured the local relationships of government and religion but also left its mark on the nation as a whole as the participation of such leaders as Jefferson and Madison elevated the Virginia struggle from a local affair to a precursor to the national debate over religion's role in government and government's role in religion.[3] Throughout, Baptists schooled themselves in the practices of partisan politics, building and mobilizing a constituency and constructing an institutional structure that generated political pressure despite their limited numbers.

At the same time that Baptists sought to expel government presence in the workings of God, Baptist churches sought to extend religious authority into what was the largely secular arena of politics. The political culture *was* a religious issue insofar as their members were concerned. While reluctant to construct a permanent political identity as a religious society, the Baptists found that the search for the appropriate boundaries between the sacred and the worldly led them into intense reflection on a diverse array of issues about their place in the emerging political culture of the new republic. As part of the larger effort to assert churches' authority over the domestic and financial aspects of their members' lives, Baptists also sought to supervise aspects of members' political activities, insisting that religious affiliation serve as a touchstone in defining relations between their members and the new nation and political culture.

To understand the distinct course that Baptists took in regard to religion and politics in the early national era, it is necessary to trace their early involvement in these issues and revisit the years preceding the Revolution. Thus, the first part of this chapter focuses on the debates over church and state in Virginia. In North Carolina, disestablishment occurred relatively quickly and with much less public debate. In part because the establishment of the Church of England was so weak and dissenters so numerous, lawmakers were able to disestablish the church in the new 1776 constitution. In Virginia, however, the process of disestablishment involved a complicated negotiation among different civil and sectarian factions that carried on for years and ultimately resulted in a far-reaching statement for religious liberty. The chapter then turns to Baptists' involvement in political debates and political culture in the early republic.

When the Virginia Baptists began a campaign to secure more legal rights, there was little indication that they stood on the brink of a massive reconstruction of the relationship between government and churches. When their meetings were being harassed and their ministers imprisoned in the 1760s and early 1770s, the Baptists began a political campaign to challenge the application of Virginia's laws governing dissenters and legal restrictions on the exercise of their faith. Their most common and most effective weapon was the petition, which not only conveyed their requests to the government but had the added benefit of mobilizing supporters into political action, if only by prompting a signature or mark on a petition. The congregational structure of Baptist churches—which made each church an autonomous body not subject to any hierarchy—potentially could have hindered political mobilization by impeding centralization and diffusing authority. Baptist leaders, though, used church networks and created new organizations to energize their expanding, but still numerically small, constituencies. Baptists were quickly able to organize effective campaigns to circulate petitions addressed to the House of Burgesses requesting the redress of grievances, petitions which might reflect the views of a small group (for instance, the Baptist church at Occaquan) or an immense one (the 10,000-name petition).

Most of the Baptist petitions submitted before the war did not question the establishment of the Church of England nor the involvement of colonial government in church matters, but asked only that the rights of dissenters be extended to their sect. They relied on the language of religious *toleration* rather than religious *liberty* and were usually piecemeal requests for specific rights that did not require a reformulation of church-state relations. These petitions accepted the idea that government could regulate religious practices and that toleration was, as North Carolina governor William Tyron suggested, "his Majestys Indulgence," a gift graciously extended by civil authorities rather than a fundamental or natural right.[4] Early petitions from 1770, for instance, requested only that Baptist ministers be exempted from militia duties like other clergy and that they not be confined to preaching in specific, authorized places. In limiting themselves to asking only for the rights of dissenters, the Baptists resembled other dissenting groups, such as the Society of Friends, the Mennonites, or the Presbyterians of a generation earlier, each of which waged campaigns for dissenters' rights.[5]

As the imprisonments and violence intensified in the early 1770s, more and more Baptists recognized the political meanings of religious belief and affiliation, and the numbers of petitions increased. Baptists from Lunenburg, Mecklenburg, and Sussex counties (all locations where ministers had been imprisoned) circulated and submitted petitions requesting that the Baptists receive the rights and protections granted to other dissenting sects under the English Toleration Act. One 1772 petition from Lunenburg County argued that the Baptists were "restricted in the Exercise of their Religion, their Teachers imprisoned under various Pretenses, and the Benefits of the Toleration Act denied them," and it asked that the Baptists receive the rights granted by that act and "be treated with the same kind Indulgence in religious Matters as Quakers, Presbyterians and other Protestant Dissenters, enjoy."[6] This sentiment was echoed (and even restated word for word) by Baptists in other counties. Another Baptist petition struggled to convey the difficult bind in which they found themselves:

> [I]f the Act of Toleration does not extend to this Colony [then] they are exposed to severe Persecution; and, if it does extend hither, and the Power of granting Licenses to Teachers be lodged, as is supposed, in the General Court alone, the Petitioners must suffer considerable Inconveniences, not only because that Court sits not oftener than twice in the Year, and then in a Place far remote, but because the said Court will admit a single Meeting-House and no more in one county.[7]

Just as Baptists campaigned for greater clarity of the rights of dissenters, the church establishment experienced a series of blows that destabilized the very idea of a government-supported church. The onset of the war and the turmoil of revolution provided an additional incentive to rethink the legal and political relationship between religion and the state when revolutionary rhetoric and wartime exigencies combined to weaken substantially the existing church establishment. This volatile context greatly intensified agitation by dissenters and enabled the Baptists to transform their campaign into a more radical one. The Baptist sect recognized the opportunity at hand and was ready to abandon old requests and embark on a bolder, more radical campaign to challenge the establishment itself, a crusade that required coalitions with other dissenting sects and even some unlikely allies.

A powerful assault on Virginia's church establishment came from the pervasive rhetoric of rights and liberty that emerged out of the imperial crisis. Frequent proclamations heralding individual rights and the centrality of personal liberty for a healthy body politic, as well as a constant dialogue about unjust taxes, put a spotlight on the church establishment. Here, it was not a distant imperial power that denied to colonists the same rights that were extended to (dissenting) Englishmen and women, but local authorities. In Virginia, the application of revolutionary rhetoric to the legal status of religion proved particularly effective not simply because of the active participation of dissenting sects such as the Baptists, but also because Virginia was home to political leaders who themselves insisted that liberty of conscience be included in the revolutionary agenda. Patrick Henry was a vocal supporter of dissenters' right to worship according to their conscience without interference from civil authorities, though he ardently supported the idea that government could and ought to support religion and religious institutions. Thomas Jefferson embraced a far more radical vision of religious liberty that included not only the freedom to worship according to one's conscience but also the right not to participate in or support any religious sect. James Madison, one of the younger members of the revolutionary contingent from Virginia, likewise emerged in the 1780s as a significant voice for liberty of conscience unfettered by government interference. The presence of such men as Henry, Jefferson, and Madison in the Virginia leadership ensured that religious liberty was in the forefront of the independent state's politics and that Virginia would be a site of lively debate.[8]

In addition to the ongoing discussions of religious liberty, there were quite material assaults on the Anglican establishment. The commencement of war dramatically destabilized Virginia's Church of England. With its obvious connection to the now proclaimed enemy of colonial liberty, the church had great difficulty distancing itself from the British cause, despite the fact that historians have found that there were twice as many patriot as loyalist ministers in Virginia. Much of the popular mistrust centered on the clergy, who were viewed with suspicion by some colonists. In the two decades prior to the war, there had been a rising tide of anticlericalism within the church, stemming in part from the prominent disputes over salaries in the 1750s and 1760s, known as the Parson's Cause, and heightened in the 1770s by some ill-timed proposals to establish an American bishop, raising the specter of English hierarchy and control. Even the Virginia clergy's apparent disinterest in the plans for an American bishop did not stem the tide of opposition. With critics complaining that the clergy were greedy, materialistic, and deceitful, it was not hard to associate them with disloyalty to the American cause. After all, Anglican ministers had taken an oath to support the Crown, and during the war many continued to read the services in their unaltered form, which included a prayer for the king and royal family. There were also a number of vocal Tories in their ranks whose political views became very public; some became a lightning rod for local conflict, so much so that some ministers were forced out of their positions by Whig threats. Moreover, the disruption of war precipitated a crisis in the number of Anglican ministers in the Upper South: Virginia lost 34 percent of its ministers due to death or exile, and North Carolina lost 29 percent. Since ordination required a trip to London, no more could be ordained during the war. Some ministers found the conflict between their religious duties and the demands of Whig allegiance (whether from their own conscience or outside pressure) so difficult to negotiate that they discontinued public worship. As the number of ministers was already insufficient for the number of parishes (profoundly so for North Carolina), the reduction of ministers meant that the churches carried on haltingly, substituting lay readers when possible. The Church of England then struggled to maintain even the semblance of an effective institution that served the whole colony and warranted its tax support and other state-sponsored privileges.[9]

The combination of the petition campaign and the growing difficulties of the Anglican Church forced the revolutionary government to rethink its relationship to the Church of England as well as the laws governing dissenting sects. In May 1776, a remarkable assemblage of Virginia statesmen, including George Mason, Patrick Henry, James Madison, Richard Henry Lee, and Edmund Randolph, met in Williamsburg to perform the work of transforming Virginia from an English colony to an American state. With the war under way in New England, the convention began the process of creating an independent civil body. On May 15, it authorized Virginia's delegates to the Continental Congress to propose that the colonies declare themselves independent of Great Britain. It then initiated the work of constructing and legitimizing a state government, creating a committee to draft a Declaration of Rights and a state constitution. To be sure, the delegates brought with them a weighty inheritance of colonial laws, traditions, and beliefs, but on paper they had a clean slate and the opportunity to construct, dismantle, or remake the structures of government as they saw fit. And, given the rising surge of public debate, the status of the church establishment and the laws governing religious practice could not escape their scrutiny.

The language of the Declaration of Rights that emerged out of the Virginia Convention in 1776 indicated a dramatic change was at hand. An early draft of the Declaration of Rights addressed the relationship between government and religion in the eighteenth article, which declared that "all men should enjoy the fullest toleration in the exercise of religion." While this seemed to fulfill the requests of early Baptist petitions, the article also included a significant exception: religious practice should be "unrestrained by the magistrate, *unless*, under colour of religion, any man disturb the peace, the happiness, or safety of society."[10] This type of broad exception to the "fullest toleration" left open the possibility of continued restrictions for dissenting sects. Indeed, disturbing the peace was a common charge that Virginia authorities leveled against Baptists. And their most fundamental practices exposed them to such charges: since their meetings swelled to hundreds and even thousands and their baptisms in local rivers continued to attract boisterous spectators, Baptists might well have been among the most vulnerable to having their worship subject to civil scrutiny. Knowing this, it is unlikely that they would be appeased by the proposed article.

James Madison, however, proposed an amendment to the article that profoundly altered the language of church-state relations. Abandoning the concept of toleration, Madison proposed liberty of conscience and freedom of worship, without limitation. His original proposal also stated that "no man or class of men ought on account of religion to be invested with peculiar emoluments or privileges." Not surprisingly, some members of the convention heard this as an attack on the church establishment, in particular, as a challenge to such long-held privileges as parish taxes and lands. Eventually, Madison had to eliminate any references to religious privileges and make no mention of the state's establishment of the church, and the final amendment read, "all Men are equally intitled to the free exercise of Religion according to the Dictates of Conscience," language that asserted the rights of dissenters without challenging the privileges of the Anglican-Episcopal Church. When the Virginia Convention issued the Declaration of Rights with the amended article, it was the strongest declaration of religious liberty yet issued from the Virginia government and a stark contrast to the government policies of the preceding fifteen years.[11]

Ultimately, however, Virginia's Declaration of Rights was simply that: a declaration. It was not a law, and it did not disestablish the Anglican Church. The only blow that it delivered to the establishment was a rhetorical one. The Virginia Convention (as a body) did not intend to attack the establishment of the Church of England or the church's legal privileges and, in fact, deliberately backed away from such an implication by eliminating any references to religious privileges. While it was a bold statement of religious liberty, the declaration was not followed by bold action in the legislature. In the first session of the legislature, lawmakers affirmed that all lands currently in the hands of the Anglican Church would remain so, and, at the same time, they suspended taxes for ministers' salaries until the next year's legislative session.[12] But this was a temporary measure that gave something to both the establishment and the dissenters and pleased neither. The Anglicans had no voluntary system in place to fill the financial vacuum left by the suspension of parish taxes. And by now, dissenters wanted more than temporary offerings. Significantly, by suspending ministerial taxes only for a limited time, confirming Anglican land titles, and continuing to legislate for the church, the new government signaled that the establishment would continue intact, if battered.

The startling announcement of a new religious policy, coupled with Virginia authorities' evident hesitation to implement it, encouraged Baptists, other dissenters, and Anglicans to try to influence the new religious order. The half step embodied in the Declaration of Rights and the absence of a clear legislative policy were enough to inspire both grand expectations and great fears. In the debates that followed, there was no shortage of proposals and few limits on hyperbole. In the remaining months of 1776, the Virginia Convention received petitions from the Baptists, the General Convention of Methodists, the German Lutheran congregation of Culpeper, Anglican clergy, the Presbytery of Hanover, Augusta's "County Committee," and several groups of "dissenters." The debate that emerged in the press in the following years was just as impressive, and what it lacked in numbers it made up for in showmanship; the papers offered commentary by such partisans as "A Preacher of the Gospel," "A Plain Dealer," and "Philoepiscopus." As raucous debates erupted in newspapers, taverns, and the new state legislature's committee for religion, Baptists were among the many sectarians who stepped forward to lobby for a solution.

The Baptists placed themselves at the forefront of these debates and called for the most radical of plans: leaving behind their requests for toleration, they now called for the government to remove itself from the religious arena. This required the elimination of the church establishment in favor of freedom of conscience. They argued that government oversight or interference corrupted the true gospel church, and they therefore rejected any legal regulations concerning their religious practice. Certainly, the imprisonments and other persecutions that had occurred in the name of the established church nurtured Baptists' beliefs about the deleterious effects of government interference in God's holy work. Recognizing the opportunity that came with the onset of war and emboldened by the Declaration, Baptists and other dissenters sought, first, to gain freedom from restrictions and, second, to eliminate the privileges given to the Anglican Church. In June 1776, the Baptist church of Occaquon submitted a petition requesting its members be relieved of the obligation to support Anglican ministers.[13] Other individuals who identified themselves simply as "Dissenters" sent petitions requesting religious equality and the elimination of the establishment. In one remarkable petition that was circulated by Baptists and gained 10,000 signatures, dissenters explained that their hopes had "been raised and confirmed by the Declaration ... with regard to equal Liberty." But, the petitioners declared, they had been denied liberty because they had been forced to pay taxes for the support of the establishment. They urged that "this as well as every other Yoke may be broken and that the Oppressed may go free."[14] Through these broader complaints, Baptists sought to highlight the fundamental problem of a church establishment and to strike a blow at the financial pillars of the Church of England.

These were audacious requests from a sect that in 1776 claimed only a small fraction of the population as members and that only three years previous had had difficulty keeping its ministers out of the local jails. But, of course, the Baptists believed that they had the cause of God on their side. God's holy work, they believed, must be free of earthly limits. This was a divine imperative, not a political maneuver. But, quite pragmatically, they discovered that they had new political leverage at the outbreak of the war and had no reservations about using it in their dealings with the government. They found that the revolutionary government needed them and that they could link the fulfillment of their religious demands to their political support. In their early petitions to the Virginia legislature, Baptists prudently identified themselves with the revolutionary cause, expressing their sympathy for the Whig position and their support for the war effort. One petition acknowledged that "however distinguished from the body of their countrymen, by appellatives and sentiments of a religious nature, they nevertheless consider themselves as members of the same community in respect to matters of a civil nature." They also allied themselves with the military efforts, agreeing that military resistance was necessary due to England's "unjust invasion, tyrannical oppressions, and repeated hostilities," and churches passed declarations specifically allowing members to take up arms. Another petition from 1776 asserted that because the colony "now contended for civil rights and liberties of mankind against the enslaving schemes of a powerful Enemy[,] [w]e [are] convinced, that the strictest unanimity among ourselves is very necessary." That said, unanimity did not come cheap: they requested that the convention remove some of the restrictions on Baptist worship and hinted that their full support of the patriot cause would be withheld until their demands were met, concluding, "[t]*hese things being granted* we will ... to the utmost of our ability promote the common cause of Freedom."[15]

In offering their full (albeit conditional) support of the patriot cause—including military service—Baptists were able to differentiate themselves from some of the other dissenting sects that occupied the margins of civil society in Virginia and North Carolina. The Mennonites and Quakers were pacifist sects that had long been conspicuous in their absence from militia duty and musters. Their refusal to participate in these rituals of the civil community, as well as other distinguishing characteristics such as speech and dress, positioned them as outsiders (a status Baptists had shared because of their unusual beliefs and practices). If Virginia and North Carolina had learned how to live with these pacifist sects during peacetime, war brought renewed scrutiny and frustration. When fighting broke out, pressure mounted for these sects to stand with the patriot population and to take up arms during the crisis. Neutrality in wartime Virginia was easily interpreted as Toryism and a threat to the American cause, and individuals who refused to bear arms, pay substitutes, or take loyalty oaths became targets for anger and, at times, abuse. Like the Quakers and Mennonites, the Baptists willfully used speech and dress to mark themselves off from the rest of the civil community, believing that they must remain separate from worldly fashions and customs. However, the Baptists' public announcements of their full support for the revolutionary position, including military service, allowed the Baptists to create a different and potentially more influential civic identity that could provide added weight to their petitions.

It was clear to the Baptists and other partisans that there was a real opportunity to influence significant questions about the new state's relationship to religion and church bodies since so many of them remained unanswered. The Declaration of Rights had laid out the principles of the revolutionary government but offered no plan for transforming the English church establishment for the postcolonial context. The war, the declining number of Anglican ministers, the vision of liberty of conscience presented in the Declaration of Rights, and the active petition campaign had all dealt serious blows to Virginia's colonial religious system, but what would replace that system remained unclear. And the new government had yet to face such questions as: what would become of the Anglican Church? Would the state continue to support religion (financially or otherwise)? If so, would the assistance be offered to all churches or all churches of a particular belief system (Christianity? the Trinity?) or a specific church exclusively? These questions were at the heart of the debates about religion between 1775 and 1786 and suggest the complex dilemmas concerning the appropriate relationship between government and religion after the disruption of the colonial arrangement.

With no clear grand plan, but plenty of vocal and adamant participants, Virginia struggled to find an answer. Dominated by zealous Anglicans (with the notable exception of deist-leaning Thomas Jefferson), the committee for religion faced the difficult task of balancing the onslaught of dissenters' petitions with the proposals of the vocal and prominent supporters of the establishment. In what would set the tone for future debates over the establishment and the legal position of religion, the discussions in the committee were rancorous, prompting Jefferson's observation that they were "the severest contests in which I have ever been engaged." The decisions of the new state's legislature raised as many questions as it answered. When the legislature voted in 1776, it agreed to exempt dissenters from taxes to support the established church, and since this placed a sudden and heavy burden on Anglican Church members during this already difficult time, the legislature suspended taxes for the church indefinitely.[16] In perhaps the most portentous section of the act of 1776, the lawmakers raised the question of a general assessment of taxes for Virginia churches, suggesting it as a possible topic for future debate. In a general assessment, taxes could be raised to aid churches, with money being distributed proportionately according to membership, a plan that would ensure ongoing financial support for the Anglican-Episcopal Church and, legislators hoped, would silence the complaints of most of the dissenters. The assembly also resolved in the first legislative session: "although the maintaining [of] any opinions in matters of religion ought not to be restrained, yet that publick assemblies of societies for divine worship ought to be regulated, and that proper provision should be made for continuing the succession of the clergy, and superintending their conduct." With language that harked back to the colonial government's explanation of its policies toward dissenters, the new government disclaimed any desire to legislate belief but left itself the opportunity to "regulate" churches and clergy and to fund certain churches: even after the passage of the Declaration of Rights, lawmakers in Virginia still perceived church activities, and religion more broadly, to be the business of government.[17]

In the sessions that followed, even while addressing the pressing needs of the war, the legislature continued to make time to address religious matters, with the different churches acting as constituencies and lobbyists. The assembly and the populace still debated a host of possible options though now with concrete proposals under review. At one end of the spectrum were those who supported the restoration of a religious establishment and restrictions on dissenters. At the other end were those who supported broad-based religious freedom. For the latter group, hopes were briefly raised in 1779 when the legislature considered a bill by Thomas Jefferson for liberty of conscience, though it was soon tabled. Between these two extreme positions were those who sought a general assessment that would provide tax assistance to all Christian churches, a proposal that became the catalyst for the Baptists' major legislative campaign. Moderate enough to be dangerous to their agenda, the assessment had the support of Patrick Henry and many Methodists and Presbyterians who had previously allied with the Baptists. Madison hoped to arouse opposition to the assessment and submitted the proposed act to the public. His tactic was successful, and those opposed to an assessment, including the Baptists, mobilized. They worked to organize their legislative efforts and created a General Committee, a representative body made up of delegates from regional associations, to speak on behalf of Virginia Baptists on church-state issues. This was a significant departure from their strictly congregational values, which eschewed hierarchal structures, but proponents hoped that the committee could act as the "political mouth" of the local churches. As Madison's tactic also aroused those who favored a general tax, petitions poured in from both sides. Rhys Isaac calculated that the anti-assessment forces submitted over eighty petitions with 11,000 names, and the pro-assessment forces mustered eleven petitions with 1,000 names. With this decisive rejection of state-supported religion, the legislature agreed to reconsider Jefferson's act. With Madison's support and political skill, the Bill for Establishing Religious Freedom was made into law in January 1786, radically altering the relationship between government and religion. The law attacked the principles of religious establishment and a general assessment and disallowed government's authority to enforce, regulate, or restrain religious belief or practice.[18]

With a successful political effort behind them and an institutional structure to sustain political activity, Baptists continued to mobilize as a political constituency in the postwar era to press for the elimination of the vestiges of state-supported religion. This goal prompted Baptists to persist in their lobbying efforts when other sects were content to withdraw. In particular, they remained disturbed by the privileges granted to the Anglican-Episcopal Church, specifically its retention of the glebe property, and after the passage of Jefferson's bill, Baptists shifted their attention to eliminating Episcopal rights to this property. These assets had not been ignored in the previous debates but had been the point of compromise repeatedly granted to the church as it faced the erosion of its other privileges. Virginia's Declaration of Rights in 1776 represented just such a compromise when it affirmed freedom of conscience and suspended religious taxation, yet at the same time confirmed the Episcopal Church's rights to its glebe lands. But the issue faded from public view in the 1780s, and most sects were willing to leave the issue be. The Baptists, however, pushed for a reevaluation of the issue of glebe lands, again circulating petitions though they received little encouragement in either civil or religious arenas. Attempting to broaden support for their efforts, in 1790 they appealed to the Methodists and Presbyterians to make a public declaration against the Episcopal property grants, a position that the ruling bodies of these sects refused to take.

Associations also took pains to keep their own members focused on this campaign and mobilized. In 1790, the United Baptist Association, which claimed a membership of fifty-five churches, asked its members to petition the General Assembly for the sale of the glebes to keep pressure on the issue. In 1793, the Virginia Portsmouth Baptist Association sought to clarify and confirm its position when it asked: "Are the People formerly called Dissenters, yet oppressed by any State Law?" And it answered, *"Yes. Namely; By an Act of the General Assembly, that invests all Parish Property in this State, in the Hands of Trustee, for the sole Use of the Protestant Episcopal Church."* Throughout the 1790s, they tested a variety of arguments to appeal to the public and to lawmakers in a campaign that was innovative, politically savvy, and ultimately successful. By the turn of the century, Baptists had mustered sufficient popular and political support, and in 1801, the legislature passed a bill declaring that glebes could be sold when the incumbent died or resigned. As Thomas E. Buckley has argued, this campaign, while typically described as the final battle in the separation of church and state in Virginia, should be understood as the commencement of evangelical involvement in political lobbying. They had successfully developed and honed the skills necessary to have meaningful influence in the political process.[19]

Not surprisingly, Baptists' fervent beliefs in the corrupting role of government drew them into the concurrent debates on the national level. Their long involvement in questions of church and state effectively positioned them to be important participants in the national debate over the Constitution in which they again attempted to influence a settlement in accordance with their beliefs. As the states debated ratification of the Constitution, the lack of a Bill of Rights guaranteeing basic liberties under the proposed federal government loomed large in much of Virginia and North Carolina. One had been proposed at the Constitutional Convention, but most Federalists believed either that such a list of rights was unnecessary as such rights were already protected, or that it was unwise since codifying a particular list might tend to limit rights to those enumerated. Southern Baptists, however, were deeply troubled by the combination of a potentially powerful centralized authority and the absence of a specific guarantee of religious liberty. In light of Baptists' struggles with the government in Virginia (and elsewhere), Baptists throughout the region were suspicious of centralized authority and wary of plans to strengthen the federal government, and even the involvement of their former ally James Madison did not assuage their apprehensions. The General Committee of Virginia explained its concerns in a later letter to then-president George Washington: "When the constitution first made its appearance in Virginia, we, as a Society, had unusual strugglings of mind; fearing that *the liberty of conscience*, dearer to us than property and life, was not sufficiently secured." The committee explained that its misgivings grew out of the Baptists' past in Virginia "when Mobs, Bonds, Fines, and Prisons were [their] frequent attendants."[20] This collective memory—already frequently repeated and circulated—inspired many Baptists to withhold their support.

In the late 1780s, the Baptists were still numerically small, but they were an important constituency and effectively worked to influence the debate, utilizing the institutional networks and political strategies that they had developed in their disestablishment campaigns. Virginia was a very important state in the national ratification effort, and Baptist leaders knew it. Baptist ministers, including John Leland, George Eve, and Aaron Bledsoe, galvanized opponents, creating a sizable enough faction against ratification to attract notice from both sides. Antifederalists in Virginia recognized that Baptists would be useful allies in blocking ratification and appealed to them by arguing that the Constitution lacked adequate guarantees of religious liberty. Federalists too sought to gain the support of the sect and worked to surmount its concerns. Reluctant to engage in direct politicking, James Madison was repeatedly warned by other Federalists in Virginia about Baptist opposition and was encouraged to seek actively to win them over. His father warned him that Baptists in the region were "generally opposed" to the Constitution and would affect the upcoming election. He received a similar friendly warning from a Baptist and revolutionary war officer, who encouraged Madison to assuage Baptist concerns about religious liberty because if that were done, they "would become friends to [the Constitution], that body of people has become Very formi[da]ble in p[o]int of Elections."[21]

Persuaded by these arguments, Madison focused on gaining the support of the Baptist ministers who led the opposition. He sent two copies of *The Federalist* to his father in Virginia and asked him to give them to ministers Leland and Bledsoe. He also corresponded with minister George Eve to counter reports that he was opposed to a Bill of Rights and had "ceased to be a friend to the rights of Conscience." He not only won over John Leland, but inspired him to solicit supporters for Madison's election as a representative to the first federal Congress in 1789. By late 1789, Madison was able to inform George Washington that most of the opposition to the Constitution in Virginia was "entirely at rest" and used the Baptists as his example, noting that "[o]ne of the principal leaders of the Baptists lately sent me word that the amendments had entirely satisfied the disaffected of his Sect, and that it would appear in their subsequent conduct."[22]

While still a small percentage of the population, southern Baptists had found a way to participate in the political arena, primarily to articulate and lobby for their vision of a separation between government and religion. But the battle over laws and government was only part of their efforts to define church-state relations. As they well knew, the relationship between religion and government involved much more than laws and restraining government's reach. Baptists expected religion to act as a touchstone for political activity; religion (through the authority of the churches) ought to guide members' relationship to the state and to the emerging political culture. As Baptists weighed in on questions of church and state and negotiated political campaigns, they became enmeshed in debates about appropriate behavior in the early republic. In this new political era, Baptists and other Americans had to learn what it would mean for them to be "republicans." In the 1790s, the new nation was still in the process of constructing a self-consciously republican political culture. Many Americans felt there was a common understanding of what republican values were—an understanding rooted in their shared Revolution. At the same time, political events and factions were demonstrating that there was no uniform opinion of the meaning of the Revolution and republicanism. The capacious language of the new republic—such as republicanism, simplicity, and virtue—was fractured in the same moment that it united different groups of people. Artisans, elites, westerners, farmers, and merchants might all construct differing notions of republicanism—and often did. Historians have studied these different formulations of political theory, focusing on categories of class and occupation, paying little attention to the role that religious affiliation played in the formation of political identity.[23] The Baptists, however, demonstrate that religion too mediated political identity and shaped a distinct experience of citizenship. Their challenge was to reconcile being a good Baptist with being a good republican, and they used their churches and associations in seeking a middle way. With their churches claiming the right to mediate members' place within republican political culture, Baptists extended religious authority into secular arenas at the same time that government's authority was being removed from religious arenas.

Given the Baptists' general enthusiasm about the revolutionary cause and their diligent mobilization to influence disestablishment and the Constitution, it is perhaps not surprising that they remained observant of the political events of the early republic. Baptists throughout the Upper South—not just those in Virginia and its Kentucky territory—scattered references to major occurrences throughout their churchbooks and association meetings. As with many sects, Baptists observed days of prayer and fasting when requested by the president or when they feared the "threatening calamities of the nation" as did the Strawberry Association in May 1794. Concerns about international turmoil increased over the 1790s as war loomed with England and France and peaked again during the War of 1812. A few churches even debated the merits of Jay's Treaty, though they left no record of a concerted political response. Evidence suggests that many Baptists in the region were Jeffersonian Republicans, but there is no indication that they attempted to use their churches for regular partisan activity. Baptists were, nonetheless, vocally enthusiastic about the election of the beloved hero of religious liberty Thomas Jefferson, and many southern Baptist churches and associations sent warm letters of congratulations upon his election and of praise and thanks as he left office.[24]

In the new republic, Baptists directly and self-consciously questioned to what degree they should participate in civil society and what their place *as*

Baptists should be in the new nation-state. These questions took up the issue of whether faith created a distinct relationship to the state and whether it designated a specific place within the political culture. Churches and associations debated a whole host of questions about the fundamentals of citizenship in relationship to religious identity. Specifically, Baptists worried about political activities that might be in conflict with their Christian identity. Many churches during the Revolution debated whether Baptists might take up arms for the rebel cause, concluding overwhelmingly that they could. In 1785, the Elkhorn Association was asked to consider "Whether it [wa]s lawful for a Christian to bear office civil or military," answering that it was, except for ministers. Similarly, one association debated what kind of oath should be taken before a civil magistrate since some believed that the standard method of kissing the Bible was sinful. Through this discourse, Baptist congregants—not simply leaders—debated and learned their relationship to civic duties, agreeing they could vote, canvass, serve in the military, take an oath, and hold office.[25]

Baptists also worried about which elements of the political culture were inconsistent with their faith and sought to limit participation where they perceived moral dangers or intemperate excesses. The political culture of the early republic had plenty of such moral and physical spaces, as political events from elections to commemorative parades became occasions for men to combine riotous festivities and contentious debate, both heightened by the consistent presence of alcohol. How to embrace the political events without the sinful components was the question that concerned a North Carolina Baptist association in 1789. It asked, "Whether a member may carry liquor to any place of an election and offer himself as a candidate and treat the people after the election?" and agreed it was disorderly conduct that ought not be allowed; members could stand for office but not entice voters with alcohol. Likewise, the watchful eye of the church followed voters on election days to ensure their good behavior, and men who allowed the norms of the world rather than the rules of the church to guide their behavior were summoned to answer for their conduct. Flat Rock Church of North Carolina, for instance, disciplined three men in 1806 for their behavior at the recent election.[26]

Celebrations of the anniversary of U.S. independence raised similar questions about negotiating American political practices. Fourth of July commemorations assumed an important role in early national political culture, though they varied from the silent (though still public) decorations of windows with a single candle to boisterous parades, musters, and barbeques. They were not simply patriotic events, but also partisan ones, in which speakers and other participants sought to align their own political beliefs with the "true" Spirit of '76. Americans in the early republic often joined politics, alcohol, merriment, and military and civic displays. Baptists did not object to the partisan element of these commemorations, but they were bothered by the other components. Many Baptists worried that observations of the Fourth of July were too often "light and spirtive" or, as one association suggestively put it, "wanton frolic[s]." To counter this decadence, the Roanoke Association recommended that Baptists "set apart the 4.th of July in each year, as a day of public thanksgiving, prayer, & praise to Almighty God, for the inestimable blessings of Liberty, and independence." The Elkhorn Association simply declared that it was not "right" for Baptists to participate in any of the barbeques on the Fourth of July.[27] To be sure, others in the early republic debated some of these issues as well. Behavior at political barbeques, parades, and elections prompted some debates in newspapers and other forums. Republican rhetoric identified citizens' virtue as crucial to the well-being and longevity of the republic, an equation that ensured anxious evaluations of public behavior, particularly at self-consciously political events. The questions by Baptists, though, were framed quite differently. They asked not on behalf of the health of the republic, but on behalf of true Christianity. For them, the issue was not what constituted good political conduct, but how faith and religious affiliation shaped right political conduct.

If Baptists withdrew from certain arenas of political culture, they were also expected to keep separate from other civic associations. In particular, the Freemasons stood out as a censurable organization that godly men should reject. Freemasonry had experienced great growth during the revolutionary era, expanding geographically and numerically and growing in prominence. Masonry claimed to be associated with the highest ideals in civic and religious life and, as historian John L. Brooke has noted, Freemasonry stood at least symbolically "at the privileged center of public culture in the new United States." Valuing selfless virtue and promoting the merits of a learned, benevolent elite, the Masons claimed to inculcate republican values in its brotherhood. And Baptist churches, as covenanted communities, shared some of the same characteristics of the Masons, including a closed membership within which members shared distinctive language, rituals, and values; even the Masons' language and ethic of fraternity in tension with larger hierarchical values and structures had much in common with Baptist churches. Perhaps it is no wonder that with these commonalities, Masonry appealed to many Baptist men since it offered many of the same benefits of fellowship, without the invasive inquiries and critiques of their behavior. Appealing or not, churches consistently maintained that Freemasonry and church membership were incompatible. Masonry, after all, demanded a powerful allegiance to a secular society and required members to privilege that identity over church fellowship to secure the secrets of Freemasonry. This was incompatible with a faith that also demanded primary loyalty, as a North Carolina association demonstrated when it agreed to excommunicate all members who joined the Masons. This issue came up with increasing frequency after the turn of the nineteenth century, and Baptists agreed consistently that they could not permit such conduct. In 1805, a Tennessee association considered how to handle Freemasons in its churches asking, "What shall a church do with a member when they know him to be a free mason, and that he attends their meetings, or is frequently in company with free masons, drinking toasts and using their Signs." In keeping with most other decisions, it agreed that if a member "persists in the practice of the Same, Cast him out." Likewise, in 1815, another association extended that prohibition to those who associated closely with them, recommending that its member churches discipline any member who displayed a "complacency" with the fraternal organization.[28] These policies came at some cost to churches since some men highly valued the social and economic benefits of Masonry and gave up church membership in favor of their civic brotherhood.

Just as it was important for Baptists to sort sinful behavior from godly in civic and political life, it was equally important for Baptists to delineate sacred space from profane space. In the Anglican South, parish churches served a wide variety of civil and religious needs. But Baptists wished to define certain spaces as exclusively religious, specifically, church lands and the meetinghouse. To that end, they designated a series of rules governing behavior in the meetinghouse during religious services and meetings of business. These rules governed everything, including how often a member could speak, how to speak, in what ways one could depart a meeting, appropriate clothing, and forbidden behaviors (including laughing, whispering, and chewing tobacco). They also disallowed the use of meetinghouses to serve the kind of multiple functions of an Anglican Church (though a few churches in the early nineteenth century made exceptions for education and allowed schools to use their buildings). The Portsmouth Association, for instance, debated whether it was "consistent for Baptist Churches to admit of political or electioneering orations at their Meeting-houses or places of publick worship?" It answered this question by again delineating firm boundaries between the sacred and secular realms—boundaries designed to protect the spiritual realm from the corruption of the secular—responding:

> In as much as the kingdom of Christ is wholy Spiritual, and by the laws and institutions of our glorious head and king, the Church and the World are, and of right ought to be seperate and distinct; we

think such a practice entirely inconsistent and nothing of the above nature should be encouraged or admitted at our Meeting-houses or places of publick worship.[29]

To allow politicking at meetinghouses risked the corruption of true religion and transgressed the divinely ordained separation between the sacred and the worldly spheres. If Baptists wished to preserve religious spaces from the influences of worldly society, they did not feel compelled to limit God's work to those spaces. Particularly in the eighteenth century, Baptists preached in fields and public squares, and they held services in houses and barns and at local rivers, an extension that virtually reversed Anglicans' designations. For Anglicans to spill religious services out of the dignity of the church building profaned the sanctity of worship, though they embraced the elasticity of roles that Sunday worship served. Baptists, on the other hand, attempted to limit non-church activities at their meetinghouses, but welcomed the opportunity to hold religious services in a variety of public places. Here, as in legal constructions of church and state, Baptists sought to keep the "world" out of religious activity, but they embraced an expansive arena for the church.

While expecting their churches to mediate members' relationship to political culture, Baptists still saw themselves as connected to, and part of, the civic community. Begun as a dissenting sect in bitter conflict with the established state church, Baptists gradually relinquished the outsider status that they had once courted and came to see their own efforts as not just consistent with, but very much part of, the republican endeavor. In a letter circulated among local churches, the Virginia Portsmouth Association begged Baptists to keep up religion in the family for a number of reasons, including the health and welfare of the republic. The association beseeched local Baptists: "if you are indeed what you profess to be, good Republicans, good Patriots...labour by all means in your power to constitute your habitations the Temples of the Lord of Hosts."[30] The duties of good republicans and good Baptists here were the same, and to do justice to one was to do justice to another. This message was subtly reinforced by the appeal to manifest religious and patriotic values within the household. The home was to be the smallest collective unit of God's kingdom on earth, a miniature of the church. This use of the home was a sectarian reflection of a common image of the home as the building block of the republic. In treatises on political theory and the body politic, the home assumed the role of the nursery of republican values and the purest representation of republican government. By co-opting this language, the Portsmouth Association conflated the republican home with the godly home (which had long been synonymous with the Baptist home).

The War of 1812 prompted renewed efforts to link Baptist and patriotic values and did so in ways that signaled increased anxiety about the need to reconcile Baptist identity with citizenship. Baptists more frequently saw the need to announce their patriotism and to position themselves explicitly as members of the national political community. Their statements echoed their revolutionary petitions but were more insistent, so much so that they appear far more defensive than in previous decades even as they proclaimed a hyperpatriotism. Association after association took space in their published minutes to lavish praise on the republic and to commiserate about current difficulties. In 1812, a Virginia association prayed that God "defend our dear country, from the power of our enemies." In 1815, another used its annual address to the churches to praise the unique liberty and national prosperity that Americans enjoyed. In 1813, the Concord Association lamented the difficulties of the crisis of the War of 1812, seeing it as without parallel in human history. In a statement praising the "flag of liberty," it proposed that churches vigilantly watch for unpatriotic sentiments among their members and "Should they discover any of her Members unfriendly to the Great Gift of heaven, our Republic form of Government, that they forthwith Exclude Such from fellowship as unworthy of the society."[31] This positioned churches to police good citizenship and political sentiments on behalf of the nation as well as Christianity. Through these declarations, Baptists not only defined themselves as part of civil society and as good citizens of the republic but colonized patriotism as a religious duty.

Just as the politics of church and state relations proved to be central components in the construction of Baptist identity, so too it proved to be a vital part of their efforts to define the realms of the sacred and the secular. The Baptists' intense self-consciousness about questions of the appropriate boundaries of the religious community also helped to define arenas of social and political life that belonged to the secular realm. Their desire to delineate the religious from the secular arose primarily to protect the spiritual realm from being corrupted by secular issues and led them to be strong proponents for the disestablishment of the Anglican Church and the complete separation of government and religion. The Baptists found that the search for the appropriate boundaries between the sacred and the worldly led them into intense reflection on a diverse array of issues about their place in the emerging political culture of the new republic. They sought to learn how a Baptist could also be a republican citizen. Through this reflection, they agreed that the rules and practices of republican politics would not be allowed to supersede the values of church membership nor circumvent the authority of the church. Their vision of the "separateness" of the sacred realm existed to give them complete autonomy over their congregants, as it had over marriage, leisure, and business practices. Vehemently defending this privilege, Baptist churches consistently expanded the realm of their activities so that very little in their members' lives could be defined as secular. This expansive reach of the churches, however, would be challenged by the issue of slavery. By the early nineteenth century, churches' involvement in the institution of slavery threatened to tear the denomination apart and forced them to choose between their vision of the sacred realm and the unity of their churches.

6

The Equity of Hereditary Slavery

In November 1788, the North Carolina Baptist church of Flat Rock deliberated on "the legality of titles" among their members. Titles were of course very significant among Baptists, who marked themselves from outsiders by their rejection of worldly titles (such as "mister," "colonel," and "mistress") and their use of "brother" and "sister"; these godly designations were to represent the essence of fellowship in the church, to mask (though not erase) the inequality of the world with the equality of souls. But on this occasion, the church at Flat Rock "Warmly Debated" whether members could compel their slaves "to Call Infants or Yong Children Master or Mistress." There were "many Debates on the Matter" in the following weeks, and in January the church members finally reached a very moderate conclusion: they did not endorse this behavior in members, but they agreed that masterly coercion of this sort would not be a matter for church discipline if and when it occurred. Member William Elliott strongly disagreed with the church's decision to ignore this behavior and demanded it reconsider the matter. Another debate, though, yielded the same agreement that the church would not take action against slave owners who forced slaves to use such titles. By February 1789, "after no small Disputation," Elliott took the unusual step of "Declar[ing] a Nonfellowship" with the church proceedings, a term that typically signified excommunication and, in this case, was certainly a challenge to the authority of the church and the morality of its decision. Elliott was censured, but he and his wife refused to countenance the judgment of the church and withdrew.[1] Far from a singular event, this conflict was one of many occurring within Baptist churches in the Upper South over the issue of slavery. Over the course of the next two decades, with slavery as a catalyst, Baptists would be forced to rethink their doctrines, world view, and relationship to the new republic.

As the Baptists set out to evangelize the Upper South, they addressed the complicated issue of slaves and slavery. Slaves were part of the audiences for Baptist preachers in the 1760s and 1770s, and, after the War for Independence, slaves began to join churches in increasing numbers.[2] This phenomenon forced Baptists into the quagmire of slavery as they constructed a coherent theology and a network of churches in a revolutionary age. The churches they built were biracial churches with white and black members. White and black evangelicals together faced the contradictions between their theology, which emphasized the equality of souls, and the institution of slavery, which reified inequality. Churches became the arenas in which southerners debated what slavery meant in an evangelical society and what religion meant in a slave society.[3]

In their ongoing efforts to claim an expansive authority for their churches and to draw a divide between their members and "the world," Baptists found themselves involved in a variety of thorny issues that ranged from the most intimate (such as sexual conduct and marriage) to the decidedly public (such as business practices and political behavior). But it was their debates about slavery that soon constituted the most serious crisis in early evangelical churches. As with all other issues facing their members, Baptist churches claimed an oversight of the relationships between, and behavior of, owners and slaves—a claim that allowed churches to intrude on the authority of white male householders and to serve as the final arbiters of the treatment of slaves. Some Baptist ministers and congregants even attempted to inscribe the theology of the equality of all souls into church policy, issuing declarations against slaveholding and creating emancipation plans. Met by hostility, these efforts rapidly created dissension within and among church congregations, so much so that in the 1790s, many Baptists began to distance themselves from antislavery statements to quell developing conflicts. Consequently, antislavery seemed to disappear from evangelical churches and from the Upper South more broadly. But, in fact, antislavery Baptists, or as they were known, "emancipation" or "emancipating" Baptists, far from going quietly, became more radical. Most vocal partisans migrated to Kentucky, making it a battleground between those for and against slaveholding and the site of a clash that would divide brethren and rupture churches. The debate over the morality of slaveholding, then, was not so much a political compromise as a hard-fought battle that divided churches, pitted old friends against one another, and ultimately marginalized the antislavery position both geographically and politically. Slavery was consequently redefined as a political issue outside the province of churches. While Baptists continued to insist on their broad authority over their members—a claim that included supervising the behavior of masters, mistresses, and slaves—they ceded the issue of the morality of slavery to the civil state when it proved too divisive.

In their efforts to define their authority, the Baptists self-consciously drew upon the parallel process under way in the nascent governmental bodies. In the early republic, the nature, structures, and powers of both state and local governments were in flux, and individuals and groups sought to define the boundaries and authority of government, a dynamic that has been explicated in the burgeoning and innovative literature on the emerging state and its political culture.[4] This process, significantly, ought not to be understood as wholly governmental or even wholly secular. There was an analogous process under way in a number of denominations, as sectarian groups sought to determine the appropriate boundaries of the religious realm and, hence, the civil realm. Here, too, these institutions sought to define and expand their authority, sometimes by limiting the authority of the state over their members and at other times seeking to create new arenas of power. A significant intersection of the different, and often competing, efforts to determine authority in the new republic was slavery, as both church and state had legitimate claims to this issue. For the evangelical Baptists of the Upper South, defining their relationship to the state and the civil realm was an imperative struggle, dictated by God, to protect the converted from the corrupting influences of worldly society—beliefs that guided the Virginia Baptists in their successful political campaign to limit state authority over religious beliefs and practices. By the 1780s, they were quite self-conscious about defining their authority against the power of government. Thus, as Americans debated how the state was defined as well as who was defining it, the Baptists intended to be a coherent voice among the clamor of voices seeking to shape civil bodies. Moreover, they wanted to use state power—and the very concept of the state—to resolve their own dilemma about the relationship between race and evangelical fellowship.

At the heart of this issue are the significance of evangelicals' opposition to slavery and their subsequent rejection of that stance. Many works have identified this compromise of early principles as a key component of evangelicals' subsequent success at gaining southern white converts. Both the Baptists and the Methodists took a similar trajectory. In the early decades of their evangelical proselytizing (1770s and 1780s for the Baptists and 1780s and 1790s for the Methodists), both sects welcomed slaves as members, extended some rights to slave members, issued statements against slavery, and in some cases, investigated ways to limit or eliminate it. Around the turn of the nineteenth century, each came to reject public declarations or actions against slavery by their churches or ministers, and by the antebellum era, they had performed a complete reversal, participating in public, explicit support for slavery. For the Methodists, this transformation has been well documented, since the hierarchical structure of the church allowed for consistent, if changing, policies. Due to the congregational structure of Baptist churches, which gave each individual church the authority to determine its own policies, this process has proven to be more difficult to trace, particularly when Virginia is studied in isolation.[5] Yet studying the anatomy of the Baptists' struggle with slavery has much to teach us about the tenacity of antislavery evangelicals, as well as the evangelicals' efforts, both conscious and unwitting, to define a division between religious authority and civil authority in the new republic.

Baptists insisted on their right to influence, and even alter, slavery in their religious communities during the revolutionary and early national eras, a claim that solidified their broader authority over members and their households. Having constructed an intrusive church authority to watch the conduct of members, Baptists brought that to bear on slave owners, at times acting in ways that benefited slave members. In one such case in June 1772, a Virginia church asked: "Is it Lawful to punnish our Servants by burning them &c in any case whatever[?]" The members quickly agreed by a unanimous vote that it was not lawful. This was not merely a theoretical question. The congregation immediately brought one of its own up on charges for burning his slave and suspended his membership until he "acknowledged his sin." This early rejection of severe physical abuse of slaves continued in the following decades, and other churches and associations took steps to limit slave owners' physical discipline of slaves in the late eighteenth century and even into the early nineteenth century. In 1808, the Tennessee Association (which advised approximately thirty member churches) considered: "Whether it be legal for members of our community having Slaves in fellowship to correct them by *whipping*[.] Yea or nay. Answered *nay* and advise members of The respective Churches, *to take the gospel rule with their slaves*, as in the 18th of Matthew." The association in this case did not consider the larger moral issue of owning human property, but it did place limits on owners' authority over their slaves. The Strawberry Association of Virginia took an interesting turn on this issue when it asked whether it was "Scriptural for one brother to whip another, a[n]swered we think not." They did not introduce race or slavery into the matter; the issue for them was appropriate conduct between spiritual brethren. Neither race nor slave status was to supersede the rules of fellowship, according to this decision.[6]

Churches similarly worked to protect slaves from other forms of abuse, including overwork and neglect. Some churches, for instance, tried to prevent slaveholders from forcing their slaves to work on Sundays. A Tennessee association addressed slave conditions more broadly when it deplored the wretched conditions under which most slaves were kept and asked its members to give to their slaves "what is first and equal," warning that "too Many lay up in that in their coffers, which of Right belongs to the Needy who labor under them." It issued this statement in 1812, well past the era of revolutionary idealism, revealing an ongoing effort to mediate the relation between owners and slaves. Some churches also sought to constrain white members' ability to separate married slaves. Abbott's Church in North Carolina voted in 1807 that brethren were not allowed to part married slaves, a rule that extended protection beyond black members. The church then agreed to write a "Letter of grievance" to other churches, reminding them to look into their "Unscriptural Sentimen[ts]."[7]

Issuing declarations against the mistreatment of slaves was one thing, but actually disciplining white members for their treatment of their slaves was quite another, and, given the relatively few charges recorded in churchbooks, congregations clearly resisted pursuing such matters publicly. One Virginia case demonstrates the potentially volatile nature of such an accusation. In 1799, based on information from people of "veracity and character," yet nonmembers, the Zoar Baptist Church brought charges against Brother Talbot for "treating an Old black servant of his with great neglect and crulty," and it sent a committee to investigate. Talbot denied the charge, but the church was not satisfied and continued its inquiry. Talbot reacted with anger at his congregation's actions and "intimated that people had better look more at home, and that he did not hold himself accountable to any one for his conduct towards his own people, and that he should treat them as he thought proper." Irritated at the invasion of his privacy, he wanted to know who reported the accusation to the church, and he refused to appear before the church, claiming infirmity.[8] To be sure, evangelical actions to protect slave members from abuse did not guarantee slave members better treatment from their owners, much less provide the range of rights that white members had. Few slaves dared to bring such charges against whites as those leveled against Talbot, perhaps fearing an unsympathetic hearing or retaliation from their owners. However, the possibility of such charges remained in these churches, providing a brake on the absolute authority of slave owners.

Not all of churches' interference benefited slaves. Just as churches sought to monitor the behavior of slaveholders, they also sought to discipline slave members, bringing them up on such charges as laziness, running away, and insubordination. In these cases, churches' actions served to buttress masters' authority, extending the surveillance into the church community and providing yet another means of disciplining slaves. Moreover, in these actions, churches invested slave owners with divine authority in their efforts to create a hard-working and obedient slave labor force; obedience was not merely a master's desire, these decisions declared, it was God's will and a Christian duty. These cases marked an essential divide between slave and free members. In the churches studied here, slaves were the only members accused of running away, and they were the great majority of those accused of disobedience or insubordination (along with a small group of white women) and of laziness. This aspect of church discipline has received a great deal of attention by historians who show how evangelical discipline supported the system of slavery and the needs of owners. This is, however, only part of the story—a notable part, certainly, yet still incomplete. Significantly, this emphasis ignores the powerful meanings of membership—to be brethren with other believers, to have the surety of knowing the "truth," and to have the dignity of being one of God's chosen people—which provided the physical and spiritual spaces to which slaves were drawn. In fact, charges like these were infrequent and occasionally provided opportunities for slaves to negotiate charges leveled against them. In Virginia, where church discipline of slaves was harshest, there were only 12 slaves accused of running away, 16 accused of disobedience, and 2 accused of laziness, out of nearly 1,200 charges in twenty-five sample churches. In North Carolina, where there were fewer slave members, out of approximately 1,100 charges in eighteen sample churches, only 1 slave was accused of laziness, 5 of running away, and 3 of disobedience (a charge that was also leveled against 8 white members). (See Tables A.4 and A.9 for more.) During these cases, slaves sometimes seized the opportunity to negotiate conflicts with their owners. A Kentucky church, while debating the case of a slave woman who ran away, agreed to consider "whether her conduct [wa]s Justifiable"; the church heard her confession and acquitted her of the charge.[9] Church discipline, then, did single out slaves for some crimes and could aid masters in their efforts to control their slaves, but it did so in a radically different context than slaves could find in any other arena.

Churches' interference in the relationship between masters and slaves had another potentially radical implication. Churches designated themselves as the arbiters of the conduct of all of their members and claimed the right to judge the treatment of slave members. By separating slave members from nonmembers, these practices made church *membership* the delineating category, thereby challenging the very foundation of the institution of slavery—that of racial difference. Within the meetinghouse and in relationships outside of the church walls, the bonds of membership, not race, were to guide behavior. This is not to suggest that race was unimportant to evangelicals; black congregants did have less power in the churches than did whites in leadership, voting, and disciplinary matters. However, race was not the primary category of importance to evangelicals. Rather, membership and nonmembership served as the most important differentiating tool between people; race and sex assumed secondary roles in organizing relations. This radical potential did not disappear in the early nineteenth century but continued to exist in tension with other beliefs and practices in the evangelical churches. There was no consistent policy to protect slave members, but churches did offer an opportunity to renegotiate the relations between master and slave, extending their domain to view, evaluate, and judge the behavior of slaveholders by a standard that was independent of the civil code.

But, as Cynthia Lynn Lyerly has argued, we do African-American evangelicals a disservice if we only ask how their religion shaped and was shaped by slavery. They were after all, more than slaves, but also spouses, parents, neighbors, lovers, friends, and believers. There were many indications that black Baptists were drawn by the same messages as their white brethren: a transhistorical identity of being heirs to the first and true Christians that (spiritually) released people from everyday realities; a powerful claim of knowing the truth in a world full of uncertainties; the often intoxicating belief that God knew them by name and was often present among them; and an egalitarian ethos that created a religious family as it masked worldly identities. One of the only recorded conversion narratives by a slave woman displayed many similarities with other Baptist narratives. Letty said she lived for many years despising religion and God's people, until one day when she was powerfully struck by her own sinfulness. She went to her brother, a convert, who warned her that she was still under the influence of the devil. Afflicted with a sense of her wickedness, she believed that she "had no friend in the world" and so turned to God. In keeping with other narratives in which converts saw a glimmer of hope that was soon lost, she came to believe that God was too angry to hear her prayers. Her despair was such that she believed "no creature was ever in my case before," and she resolved to run into a river, perhaps to drown. Instead, she threw herself prostrate to the ground, and like many fellow evangelicals in the throes of conversion, suddenly knew the words that would provide her deliverance. For Letty, those words were "inherit the kingdom prepared for you from the foundation of the world" (Matthew 25:34), and with the knowledge that those words were said for her, she experienced the "Heavenly rapture" that later she shared with her fellow converts. The promise of being an heir to God's kingdom may have had distinct resonances for Letty, but this could be as easily an awe-inspiring prospect for all those who found themselves humbled by their sinfulness.[10]

The belief in the equality of all souls was a powerful concept that Baptists conscientiously struggled to understand. God, as they often declared, was no respecter of persons, a belief which created a spiritual space that suspended the realities of slavery. Slaves could enter that space when moved by a presence within themselves and their own belief or through the power of another's words. The Baptist belief that words could penetrate the soul and alter one's connection to the divine proved appealing to slaves. Moreover, in these churches, slaves (and other members) shaped the theological belief in the equality of souls into practical and meaningful opportunities to influence their own families and communities and used it to claim an identity as part of a shared biracial community of God's faithful; in so doing, they disrupted the institution of slavery in ways that were mundane, daily, constant, and therefore significant. Baptist churches and faith did not ignore slavery; they were important sites in which it was contested and constructed.

While churches consistently intervened in the behavior of masters and slaves, the issue of slavery itself proved to be deeply problematic. In the late eighteenth and early nineteenth centuries, Baptists' efforts to reach consensus on the morality of slaveholding threatened to divide the young denomination permanently. Baptist theology itself forced congregants and churches to face the question directly. In particular, the Baptist belief in the equality of souls conflicted with the social practices of their communities, their churches, and, for slave owners, their homes. Baptists commonly cited New Testament doctrines to articulate a vision of believers that valued a relative egalitarianism over "earthly" divisions of gender, race, and status. Baptists insisted that their mission was to strive for a pure covenanted community that rooted out all sin. Other churches (such as the Presbyterian Church and the Anglican-Episcopal Church) did not expect human society to approach the perfection of the heavenly realm, but evangelical Baptists could not accept such distinctions and sought to create a godly haven in an imperfect world. This required church congregations to confront the presence of slavery in their midst. How to reconcile their theology with the reality of slaves and slave owners in their churches became the subject of frequent and often intense debate. In the 1780s and 1790s, that debate was only beginning, and no clear consensus had yet emerged.

In the years immediately following the War for Independence, some Baptists came to believe that the doctrine of the equality of all souls before God necessitated the abolition of slavery. In the 1780s and 1790s, a number of Baptist churches and associations made a brief and wavering commitment to antislavery. A wavering commitment is, of course, a contradiction in terms, but contradiction perhaps best captures white Baptists' struggles with slavery. One of the earliest debates came in 1785 (a year after the Methodists issued and quickly repealed a bold antislavery policy) when the Baptist General Committee of Virginia took up the issue of slavery. This committee of church representatives was explicitly and exclusively intended to be the "political mouth... to the State Legislature" regarding the disestablishment of the Anglican-Episcopal Church. Despite its narrow charge, the committee repeatedly issued declarations against slavery to be circulated among its member churches. The 1785 meeting, when the General Committee first debated slavery, resulted in a statement that avowed "hereditary slavery to be contrary to the word of God." Whereas the recent Methodist Conference had more definitively laid out its position rejecting slaveholding and formulating plans for ministers and the laity to emancipate their slaves within a year, the Baptist position was more moderate. In defining slavery in opposition to God's word, it implied that holding slaves could be, and even ought to be, defined in the churches as an excommunicable offense, but it left any such conclusions unstated.[11]

In 1790, the General Committee took a more forceful stand when the attendees again considered the "equity, of Hereditary Slavery." The assigned subcommittee had difficulty formulating a statement so it deferred to the leadership and words of minister John Leland. Leland submitted a resolution that the General Committee then issued in its minutes:

> Resolved, That slavery, is a violent deprivation of the rights of nature, and inconsistent with a republican government; and therefore recommend it to our Brethren to make use of every legal measure, to extirpate the horrid evil from the land, and pray Almighty God, that our Honourable Legislature may have it in their power, to proclaim the general Jubilee, consistent with the principles of good policy.

With this statement, the General Committee broadened the position from which it attacked slavery; having already found slavery at odds with the word of God, it also declared slavery contrary to republicanism and natural rights. Indeed, it was this latter, more secular assault that dominated this second statement against slavery. And it boldly encouraged Baptists to take legal steps to eliminate slavery, though it again avoided drawing the logical conclusion that slaveholding must therefore be a sinful act that required church intervention. Significantly, because Baptists valued consensus, it is likely that most, if not all, of the forty-two ministers and church representatives in attendance would have had to agree to this declaration before it could be passed. The committee's minutes were published for wide circulation among the represented churches and other associations in Virginia, North Carolina, and Kentucky.[12]

As this document circulated, the decentralized nature of Baptist institutions ensured that these antislavery resolutions would be the subject of great debate and likely strong opposition. Since each church was an independent, covenanted body, each could formulate its own rules and policies regarding slavery. At the same time, Baptists valued consensus and continuity, which promised the converted relative harmony and gave them confidence in the godliness and purity of their practices. To ensure this stability, Baptists relied on specific structures and practices to maintain continuity across time and across churches. In particular, regional associations played an important role here as they guided churches on thorny issues of theology, practices, and discipline and then circulated published minutes of their debates and decisions to their churches and other regional associations. Church representatives thus had a chance to consider and debate a host of questions, bringing their collective judgment to bear and distributing their conclusions to member churches and to other associations that might be faced with the same problem. While information on a variety of issues such as heresies, price setting, Freemasonry, and consanguineous marriage commonly circulated, no topic excited the backlash which antislavery resolutions did.

In 1790, when the General Committee circulated its strong statement against slavery, the clamor from some quarters was so loud and immediate that the following year the committee had to reconsider that statement and the one from 1785. Indeed, some church representatives were so disturbed by the resolution of 1790 that they also requested that the association entertain the question of whether it had deviated from its original design. Seeking greater agreement among Virginia Baptists, the General Committee agreed that the antislavery policy should be "again referred to the district association, and from thence to their respective churches for their consideration, desiring them to take the matter into consideration, and shew their opinion on this subject to the general committee." By returning the issue of slavery to local associations and their member churches, the representatives hoped to signal the committee's respect for the appropriate lines of communication (from independent churches to representative bodies) and for the authority of the churches. Finally, since the committee's consideration of the morality of slavery appeared to have inadvertently raised the specter of oppression from a centralized body, the representatives took pains to assure their member churches that they did not consider themselves a supervisory committee and that their sole goal was to promote the political liberty of the sect.[13]

In asking the churches and regional associations to discuss the issue of slavery and send back their views, the General Committee hoped to see a consensus emerge. Divisions, however, emerged instead. The Strawberry Baptist Association agreed to advise the General Committee "not to Interfere" in slavery. The Roanoke Association was quite troubled by this issue, explaining that its members wished to be governed by the "spirit of humanity" and acknowledging that they were "not unanamously clear in [their] minds whether the God of nature ever intended, that one Part of the human species should be held in an abject state of slavery to another part of the same species." Nonetheless, the association did not believe that the General Committee should meddle in slavery, citing concerns about how slaves would support themselves as well as the general complexity of the issues.[14] The Ketocton Association was apparently unconvinced by the General Committee's nod to congregational autonomy and went so far as to suggest that the General Committee was "dangerous to the liberties of the Churches." It was two years before the General Committee came to any type of agreement. When it did, it not only radically departed from its own position of just a few years previous, it also signaled a major transformation in the Baptists' understanding of religious and civil authority. In 1793, the committee again debated hereditary slavery and voted "by a majority (after considering it a while) that the subject be dismissed from this committee, as believing it *belongs to the legislative body.*"[15] This was a remarkable rejection of contemporary Baptist theology and practice. Baptists intended to build a distinct society within society, a community that would maintain broad authority over its congregants' lives to ensure the righteousness of each individual and the purity of the church. Churches thus positioned themselves alongside civil authorities when they claimed a jurisdiction over marriage, price regulation, civil disputes, and civic behavior, and while they did not reject the authority of the state, they did seek to assert the primacy of the church in determining Christian behavior. Yet now some Baptist leaders were willing to sacrifice a major issue to the civil state, defining it as outside of the province of the churches and more properly the concern of the government.

While the General Committee backed away, other Baptists continued to press the issue. John Leland was clearly not persuaded by opponents to the antislavery position, and he worked to galvanize southern Baptists. In the same year that he wrote the General Committee's statement, he published his own essay in which he decried the evils of slavery and the slave trade, which he denounced as "the horrid work of bartering spirituous liquor for human souls." Leland objected to the legal structures of slavery that eliminated a slave's ability to testify in court against a white person, leaving the slave no legal redress if abused; he also complained of federal law which, under the Constitution, decreed that slaves were "possessed of 3 fifths of a man, and 2 fifths of a brute." Using language that presaged rhetoric by antebellum abolitionists, Leland warned that "the whole scene of slavery, is pregnant with enormous evils. On the master's side, pride, haughtiness, domination, cruelty, deceit and indolence; and on the side of the slave, ignorance, servility, fraud, perfidy and despair."[16] Shortly after the publication of this essay, Leland moved with his family to New England, and a leading voice for antislavery in the region was lost.

Other Baptist ministers and unordained leaders shared Leland's antislavery beliefs and attempted to unite brethren in the region against slavery, working against the emerging coalition of evangelicals who wished to define slavery as a civil issue. As representatives of their churches to regional associations, church leaders worked together to issue statements against slavery on behalf of their churches. In 1796, the Portsmouth Baptist Association, representing some twenty-two churches, complained of the "Covetousness [that] leads Christians, with the people of this country in general, to hold and retain, in abject slavery a set of our poor fellow creatures *contrary to the laws of God and nature.*" Churches and associations also tried to initiate debate and so posed "queries" for congregations and associations. In 1796, the Kehukee Association, which represented churches from North Carolina and Virginia, proposed to debate: "*Whether Negro Slavery be Lawful in the Sight of God or not.*" Happy Creek Church of Virginia wanted its regional association to take up the issue of slavery as well, asking: "Can the present practice of holding Negroes in slavery be supported by scripture and the true principles of a republican government?" But it was disappointed when the association "refused to take it up, considering it as an improper subject of investigation in a Baptist Association, whose only business is to give advice to the Churches respecting religious matters, and considering the subject of this query to be the business of government, and a proper subject of Legislation."[17]

For many Baptist activists, antislavery agitation was one radical effort among many to limit the authority of slave owners and to reshape the institution of slavery. In the early 1790s, as the General Committee was backing away from its public opposition, minister David Barrow worked to ameliorate slavery, seizing and creating opportunities to highlight slavery's injustices to his brethren. When the Virginia Portsmouth Association was asked to consider whether an unnamed male slave could remarry after his wife was forcibly removed to a great distance, the representatives debated it for so long that it was referred to the following yearly meeting. Here too, they engaged in an extensive debate before the question was withdrawn for unnamed reasons. Barrow was one of a three-member committee that was authorized to construct a substitute question. Barrow and his fellow committee members submitted: "What ought Churches to do with Members in their Communion, who shall either directly, or indirectly separate married Slaves, who are come together according to their custom as Man and Wife?" From judging the appropriate behavior of one particular slave, Barrow and his committee asked a far broader question about the behavior of slave owners, a question with the potential to limit owners' ability to sell, lend, or will their married slaves.[18]

While ministers' names were most frequently identified with antislavery, the laity played a crucial role in driving the issue of slavery to the center of debate within congregational life. In late eighteenth- and early nineteenth-century churches, laypeople not only had the right, but also the responsibility to secure the "purity" of the covenanted community, and therefore they could, and did, raise questions for debate, propose new rules, and instigate disciplinary proceedings.[19] Antislavery Baptists took advantage of this opportunity to agitate on the immorality of slavery. Just before a major conflict over slavery erupted in his church, Brother Palmer charged Brother and Sister Stephens of mistreating their slave Nancy, an act that required a church inquiry into their home. After the couple was acquitted of that charge, Palmer brought similar charges against them six months later, forcing another investigation. Similarly, Brother Samuel Richardson asked his congregation to debate whether slavery could be justified by scripture or was consistent with republican government. Women were often restricted from raising formal queries, but they too became important actors in the local dramas. Antislavery women often outnumbered antislavery men, creating a sizable enough faction to disrupt the working of churches. In South Fork Church, when members of the antislavery faction declared themselves, they included six men (including the minister) and ten women. By exiting their church en masse, these individuals were able to hinder the remaining body's ability to function. The actions of the laity belie the idea that antislavery was promoted primarily by the ministers, who were alienated from the mainstream views of their congregants, an argument that has encouraged scholars to conclude that evangelical antislavery never ran deep and quickly dried up from lack of support. To be sure, ministers who used their positions and pulpits to attack slavery became more notorious in their communities, but laymen and laywomen acted as well to force congregations to debate slavery and to shelter those ministers who took public stands against slaveholding.[20]

In the 1780s and 1790s, some antislavery Baptists wanted to move beyond general statements of opposition and sought to promote bolder action among their brethren, though they still worked within the confines of consensus building. Pushed by antislavery agitation on the part of Happy Creek and Bent Creek churches, the Ketockton Association in Virginia circulated a plan for gradual emancipation. The Dover Association also believed that, along with its member churches, it should create a plan to emancipate their slaves gradually and asked people to aid abolition efforts. Moved by revolutionary spirit and egalitarian theology, some individual Baptists, such as ministers George Smith, Hampton Pangburn, and David Barrow, as well as a number of laypeople, including the very wealthy planter Robert Carter, manumitted their slaves. It is impossible to know how many individuals manumitted slaves under the influence of Baptists' arguments, but it is clear that even ardent antislavery Baptists did not seek bold collective action before 1800. They did not, for instance, attempt to make slaveholding an excommunicable offense, and emancipation plans were circulated, not mandated. Some sects in the region offered models for stronger action. In the 1760s and 1770s, the Society of Friends, who in the early eighteenth century had reluctantly tolerated slaveholding among their brethren, took aggressive steps to eliminate it, agreeing to expel Friends who refused to manumit their slaves. The Methodists, too, briefly attempted to purge slaveholding among their ministers and members. In 1784, the Methodist Annual Conference decreed that ministers could not participate in the slave trade and must free their slaves where it was legal to do so. Emboldened, church leaders agreed a few months later that members must emancipate their slaves, though local Methodists reacted with such immediate hostility that these new polices were suspended within a few months. Such an effort on the part of the Baptists might have been easier to attempt (and sustain) because of the congregational structure that empowered individual churches to pass their own rules. Ironically, it may have been the Baptist ethic of consensus building—to compensate for the lack of institutional structures creating unity—that limited rather than expanded possible strategies.[21]

Beginning in the 1790s, this debate shifted geographically and rhetorically into new territory. Many devoted antislavery Baptists—both ministers and laypeople—moved west, including many of the leaders of the antislavery contingent, and "western parts," or what would become Kentucky, quickly became the battleground between Baptist pro- and antislavery factions in the Upper South. The West seemed to offer more opportunity for those whom Ronald Hoffman has called "the disaffected." Just as political dissenters, tax revolters, and land squatters had sought refuge in the western fringes of white settlement in the late eighteenth century, so antislavery Baptists sought a greater chance to create their vision of a godly society. The West was an exciting prospect for many evangelicals. It offered them the opportunity to shape community at its broadest level. To be sure, the Baptists were strong believers in the separation of political and church authority and did not envision a western theocracy or even an evangelical version of a church establishment. Nonetheless, the promise of the West lay in the possibility of creating pure covenanted communities in a region unfettered by a church establishment or a society that was hostile to evangelicals. It promised not just the financial and personal opportunities that drew so many migrants westward, but also a spiritual hope to have church and faith precede, and ultimately guide, state and society. It seemed to be a wilderness free of such abhorred social conventions as dancing schools, theaters, gaming, and, for antislavery Baptists most significantly, slavery. David Barrow saw Kentucky as idyllic farmland with rich soil, fatted calves, and hard-working settlers in a land "entirely exempt from the horride course of negro slavery." For men like Barrow, antislavery ideals joined with financial incentives in their decision to migrate. Kentucky farmland, Barrow explained in his departure letter, would allow him to do justice to his ministry and support his family without having to turn to the unsavory practices of speculation or slaveholding. With high expectations of a better life in a better land, antislavery Baptists, such as Barrow, William Hickman, and Carter Tarrant, moved their families and made their homes in Kentucky. This migration, though, spatially marginalized the debate over slavery to this frontier region: after 1800, debate virtually ceased in Virginia, North Carolina, and Tennessee churches and district associations.[22]

The consolidation of the emancipating Baptists, however, did not lead to an easier path because there they met with an increasingly intransigent antiemancipation faction that was determined to eliminate evangelical debate about slavery. The West, of course, also beckoned to those who saw slavery as a significant and desirable tool for financial success. In the 1780s and 1790s, Virginians journeyed over the Cumberland Gap in pursuit of many kinds of opportunities; cheap land, a growing economy, and an underdeveloped legal system all made Kentucky a playground for those hoping to make their fortunes. Some of these migrants, Baptists and non-Baptists alike, saw slave owning as the foundation of their economic strategy. Given the demands of colonization and the chaotic land tenure system, slaves served as a valuable asset in quickly clearing land and planting and harvesting crops. That was certainly Jacob Creath's expectation when he moved to Kentucky in 1803. Like Barrow, he was a minister struggling to support his family, but, unlike Barrow, Creath hoped Kentucky would allow him to compete effectively as a small slave owner. And there were many who shared his expectations: as early as 1792, there were already over 11,600 slaves in Kentucky. By 1800, that number had more than tripled to nearly 36,000.[23] Kentucky then combined antislavery sentiments born of evangelical and revolutionary optimism, hopes of greater fortune, and the absence of strong civil authority, all in a region fiercely claimed by competing groups. This combination proved explosive in both the civil and religious arenas.

In the civil arena, Kentucky was home to intense debates over emancipation in the 1790s, particularly during the two campaigns preceding its two constitutions (1792 and 1799). In both campaigns, slavery proved to be the most divisive issue and one that incorporated other large questions of political representation, economic development, tax structures, population growth, class structure, and, at its broadest level, the future of Kentucky society. If the stakes were high, the possibilities were many, particularly before the ratification of the first constitution. Emancipationists had settled in considerable numbers, feeling that western territories were a good place to work for emancipation because of the relatively weak slave structure. Slavery proponents, on the other hand, saw the constitution as the key opportunity to determine the value of their property (slaves and land) and their place in the developing local economy. While these groups did not neatly align with religious affiliation, the evangelical churches, as Joan Wells Coward argues, provided the core of antislavery activism during the debates of 1791 and 1792. Seven ministers, all opposed to slavery in some measure, were elected to serve at the convention. The Elkhorn Baptist Association even attempted to influence the delegates and drew up a memorial address to the convention on the topics of slavery and religious liberty. But these efforts by evangelicals failed dramatically. Not only did they not weaken or eliminate slaveholding, proslavery leaders were able to pass constitutional protection of slave property.[24]

While the passage of the proslavery article was a substantial blow to the antislavery movement, emancipation again emerged as a legitimate political agenda during debates in the late 1790s about whether Kentucky should create a new state constitution. A provision of the 1792 constitution provided for such a prospect, and antislavery activists were one voice among many that sought a constitutional convention. However, even in the few years between the 1792 constitution and the 1798 campaign, antislavery opportunities had declined in Kentucky. With Ohio lands opening up after the Battle of Fallen Timbers, some devout emancipators migrated westward, while the constitutional protection of slavery had made Kentucky a more appealing place for slaveholders. Indeed, antislavery was such a controversial stance during these debates that some supporters of a constitutional convention downplayed the possibility of any reconsideration of slavery and even accused their political opponents of raising the issue to discredit a new convention. Nevertheless, emancipation was a political issue in this process, and again, evangelicals, including Presbyterian minister David Rice, were a leading voice. In this case, the antislavery activists won the battle but lost the war. They succeeded in calling for a constitutional convention, but their opponents waged a determined and ultimately successful effort to control the convention. The election of delegates proved to be a fierce contest that pitted Governor James Garrard, a Baptist preacher opposed to slavery, and his supporters against some of the most prominent Kentucky politicians, including George Nicholas and John Breckinridge. It exposed regional fault lines as Lexington emerged as largely antislavery while the Bluegrass region was solidly proslavery, and it engulfed national debates over the Alien and Sedition Acts when antislavery activists attempted to capitalize on Kentucky's opposition to those despised acts. Profound divisions emerged in the counties of Montgomery, Logan, and Mason. But ultimately the majority of voters were unwilling to reconsider the issue of slavery and elected proslavery representatives who ensured that the 1799 constitution kept the divisive guarantee of slave property.[25]

Even as opportunities were being closed off in the political arena, conflicts over slavery erupted again in the religious realm. Frustrated that other members of their sect were dragging their feet, some antislavery Baptist ministers and churches began to abandon the moderate consensus model, preaching outright emancipation and refusing to remain in churches and associations with slaveholders or those who tolerated slaveholding. Rollings Fork Church of Kentucky transitioned from agitation to separatism in just seven years. In 1789, the church asked its association to consider whether it was "lawful in the sight of God for a member of Christ's Church to keep his fellow creature in perpetual slavery?" Since the church had only been admitted to the association in the previous year, the other representatives may have considered the controversial question unnecessarily aggressive; in any case, the other attendees were in no mood to debate such a topic and so, while conceding that the matter was critical, they ruled that it was improper for them to consider. By 1796, the Rollings Fork congregation was frustrated enough by the association's refusal to take a stand on the topic that it withdrew. The solidly antislavery church at Mill Creek took similar action in 1794, withdrawing from its association when the group refused to consider a query about slavery.[26]

After the turn of the century, an increasing number of emancipating Baptists proclaimed in word and deed that quiet coexistence with slavery was itself a sin and that they would no longer live with that transgression. Insisting that they wanted to worship in churches that wholly reflected their doctrine and were untainted by anti-emancipation beliefs, they began to create new churches specifically organized around antislavery principles. Minister Carter Tarrant, a vocal proponent of emancipation, joined minister John Sutton in forming the New Hope Church specifically for antislavery Baptists. Antislavery members of the church at Clover Bottom sought such an opportunity and asked the other members to dismiss them so they could join a church that supported emancipation. In what was an even more shocking move to their fellow brethren, by 1804, ministers such as David Barrow and Carter Tarrant began to use their pulpits to preach emancipation as a moral necessity. While these early sermons did not survive, complaints about them suggest that their position was adamant, blunt, and, perhaps worst of all, spoken to audiences that were increasingly biracial. As Ellen Eslinger demonstrates, while relatively few African Americans joined Kentucky churches before 1800 (considerably fewer than had joined Virginia churches), a growing number of slaves sought membership during the revivals that began in 1800. Whether influenced by the mounting number of slaves in their churches or by disappointment that Kentucky was looking progressively more like the slaveholding Virginia that they had left behind, these emancipators adopted a new stand that more aggressively and publicly challenged their Baptist brethren.[27]

This newly radicalized antislavery faction quickly clashed with equally intransigent anti-emancipation Baptists. In this new conflict, which spread through much of Kentucky, neither side sought unanimity or consensus; each sought to identify godliness with its own position and sin with the other. Anti-emancipation Baptists rejected out of hand the idea that slaveholding was a sin that required church discipline; in this, they repeated arguments from the earliest debates over a Baptist position on slavery. But they went even further. They now sought to make an *antislavery* stance an actionable offense that required church discipline. As these individuals sought to reframe the debate about emancipation and evangelicalism, they aimed at the most prominent of the antislavery Baptists: the ministers. In 1805, David Barrow found himself at the center of a controversy that would divide associations and churches and would force long-time colleagues to turn against him and one another. Barrow was not new to the debate and had in fact been a voice against slavery for some decades. He freed his own slaves in the 1780s and publicly spoke against slavery in several venues, including in a published letter announcing his departure to Kentucky. His public antislavery beliefs appeared to be no barrier to active leadership in either Virginia (where he remained until the late 1790s) or in Kentucky. Upon his arrival in Montgomery County, Kentucky, he became pastor to three churches and was frequently called to leadership in the regional associations where he served on committees, as association moderator, and as the voice of the association in sermons and circular letters.[28]

By 1805, however, Barrow's decades-long attack on slaveholding and slaveholders had become a thorn in his ministerial brethrens' side. At the next two meetings of the North District Association, representatives from another association came and charged Barrow with "Meddling with emancipation" and "preaching the doctrine of emancipation, to the hurt and injury of the feelings of the brotherhood." These charges were unprecedented, and the unusual method of bringing charges to an association (which had no authority to discipline individual Baptists) rather than to Barrow's church suggests that his accusers thought they would have a more sympathetic audience in this body, and also reveals their drive to see action taken. The strategy proved to be an effective one: the North District Association agreed to consider the charges and rebuked emancipationists in its annual circular letter to the churches. The association warned the brethren against people who professed godliness and yet were "so far deluded, that their printing, preaching, and private conversation, go to encourage disobedience in servants, and a revolution in our Civil Government." In 1806, it required Barrow to be "tried" before a committee of five ministers. Rather than exhibit remorse and repentance, Barrow spoke, as the meeting minutes report, "in justification of his conduct on that subject, and brother Barrow manifest[ed] no disposition to alter his mode of preaching, as to the aforesaid doctrine." The representatives then took the extraordinary step of expelling him from his seat in the association.[29]

The drama of Barrow's trial and expulsion sent shock waves through the region's churches and associations. A prominent and celebrated leader, Barrow was baptized among the first generation of evangelical Baptist converts, before quickly joining the ministry. He was a veteran of the Revolutionary War, and he was a hero to this cohort of southern Baptists because of his engagement in another kind of battle. He was a survivor of the religious persecution of the 1760s and 1770s, having been nearly drowned by some men during a preaching appointment. No doubt, the badge of having suffered for the cause of Christ followed Barrow into his pastorates at various Virginia and Kentucky churches and contributed to his frequent calls to leadership, but it did not insulate him from attack once the conflict heated up. As news of Barrow's expulsion spread throughout the region, Baptists lined up to take sides in this increasingly polarized debate, and the next thirty-six months witnessed a bitter and rancorous dispute. The North District Association did not stop at expelling Barrow; it also sent a committee to his church to instigate discipline there. Proslavery Baptists took heart from this ruling and acted against emancipationists in their midst. Churches dismissed their antislavery ministers and revoked their right to preach. Emancipationists left churches to set up new ones. Proslavery majorities excommunicated pro-emancipation minorities. Ministers on both sides denounced congregants and colleagues. Hostage to these two adamant positions, many churches in Kentucky broke apart. Minister John Sutton left his church, Clear Creek, to join an antislavery church; the following month, Clear Creek expelled him for that action and for speaking contemptuously of other ministers. South Fork Baptist Church's minister declared himself an "amanspater," and within seven months the church had divided and the emancipationists left the congregation.[30] Similar conflicts divided such churches as Lick Creek, Bracken, Clear Creek, Hillsborough, and Clover Bottom, and this controversy extended across the Kentucky counties of Woodford, Bracken, Washington, Clarke, Shelby, Fleming, Montgomery, Barren, Jefferson, Hardin, and Warren, among others.

Forks of Elkhorn Church provides a window into the demise of these church communities. Formed in 1788, Forks of Elkhorn was biracial (like most southern churches) and even included some slaves who were owned by the governor. The church had faced normal theological, procedural, and disciplinary issues: in the years preceding the conflict over slavery, the church considered such matters as the proper time for the Lord's Supper, its method of receiving new members, the Son of God's equality with the Father, and the discipline of members for such offenses as lying, drinking to excess, gambling, adultery, fighting, fraud, spousal abuse, and disobedience to a master. And, like other churches in the region, Forks of Elkhorn was swept into the divisive debate about slavery and emancipation. Its minister, William Hickman, was one of the early opponents of slavery. It appears likely that some white members of the church were equally uncomfortable with slavery or, at the very least, with how their white brethren treated their slaves, as evidenced by Brother Palmer's accusations against Brother and Sister Stephens for mistreating their slave.

The church polarized over this issue between 1806 and 1807 when the majority began to reject the antislavery minority led by Hickman. In May 1806, the church asked whether "Baptist Preachers are authorized from the word of God to Preach Emancipation" and soon agreed with the recent ruling of the Elkhorn Association that ministers should not meddle in this "political Subject." The church again confronted Hickman when he allowed the recently excommunicated abolitionist minister Carter Tarrant to preach at his home. By September of the next year, tension had built in the church, and it reached a climax when Hickman went on the offensive, informing "the Church that he was distressed on account of the practice of Slavery as being tolerated by the members of the Baptist Society, therefore declared himself no more in Union with us, or the Elkhorn Association." The church responded to his withdrawal by excluding him. Other members who agreed with Hickman also formally withdrew or simply stopped attending the church. Brother Sisk took the opportunity to withdraw from the church at the same meeting and was likewise excluded. Lewis Palmer was called to task for absenting himself. In response, he charged the church with "acting tyrannically in expelling her former Pastor," an accusation that got him excommunicated. While other members who stopped attending church meetings chose not to give a reason, one woman's declaration rocked the church, not simply for her words but also for who and what she was. Winney was a slave (owned by a Baptist woman) who had converted to Christianity and been admitted to the church. Her conversion and faith, she explained, convinced her that no true Christian would own slaves, and she said as much, condemning slavery as well as slaveholders. Winney avowed that she had "once thought it her duty to serve her Master & Mistress but since the lord had converted her, she had never believed that any Christian kept Negroes or Slaves." Furthermore, she contended that there were "thousands of white people Wallowing in Hell for their treatment to Negroes[,] and she did not care if there was as many more." (Ironically, it was likely the church's horror at her words that inspired the church clerk to record Winney's declarations in greater detail than white emancipationists' statements.) In linking her religious conversion directly to her defiant stand against slavery and slaveholders, Winney embodied what many southerners feared most about evangelicalism. Doctrines such as the equality of all souls together with practices that downplayed social distinctions seemingly threatened to disrupt the slave system, a charge that many evangelicals had worked hard to counter. The Forks of Elkhorn Church made it clear that Winney's statements were unacceptable by expelling her from the church one month after she leveled the accusations.[31]

The polarization of Baptists on the question of slavery was soon felt on an institutional level as a vocal coterie of emancipationist Baptists in Kentucky agreed to unite in their own association. In 1807, David Barrow joined other antislavery Baptists in creating the "Baptized Licking-Locust Association, Friends of Humanity." In their first meeting, they welcomed representatives from nine small churches and most of the prominent Baptist abolitionists in the region. The representatives indicted slave owning in general and Christian slave ownership in particular. They rejected the stance of other Baptists, explaining, "We are now distinguished from our former brethren, by reason of our professed abhorrence to unmerited, hereditary, perpetual, absolute unconditional Slavery." Seeking to highlight the discordance of Christianity and slaveholding, they marveled that "(strange as it may appear in other nations and to future generations,) there are professors of christianity in Kentucky, who plead for [slavery] as an institution of the God of mercy; and it is truly disgusting to see what pains they take to drag the holy scriptures of truth, into the service of this heaven daring iniquity." Slave apologists, they continued, use erroneous scriptural justifications for slavery, such as the curse of Noah or Philemon's servant, Onesimus. In rejecting these justifications, the emancipators challenged an increasingly common Baptist practice, which was to "exchange the word slave for servant," a rhetorical turn, they argued, that obscured the reality of the system and allowed appeals to biblical discussions of the duties of servants. They criticized those ministers who remained silent on the issue of slavery and laypeople who were opposed to slavery but remained in fellowship with slaveholders. And they publicly denounced their former brethren by naming the associations that countenanced this obscenity. They identified the Bracken, Elkhorn, and North District Associations as having issued "cruel censures against the Friends of Humanity[.] Blinded by covetousness and intoxication with the cup of Babylon, they call evil good and good evil." With these ringing denouncements of their former brethren, the Licking-Locust Baptists signaled that there was no room for negotiation or compromise in this showdown between good and evil.[32]

For these emancipation Baptists, the evils of slavery required that they combine their political and religious identities. Rejecting the anti-emancipationists' bifurcation of religious and civil responsibilities, they embraced a dual identity as citizens and as Christians, insisting that each required them to take an active position to end slavery. "As a political evil," they declared, "every enlightened wise citizen abhors it; but as it is a sin against God, every citizen is in duty bound to testify against it." They scorned those who tried to defer this issue to the civil state, "as if the church was beholden to the world for assistance in matters of religion, and had no king nor constitution of her own, and as if the laws of Kentucky constrained men to commit wickedness in the land, a stigma on our constitution." Carter Tarrant also embraced his civil identity when in his own speeches and writings about slavery he insisted that it was his constitutional right as a "free citizen" to speak on this topic. His views, he argued, were entirely in keeping with both the Constitution and the Bible. And, with mock concern that his opponents appeared unacquainted with the Constitution, he repeated a few passages he found relevant; in addition, calling upon a series of civil "proof texts" to stand alongside his biblical ones, he quoted liberally from Thomas Jefferson's *Notes on the State of Virginia* and one of Jefferson's speeches on the close of the international slave trade to demonstrate the justice of his cause. In his appeal to "republican principles," he reminded his listeners that the Revolution and the Bill of Rights demanded liberty as a birthright: "Your late gallant struggles with British fury, adamantly declare that you mean to maintain those rights sacred and inviolate . . . but oh!

how horridly have we abused this liberty." African Americans, he argued, had "never forfeited their natural right to liberty, and that an attempt to take it from them is a violation of nature, reason, philosophy and the word of God." Seamlessly combining religious and political language that authorized his brethren's antislavery actions, Tarrant declared simply, "We are republicans and will hear who we please, even the Pharisees." These references did not necessarily display a sophisticated engagement with contemporary political theory, but they were a consistent component of emancipating Baptists' speeches and writings, and they allowed these individuals to mark themselves as true republicans, as well as true Christians.[33]

Both sides of this sectarian debate, then, self-consciously appealed to the state in their arguments. Emancipationists saw their cause as one with that of republican government. "Republican principles" mirrored Christian principles; the Bill of Rights and the Constitution reiterated the message of the Bible. These twin authorities presented a unified message in regard to slavery that made easy the path to good principles and to right action. For the anti-emancipationists, the state served a very different role, one that established a distinct authority for human behavior. For these Baptists, the boundary between church and state became of supreme importance because it allowed them to mark slavery as a "political" and "legislative" matter and, therefore, not their concern. Drawing upon a well-established rhetoric that divided the sacred from the profane, these Baptists used the boundary to delineate the limits of their authority, and, in the process, they saved themselves and their sect the difficulty of reconciling egalitarian theology with the profound inequities of slaveholding. They drew upon this rhetoric, but they could not incorporate it wholly. Originally, this effort to delineate the religious from the secular arose from the desire to protect the spiritual realm from being corrupted by secular authorities. It was, in other words, more concerned with defining the limits of government than with churches or religion. But the anti-emancipationists argued that unity among the churches required them to relinquish their jurisdiction over slavery to the secular powers that they usually mistrusted. For them, slavery was a "legislative concern" outside of the province of the church, a designation unshaken by churches' regular involvement in business disputes, price setting, and politics. It was this compromise that won in the debate over slavery. Even the Elkhorn Association, which had publicly opposed slavery in 1791 at the Kentucky Constitutional Convention, joined its sister associations in designating slavery a political issue in 1805.[34]

As this settlement emerged as the dominant Baptist practice, Baptists healed the rifts in their churches and associations quite rapidly with the aid of significant shifts in their population. The Kentucky emancipationists lost a number of their most prominent leaders, losses that, given their small numbers and the hostility of some of the population, must have been profoundly felt. A number of these individuals died during these years. They had been part of the cohort of Baptists converted in the 1770s and 1780s as young adults, and by 1810, many of them were in their sixties and seventies. David Barrow, for instance, died in 1819 at the age of sixty-six. Likewise, seventy-three-year-old George Smith died in 1820; his younger brother George Stokes Smith had died in 1810, and fifty-one-year-old Carter Tarrant died in 1816. Some of the younger generation, including Joshua Carman (who had founded an early emancipation church), Donald Holmes, and Thomas Whitman, gave up on Kentucky altogether, often moving to Ohio and Illinois. There was enough migration out of Kentucky that another Friends of Humanity Association was established in Illinois in 1822, explicitly following the model established by the Kentucky society.[35]

Many of the remaining emancipationists finally accepted the now established definition of slavery as a "civil" matter and returned to their churches. A significant step toward this reconciliation occurred in March 1808 with Carter Tarrant's published announcement in the *Kentucky Gazette* that there would be an attempt to form a secular abolition society in which "No religious acknowledgement" was necessary. Later that year, the Kentucky Abolition Society was founded. After that year, participation in the Friends of Humanity declined precipitously, so much so that a prominent Baptist historian, who had traveled through the region to research a book published in 1813, believed that they had dissolved. Friends of Humanity finally disbanded in 1820, just months after the death of David Barrow. The decline of this association provided an incentive for emancipationists to return to their old churches; these churches were also eager to heal the rifts, and they not only accepted the former members but quickly restored them to their former positions. Elijah Davidson, who had declared "nonfellowship" with his church in 1808, returned two years later; just two months after his readmission, he was appointed treasurer of the church, and in 1812, the church elected him as a deacon. In the following years, other emancipating members drifted back. In February 1814, a former preacher in the church, John Murphy, returned with his wife, Rachel; two months later, the church restored his license to preach. Other churches, including South Fork, Forks of Elkhorn, and Bracken, also experienced these years as a period of reconciliation. Indeed, even the abolitionist slave Winney had her membership restored in 1812.[36]

The brokered compromise with slavery after 1810 meant that Baptists no longer would debate the morality of the institution of slavery; instead, churches that were so inclined would consider only specific cases to ameliorate some aspects of slavery. Individual incidents involving slaves and owners would continue to be adjudicated in churches, and these matters would be accepted, investigated, and determined entirely on the local level without implying or leading to broader reevaluations of the institution itself. The deliberations of the Concord Association in 1812 reveal the contours of this settlement. In a circular letter distributed to member churches and other associations, Concord gave advice on good "family discipline," first evaluating husbands', wives', and children's duties, before turning reluctantly to "servants." The association explained that "on this subject we dwell with unpleasant sensations," and it avoided any use of the terms "slaves" or "slavery," or even designations of race, such as "blacks" or "Negroes." But, even at this date, the representatives did acknowledge slavery to be "an evil [as] all agree, but how to Remedy it none can devise." Rather than take up that issue, the association settled for instructing masters to use moderation in exercising authority over their slaves and to be just in what they distributed to their slaves. White members who failed to exercise moderation, separated married slaves, or denied their slaves' basic needs faced the possibility that they could be called before their churches to answer for their conduct. But no longer would Kentucky churches and associations debate the larger issues of slavery and slaveholding. Now, following the practices common to other southern states, they would, at best, seek to mitigate some aspects of slavery for individual black members.[37]

For fifty years, since the arrival of the Separates and the rapid growth of converts and churches, Baptist churches had claimed a broad jurisdiction over all aspects of their members' lives. Baptists believed that they answered a divine calling to build covenanted churches of the faithful, and they asserted godly authority wherever they could. They demanded the right to judge each other's business practices, land disputes, parental decisions, leisure activities, and marital relations. In this context, it was natural that churches would insist on their right to monitor master-slave relations and to debate the morality of slaveholding. But efforts to resolve the contradictions between the belief in the equality of all souls and the presence of slaves and slaveholders in their churches threatened to tear the denomination apart. To stem the developing crisis, Baptists redefined slavery to be a civil rather than a moral and religious issue. This solution meant that individual cases involving specific slaves and masters would remain within the purview of the local church, but that Baptists would relinquish any authority over the question of slavery as an institution. For the first time, they defined an issue as being outside the province of the churches and exclusively the concern of the civil government. Thus, the separation of church and state—often understood as a legal delineation enacted during the revolutionary era—was not a straightforward process, nor was it strictly legal. It was, instead, the political and legal face of a broader reconceptualization of secular and sectarian bodies in the postrevolutionary era. In other words, as debates over slavery reveal, it was a reconstruction of civil and religious authority. At the same time that civil authorities embraced a new relationship between religion and government, church members too sought to define the appropriate boundaries between the religious and civil realms in the early republic, a shift that required they welcome the presence and authority of the state over an issue that had been a church matter and that they reshape their understanding of religious authority.

Conclusion

Evangelical Baptist churches in the late eighteenth- and early nineteenth-century South served as both religious and civil bodies. As religious bodies, they galvanized southerners as no church had previously, marking the transformation of the region into a profoundly evangelical society. Their combination of enthusiastic worship and an emotional rather than doctrinal style appealed to both white and black southerners. Baptist churches also served as civil organizations, regulating marriages, supervising migrating individuals, monitoring prices, and arbitrating business, land, and interpersonal disputes. That these church congregations performed civil as well as spiritual tasks has significant implications for our understandings of both religion and the developing state in the new nation. The demarcation of the province of churches and the province of secular authorities shaped not only physical spaces, but also legal codes and constructions of social authorities and power. In the late colonial and revolutionary eras, the struggles of the state-established Church of England and the dramatic changes in the legal relationship between church and state destabilized these definitions as well as the boundary between religion and the civil arena. The Baptists were one of many groups trying to influence the postrevolutionary redefinition of the relationship between religion and the civil realm, and they became an important voice both in local concerns and in state and national political discussions. Baptists' positions in these debates were not wholly consistent: despite having churches assume civil functions, they were in fact strong proponents for the "complete" separation of church and state. Ironically, as Baptists withdrew from civil institutions in order to preserve the purity of their religion, they recreated those structures internally. In disestablishment, legislators quickened the process of removing religion from the purview of the state; with their policies, by contrast, the Baptists brought the state into religion.

In replicating civil structures and services, southern Baptist churches tutored their members in the ways of government. Southerners in the late eighteenth century, particularly those in the western regions, tended to be suspicious of centralized authority and institutions. The Baptists appealed to individuals who were wary of centralized power and hierarchical structures because of the congregational organization of the sect. Each church had the authority to choose its own leaders, rules, and policies, without being subject to any higher body. While Baptists did create regional associations to discuss policies and theological questions, the associations were frequently forced to defend their existence and to avow that they served only an advisory, never a supervisory, role. In theory, each church was an autonomous unit. In practice, however, Baptist churches in the Upper South between 1765 and 1815 proved very consistent in their policies, rules, and even discipline codes and practices. Despite the climate of suspicion regarding the centralization of power and institutions in general, Baptists created a remarkably stable institution that successfully, and even easily, reproduced itself in successive western settlements, creating new churches that exhibited older eastern values and policies. They gradually organized as a confederation of congregations with substantial power over congregants and a consistent code of discipline. Yet, by maintaining the independence of each individual church, the Baptists constructed an institution that masked its own structure. Individual members participated in—and were subject to—a powerful and voluntary institution that mimicked the duties and structures of government but appeared to be democratically and locally run.

In addition to mediating civil disputes, Baptists allowed churches to regulate their marital and family relations and master-slave relationships, giving churches an influential voice in the household. Members' conduct was always subject to the scrutiny and judgment of their brethren, guaranteeing that no matter could be defined as private. Their interventions in marital disputes, child rearing, and sexual misconduct gave churches sway over the most mundane and the most significant events of family life. Likewise, the behavior of masters and mistresses came under the scrutiny of the churches as churches investigated charges of mistreatment, overwork, and the separation of married slaves. By intervening in these matters, churches claimed an authority in the household that at times superseded that of the white, male householder.

Moreover, they positioned themselves to arbitrate gender and racial norms, investing their rules and policies with divine sanction.

In claiming a sweeping purview for churches, Baptists and other evangelicals carved themselves a lasting social, not simply spiritual, authority, asserting their rights over a remarkably broad range of individuals, behaviors, and spaces. Seeing themselves as gloriously different from their peers, they were willing to consider and craft gender conventions and norms that at times were at odds with the larger society. In Baptist stories of their early era, characteristics associated with manhood and womanhood were often inverted, such that women were praised for their indomitability and men for their meekness. Lauding these sex-specific traits (rhetorically) reduced the difference between men and women. Insofar as they wished to live within the doctrine of the equality of all souls, Baptists moved toward creating the model of the genderless believer.

Outside of the realm of the heroic canon, the lessons that emerged out of day-to-day life within a Baptist church community proved more diverse and more complicated: the avenging hand of justice did not always come in time to vindicate the faithful, and the practices of gender identity were sometimes contradictory. White men most often occupied the positions of authority. They were the vast majority of ministers and most of the exhorters, and as a group, they consistently had a full array of rights within the church. Some historians have argued that there was a double standard in church discipline that scrutinized white women and slaves more heavily and that ultimately sanctified gender and racial hierarchies that placed white men on top.[1] However, these churches reveal that, in actuality, discipline fell hardest upon white men. While only about a third of the membership, they were subject to nearly 60 percent of all accusations. White men had the lowest excommunication rate after they were accused of a crime, but with the sheer weight of the accusations against them, they were expelled more often than were white women, slave men, and slave women combined. Moreover, the amount, type, and intensity of scrutiny may have made church investigations the hardest to bear for white men. Common charges, such as gambling, gaming, wrestling, and drinking, struck hard at conventional forms of male sociability. And in a culture that exalted the independence of the (white male) citizen/householder, Baptist men endured the scrutiny of their fellow members into their business practices, families, and treatment of slaves. They could not claim the sovereign authority that many southern planters happily asserted, but instead had to agree to submit to the scrutiny of the other members of the church. In this context, it is not surprising that white men's membership numbers did not hold steady against women's and black men's.

Women too had to submit to the authority of the brethren, but, given powerful cultural expectations of female submissiveness, this expectation of obedience would likely not have felt as foreign to them. Moreover, in a variety of ways, churches offered women some forms of protection and empowerment. They recognized women as crucial to the development of the sect and as the instruments of God's holy work, and they authorized their participation in church discipline, the central work of the church body. By the turn of the century, women may have lost opportunities to exhort and act as deaconesses, but churches continued to offer women opportunities to enact their values, structure community, and claim a (however circumscribed) public authority. Churches also influenced families in ways that could benefit women. They recognized women as joint heads of household and sometimes supported women's independent actions, whether it was seeking membership despite their husbands' objections or other individual negotiations between husbands and wives. Even in providing something as mundane as an accessible arena for economic disputes, churches offered women protections and options that could be difficult to find in that time and place. This is not to say that women joined churches for these practical or empowering elements, but they were likely a welcome part of church membership. They also indicate that we need to avoid using antebellum studies to understand gender practices of the late eighteenth and early nineteenth centuries. With most studies of the evangelical gender roles focusing on the antebellum period, the dominant model of evangelical white womanhood suggests that white women were invested with special spiritual qualities that well positioned them to raise children in the nurture of the Lord, infuse the home with Christian love, and act as domestic guardians of religious values, but should otherwise submit to a subservient place in the domestic hierarchy. Indeed, some historians have argued that churches served to sacralize gender inequality and to bolster the authority of husbands and fathers. However, as this volume and Lyerly's study of Methodism indicate, such themes and messages were largely absent before 1815.[2] During this era, parents were still identified together as responsible for children and domestic worship, and there are few indications that women were seen as invested with peculiar or exceptional forms of spirituality. Instead, in keeping with the ideal of the morally courageous and independent woman lauded in early Baptist stories, churches supported and sanctified female members' efforts to claim a religious identity of their own and their individual relationships to God and the church community. These were churches far more in pursuit of a spiritual agenda than of social hierarchies, and when it served this agenda to disrupt gender norms, they generally did so.

The issue of slavery proved to be a significant stumbling block for Baptists. There was an essential tension in eighteenth-century churches between the bonds of fellowship and the existence of slavery. While other tensions were able to be negotiated within churches, slavery ultimately proved too volatile as two equally resolute factions clashed. The contest was first contained geographically, and when that too proved explosive, Baptists confined it rhetorically, by creating a powerful redefinition with far-reaching consequences. By 1808, churches and associations agreed that slavery would no longer be considered a religious issue, but would instead fall under the jurisdiction of civil authorities, and they ceased any substantive protests of slavery. Thereafter, a church's intervention could only occur on a local level through voluntary oversight of the behavior of individual owners and slaves. The significance of this compromise would be difficult to overstate. Baptists' world view, after all, had posited a chasm between themselves and the world, a divide that allowed them to live outside of time and the norms of sinful society as God's holy remnant. To incorporate state authority into their resolutions was to defer to it; it was to acknowledge that the state had a jurisdiction upon which even the covenanted church could not encroach. Despite the cost, this settlement did not resolve the essential contradiction between an egalitarian theology and the acceptance of slavery and slaveholders within evangelical churches.

In the antebellum era, churches continued to contain black and white congregants, but the gap between black and white religious experiences grew. White ministers increasingly preached separate messages for their slave congregants that prescribed appropriate behavior, and large churches divided so that white and black congregants met separately. But despite these very real limitations which churches placed upon slave members, and the racism of many church policies, evangelical churches remained the only institution in which slaves could seek redress of their grievances, experience the social sanction of their marriages, and learn a language in which to safely express their hopes for freedom and redemption. As white Baptists increasingly came to actively support slavery and black Baptists found communal methods to resist slavery, each did so using evangelical language and, more remarkably, often did so in the same churches.[3] By the antebellum era, evangelical religion had come to permeate not only southern institutions, but the language and beliefs of those seeking to impose order and those seeking to unsettle it. Hereafter, the question would not be *whether* evangelicalism but *which* evangelicalism.

Appendix

Tables A3–A9 and 3.1 are based on discipline cases of *specific* charges in 78 churches in Virginia (25 churches), North Carolina (18 churches), Kentucky (18 churches), and Tennessee (19 churches). The earliest Virginia church minutes included here begin in 1766, the North Carolina minutes in 1772, the Kentucky minutes in 1786, and the Tennessee minutes in 1785, though most Tennessee records date from after 1794. These tables do not include unspecified charges of disorder, misconduct, or dispute; they also do not include nonattendance and not hearing the church, charges that were often leveled at the end of an unsatisfactory disciplinary proceeding and therefore can mask the primary offense.

TABLE A.1. Membership Numbers of Sample Churches by Sex and Race

Church	State	Date of Roll[a]	Total	White Men	White Women	Black Men	Black Women	Unknown
Chesterfield	Va.	1773	20	7 (35.0%)	12 (60.0%)	0	1 (5.0%)	0
Albemarle	Va.	1799	129	23 (17.8%)	33 (25.6%)	33 (25.6%)	40 (31.0%)	0
Broad Run	Va.	1801–1816	97	18 (18.6%)	28 (28.9%)	24 (24.7%)	27 (27.8%)	0
Hartwood	Va.	1806–?	136	32 (23.5%)	51 (37.5%)	27 (19.9%)	20 (14.7%)	6 (4.4%)
Providence	Ky.	1781	43	16 (37.2%)	25 (58.1%)	0	0	2 (4.7%)
Severn's Valley	Ky.	1796	41	16 (39.0%)	23 (56.1%)	1 (2.4%)	0	1 (2.4%)
Marble Creek	Ky.	1800–?	154	45 (29.2%)	61 (39.6%)	18 (11.7%)	30 (19.5%)	0
Burks Branch	Ky.	1801–1815	150	54 (36.0%)	88 (58.7%)	2 (1.3%)	6 (4.0%)	0
Flat Rock	N.C.	1796	89	29 (32.6%)	56 (62.9%)	2 (2.2%)	2 (2.2%)	0
Yeopim	N.C.	1798	85	33 (38.8%)	40 (47.1%)	5 (5.9%)	5 (5.9%)	2 (2.4%)
Wheeleys	N.C.	1807	155	54 (34.8%)	81 (52.3%)	9 (5.8%)	11 (7.1%)	0
Bent Creek	N.C.	1817	71	31 (43.7%)	37 (52.1%)	2 (2.8%)	0	1 (1.4%)
Red River	Tenn.	1791–1803	99	41 (41.4%)	57 (57.6%)	0	1 (1.0%)	0
Dixon's Creek	Tenn.	1805	81	36 (44.4%)	32 (39.5%)	3 (3.7%)	8 (9.9%)	2 (2.5%)
Mill Creek (Davidson Co.)	Tenn.	1797	102	26 (25.5%)	36 (35.3%)	19 (18.6%)	18 (17.6%)	3 (2.9%)
Spring Creek	Tenn.	1814	52	20 (38.5%)	31 (59.6%)	0	0	1 (1.9%)
Total			1504	481 (32.0%)	691 (45.9%)	145 (9.6%)	169 (11.2%)	18 (1.2%)

Sources: Membership lists drawn from each churchbook.

[a] Some membership lists identified the individuals currently in the church. Other lists were cumulative, adding the name of each newly admitted member; these lists then show how many members were admitted in a particular time period but not the number of members in the church at any one time. Those latter lists are marked here with a span of years and when the list was concluded, if known.

TABLE A.2. Membership Changes over Time in Sample Churches

Church	State	Date of Roll[a]	Total	White Men	White Women	Black Men	Black Women	Unknown
Albemarle	Va.	1773	48	25 (52.1%)	21 (43.8%)	1 (2.0%)	1 (2.0%)	0
Albemarle	Va.	1799	129	23 (17.8%)	33 (25.6%)	33 (25.6%)	40 (31.0%)	0
Broad Run	Va.	1762–1801	217	87 (40.0%)	95 (43.8%)	13 (6.0%)	21 (9.7%)	1 (0.5%)
Broad Run	Va.	1801–1816	97	18 (18.6%)	28 (28.9%)	24 (24.7%)	27 (27.8%)	0
Marble Creek	Ky.	1787	19	11 (57.9%)	8 (42.1%)	0	0	0
Marble Creek	Ky.	1787–1800	126	46 (36.5%)	57 (45.2%)	8 (6.3%)	15 (11.9%)	0
Marble Creek	Ky.	1800–?	154	45 (29.2%)	61 (39.6%)	18 (11.7%)	30 (19.5%)	0
Red River	Tenn.	1791	16	8 (50.0%)	8 (50.0%)	0	0	0
Red River	Tenn.	1791–1803	99	41 (41.4%)	57 (57.6%)	0	1 (1.0%)	0
Red River	Tenn.	1803–1814	276	98 (35.5%)	153 (55.4%)	8 (2.9%)	17 (6.2%)	0

Sources: Membership lists drawn from each churchbook.

[a] Some membership lists identify the individuals currently in the church. Other lists were cumulative, adding the name of each newly admitted member; these lists then show how many members were admitted in a particular time period but not the number of members in the church at any one time. Those latter lists are marked here with a span of years and when the list was concluded, if known.

TABLE A.3. Charges Leveled in Disciplinary Cases, 1760–1815[a]

	White Men	White Women	Slave Men	Slave Women	Other or Unclear[b]	Total
1760–1785	183 (57.7%)	85 (26.8%)	34 (10.7%)	5 (1.6%)	10 (3.2%)	317
1786–1800	540 (61.2%)	197 (22.3%)	83 (9.4%)	40 (4.5%)	23 (2.6%)	883
1801–1815	1668 (58.9%)	488 (17.2%)	371 (13.1%)	223 (7.9%)	83 (2.9%)	2833
Total	2391 (59.3%)	770 (19.1%)	488 (12.1%)	268 (6.7%)	116 (2.9%)	4033

Sources: Church Minutes of Abbott's Baptist Church; Albemarle Baptist Church; Bear Creek Baptist Church; Bent Creek Baptist Church; Bethel Hill Baptist Church; Bethlehem Baptist Church; Boar Swamp Baptist Church; Boone's Creek Baptist Church; Brashear's Creek Baptist Church; Broad Run Baptist Church; Brock's Gap Baptist Church; Bryan's Station Baptist Church; Buck Marsh Baptist Church; Burks Branch Baptist Church; Cashie Baptist Church; Chappawamsic Baptist Church; Cherokee Creek Baptist Church; Chesterfield Baptist Church; Church on the Twins; Cove Creek Baptist Church; Dandridge Baptist Church; Davis Baptist Church (published); Dixon Baptist Church (published); Dumplin Creek Baptist Church; Flat Rock Baptist Church; Forks of Elkhorn Baptist Church; Frying Pan Baptist Church; Garrison Fork Baptist Church; Goose Creek Baptist Church; Graves Creek Baptist Church; Great Cohary Baptist Church; Hartwood Baptist Church; Jersey Baptist Church; Little Beaver Creek Baptist Church; Lower Banister Baptist Church; Marble Creek Baptist Church; Matrimony Baptist; Meherrin Baptist Church; Mill Creek Baptist Church (Frederick County and Berkeley County, Va.); Mill Creek Baptist Church (Shenandoah County and Page County, Va); Mill Creek Baptist Church (Davidson County, Tenn.); Mill Swamp Baptist Church; Miller's Cove Baptist Church; Morattico Baptist Church; Mount Hermon Baptist Church; Mountain Island Baptist Church; Mount Olivet Baptist Church; Mount Tabor Church (published); New Hope Baptist Church; Newfound Baptist Church; Paw Paw Hollow Baptist Church; Providence Baptist Church (Clark County, Kent.); Providence Baptist Church (Davidson County, Tenn.); Red Banks Church; Red River Baptist Church (published); Reddies River Church; Salem Baptist Church; Saline Baptist Church; Sandy Creek Baptist Church; Severn's Valley Baptist Church; Shawnee Run Baptist Church (published); Sinking Creek Baptist Church; Six Mile Baptist Church; Smith's Creek Baptist Church; South Fork Baptist Church; South Quay Baptist Church; Spring Creek Baptist Church; Tate's Creek Baptist Church; Tomahawk Baptist Church; Tom's Creek Baptist Church; Upper King and Queen Baptist Church; Waller's Baptist Church; Waterlick Baptist Church; Well's Chapel Baptist Church; Wheeley's Primitive Baptist Church; Wilson Creek Primitive Baptist Church; Yeopim Baptist Church; and Zoar Baptist Church.

[a]This table demonstrates the accusations leveled against church members, not the number of accused. Some individuals had multiple offenses charged to them.

[b]This category includes very small numbers of free blacks. It also includes individuals whose race, status, or sex cannot be identified due to poor handwriting, incomplete references, unusual naming practices, or when white members in the church had a surname that matched a slave member's name (e.g., Brother Thomas).

TABLE A.4. Thirty Most Common Charges and the Accused

Charge	Total	White Men	White Women	Slave Men	Slave Women	Other or Unknown
1. Drinking to excess	800	682 (85.3%)	36 (4.5%)	55 (6.9%)	9 (1.1%)	18 (2.3%)
2. Lying	252	92 (36.5%)	67 (26.6%)	46 (18.3%)	41 (16.3%)	6 (2.4%)
3. Fighting	198	166 (83.8%)	3 (1.5%)	20 (10.1%)	7 (3.5%)	2 (1.0%)
4. Ill language[a]	181	119 (65.7%)	51 (28.2%)	3 (1.7%)	7 (3.9%)	1 (0.6%)
5. Mistreating spouse or family member[b]	155	63 (40.6%)	49 (31.6%)	19 (12.3%)	12 (7.7%)	12 (7.7%)
6. Adultery[c]	137	14 (10.2%)	17 (12.4%)	55 (40.1%)	43 (31.4%)	8 (5.8%)
7. Theft	136	22 (16.2%)	11 (8.1%)	64 (47.1%)	30 (22.1%)	9 (6.6%)
8. Fornication[d]	133	23 (17.3%)	75 (56.4%)	12 (9.0%)	22 (16.5%)	1 (0.8%)
9. Withdrawing from church or schism[e]	121	62 (51.2%)	32 (26.4%)	10 (8.3%)	11 (9.1%)	6 (5.0%)
9. Swearing	121	82 (67.8%)	8 (6.6%)	17 (14%)	8 (6.6%)	6 (5.0%)
11. Criticizing church or minister	101	68 (67.3%)	22 (21.8%)	8 (7.9%)	1 (1.0%)	2 (2.0%)
12. Gaming or gambling[f]	89	81 (91.0%)	2 (2.2%)	6 (6.7%)	0	0
12. Violating church disciplinary rules[g]	89	58 (65.2%)	30 (33.7%)	1 (1.1%)	0	0
14. General sexual misconduct[h]	88	28 (31.8%)	25 (28.4%)	19 (21.6%)	10 (11.4%)	6 (6.8%)
15. Keeping bad or worldly company (outside of the home)[i]	85	54 (63.5%)	25 (29.4%)	2 (2.4%)	0	4 (4.7%)
16. Participating in dancing, balls or dancing schools[j]	84	36 (42.9%)	35 (41.7%)	4 (4.8%)	6 (7.1%)	3 (3.6%)
17. Moving without letter of dismissal	83	40 (48.2%)	37 (44.6%)	1 (1.2%)	3 (3.6%)	2 (2.4%)
18. Anger	82	66 (80.5%)	12 (14.6%)	1 (1.2%)	2 (2.4%)	1 (1.2%)
19. Not properly governing home and family[k]	71	46 (64.8%)	24 (33.8%)	1 (1.4%)	0	0
20. Joined or communed with another faith	69	22 (31.9%)	44 (63.8%)	0	2 (2.9%)	1 (1.4%)
21. Misconduct related to land, money, or property	64	56 (87.5%)	7 (10.9%)	0	0	1 (1.6%)
22. Misconduct in trade or contract	56	46 (82.1%)	6 (10.7%)	4 (7.1%)	0	0

(continued)

TABLE A.4. *(continued)*

Charge	Total	White Men	White Women	Slave Men	Slave Women	Other or Unknown
23. Slander[l]	51	27 (52.9%)	17 (33.3%)	5 (9.8%)	1 (2.0%)	1 (2.0%)
24. Not paying debts[m]	50	45 (90.0%)	4 (8.0%)	0	0	1 (2.0%)
25. Breaking the Sabbath	41	33 (80.5%)	2 (4.9%)	5 (12.2%)	0	1 (2.4%)
26. Making false accusations[n]	41	24 (58.5%)	9 (22.0%)	4 (9.8%)	2 (4.9%)	2 (4.9%)
27. Assault	40	29 (72.5%)	6 (15.0%)	2 (5%)	0	3 (7.5%)
28. Bigamy	40	5 (12.5%)	7 (17.5%)	15 (37.5%)	8 (20.0%)	5 (12.5%)
29. Fraud	40	36 (90.0%)	2 (5.0%)	0	0	2 (5.0%)
30. Running away	39	0	0	28 (71.8%)	11 (28.2%)	0
Total	3537	2125 (60.1%)	665 (18.8%)	407 (11.5%)	236 (6.7%)	104 (2.9%)

Sources: See sources for Table A.3.

[a] Includes bad language; ill words; rough language; speaking harshly; murmurs; speaking out of the way; speaking reproachfully of member; disorderly speaking; unbecoming talk; talking more than becomes a Christian; talking too free; and insults. This category does not include allegations of profane language or blasphemy, which Baptists considered more serious offenses.

[b] Includes such charges as abused son's wife; disorderly conduct to wife and family; irregular conduct to wife; misconduct to mother; unbecoming conduct to husband; jealous of husband; left husband's bed; refusing subjection to husband; desertion; and whipped wife.

[c] Adultery was a different charge than fornication and indicated that at least one of the participants was married.

[d] Fornication (which includes the charge of bastardy) often was leveled against individuals who subsequently married but had a child before nine months had elapsed.

[e] Refers to individuals accused of leaving the church in anger or spirit of defiance, requesting excommunication, or declaring nonfellowship with the church. In this table, criticizing the church or minister and joining another faith are counted separately.

[f] Includes attending a shooting match or horse race; offering to bet; playing cards; playing fives; and pitching dollars.

[g] Includes charges of not taking gospel steps; going to law; reporting members' misbehavior outside the church; hard spirit in dispute with a member; and refusing reconciliation with a disciplined member.

[h] Includes all charges of sexual misconduct that did not explicitly include sexual relations, including acting too great with a certain woman; too familiar with a woman, not his wife; making too free with a married man; whispering to a young man; kissing; and whoring.

[i] Includes charges of attending unbecoming gatherings; attending a frolick; going out with soldiers; belonging to the Freemasons or other worldly societies; going to a play or racing party; and mixing with the world. It does not include attending balls (see number 16) or having bad company in one's home (see number 19).

[j] Includes those who sent their children (usually their daughters) to balls or dancing schools.

[k] Includes not governing children; neglecting family worship; and allowing disorder such as dancing, fiddling, gambling, "riots," or a disorderly corn shuck in their homes.

[l] See also making false accusations (number 26).

[m] Does not include charges of not paying *church* assessments or tithes.

[n] While this is similar to slander, Baptists leveled this charge against those who tried to initiate church disciplinary procedures without just cause.

TABLE A.5. Outcome of All Charges by Sex, Race, and Status, 1760–1815

Sex/Race	Acquitted	Gave Satisfaction & Restored	Admonished & Restored	Censured or Suspended	Expelled or Excommunicated	Other/Unclear[a]	Total
White Men	109 (4.6%)	704 (29.4%)	65 (2.7%)	343 (14.3%)	1064 (44.5%)	106 (4.4%)	2391
White Women	33 (4.3%)	112 (14.5%)	21 (2.7%)	114 (14.8%)	459 (59.6%)	31 (4.0%)	770
Slave Men	12 (2.5%)	43 (8.8%)	12 (2.5%)	52 (10.7%)	352 (72.1%)	17 (3.5%)	488
Slave Women	6 (2.2%)	12 (4.5%)	10 (3.7%)	16 (6.0%)	213 (79.5%)	11 (4.1%)	268
Free Black Men	0	1 (11.1%)	0	0	6 (66.7%)	2 (22.2%)	9
Free Black Women	1 (20%)	0	0	0	4 (80.0%)	0	5
Unknown	3 (2.9%)	15 (14.7%)	3 (2.9%)	10 (9.8%)	64 (62.7%)	7 (6.9%)	102
Total	164 (4.1%)	887 (22.0%)	111 (2.8%)	535 (13.3%)	2162 (53.6%)	174 (4.3%)	4033

Sources: See sources for Table A.3.

[a] This includes cases when charges were not mentioned again, cases which were not completed by the church because the accused died or moved to another church (where the matter would be completed), and cases in which the church records were incomplete.

TABLE A.6. Outcome of Discipline: Patterns across Time

	Acquitted	Gave Satisfaction & Restored	Admonished & Restored	Censured or Suspended	Expelled or Excommunicated	Other or Unclear	Total
1765–1785							
White Men	3 (1.6%)	14 (7.7%)	4 (2.2%)	72 (39.3%)	89 (48.6%)	1 (0.5%)	183
White Women	2 (2.4%)	4 (4.7%)	2 (2.4%)	26 (30.6%)	49 (57.6%)	2 (2.4%)	85
Slave Men	0	1 (2.9%)	0	12 (35.3%)	21 (61.8%)	0	34
Slave Women	0	0	0	1 (20.0%)	4 (80.0%)	0	5
Other or Unknown	0	1 (10.0%)	0	1 (10.0%)	8 (80.0%)	0	10
Total	5 (1.6%)	20 (6.3%)	6 (1.9%)	112 (35.3%)	171 (53.9%)	3 (0.9%)	317
1786–1800							
White Men	23 (4.3%)	158 (29.3%)	14 (2.6%)	78 (14.4%)	236 (43.7%)	31 (5.7%)	540
White Women	9 (4.6%)	32 (16.2%)	12 (6.1%)	30 (15.2%)	102 (51.8%)	12 (6.1%)	197
Slave Men	3 (3.6%)	14 (16.9%)	2 (2.4%)	17 (20.5%)	43 (51.8%)	4 (4.8%)	83
Slave Women	3 (7.5%)	0	0	4 (10.0%)	30 (75.0%)	3 (7.5%)	40
Other or Unknown	1 (4.3%)	0	0	3 (13.0%)	16 (69.6%)	3 (13%)	23
Total	39 (4.4%)	204 (23.1%)	28 (3.2%)	132 (14.9%)	427 (48.4%)	53 (6.0%)	883
1801–1815							
White Men	83 (5.0%)	532 (31.9%)	47 (2.8%)	193 (11.6%)	739 (44.3%)	74 (4.4%)	1668
White Women	22 (4.5%)	76 (15.6%)	7 (1.4%)	58 (11.9%)	308 (63.1%)	17 (3.5%)	488
Slave Men	9 (2.4%)	28 (7.5%)	10 (2.7%)	23 (6.2%)	288 (77.6%)	13 (3.5%)	371
Slave Women	3 (1.3%)	12 (5.4%)	10 (4.5%)	11 (4.9%)	179 (80.3%)	8 (3.6%)	223
Other or Unknown	3 (3.6%)	15 (18.1%)	3 (3.6%)	6 (7.2%)	50 (60.2%)	6 (7.2%)	83
Total	120 (4.2%)	663 (23.4%)	77 (2.7%)	291 (10.3%)	1564 (55.2%)	118 (4.2%)	2833

Sources: See sources for Table A.3.

TABLE A.7. Excommunication Numbers and Rates of Ten Most Common Charges

Charge	All Groups	White Men	White Women	Slave Men	Slave Women	Other or Unknown
1. Drinking	331 (41.3%)	269 (39.4%)	16 (44.4%)	31 (56.4%)	5 (55.6%)	10 (55.6%)
2. Lying	169 (67.1%)	50 (54.3%)	43 (64.2%)	38 (82.6%)	33 (80.5%)	5 (83.3%)
3. Fighting	81 (40.9%)	68 (41.0%)	2 (66.7%)	8 (40.0%)	3 (42.9%)	0
4. Ill language	79 (43.6%)	47 (39.5%)	26 (51.0%)	1 (33.3%)	5 (71.4%)	0
5. Mistreating spouse or family member	92 (59.4%)	32 (50.8%)	25 (51.0%)	14 (73.7%)	11 (91.7%)	10 (83.3%)
6. Adultery	126 (92.0%)	11 (78.6%)	17 (100%)	50 (90.9%)	40 (93.0%)	8 (100%)
7. Theft	96 (70.6%)	12 (54.5%)	4 (36.4%)	52 (81.3%)	19 (63.3%)	9 (100%)
8. Fornication	113 (85.0%)	17 (73.9%)	63 (84.0%)	12 (100%)	20 (90.9%)	1 (100%)
9. Withdrawing from church or schism	103 (85.1%)	49 (79.0%)	28 (87.5%)	10 (100%)	11 (100%)	5 (83.3%)
10. Swearing	81 (66.9%)	54 (65.9%)	2 (25.0%)	13 (76.5%)	7 (87.5%)	5 (83.3%)
Total	1271 (56.9%) (N = 2234)	609 (46.0%) (N = 1325)	226 (64.8%) (N = 349)	229 (76.1%) (N = 301)	154 (81.1%) (N = 190)	53 (76.8%) (N = 69)
Total [excluding drinking]	940 (65.6%) (N =1434)	340 (52.9%) (N = 643)	210 (67.0%) (N = 313)	198 (80.5%) (N = 246)	149 (82.3%) (N = 181)	43 (84.3%) (N = 51)

Sources: See sources for Table A.3.

Note: For overall numbers of charges in each category and types of accusations included in each category, see Table A.4.

TABLE A.8. Charges concerning Families and Households (except Slaves)

Charge	White Men	White Women	Slave Men	Slave Women	Other or Unknown	Total
Adultery	13 (9.6%)	17 (12.5%)	55 (40.4%)	43 (31.6%)	8 (5.9%)	136
Fornication	23 (17.3%)	75 (56.4%)	12 (9.0%)	22 (16.5%)	1 (0.8%)	133
Desertion of spouse or family	9 (17.3%)	14 (26.9%)	15 (28.8%)	7 (13.5%)	7 (13.5%)	52
Allowing revelry or disorder in the house or family	34 (66.7%)	16 (31.4%)	1 (2.0%)	0	0	51
Bigamy	5 (12.5%)	7 (17.5%)	15 (37.5%)	8 (20.0%)	5 (12.5%)	40
Not governing or raising children properly[a]	19 (57.6%)	14 (42.4%)	0	0	0	33
General disorderly conduct to family members[b]	13 (41.9%)	14 (45.2%)	0	4 (12.9%)	0	31
Fighting with spouse or marital discord	10 (40.0%)	8 (32.0%)	2 (8.0%)	1 (4.0%)	4 (16.0%)	25
Spousal abuse	19 (95.0%)	0	1 (5.0%)	0	0	20
Unlawful or inappropriate marriage[c]	4 (30.8%)	6 (46.2%)	1 (7.7%)	2 (15.4%)	0	13
Assaulting or abusing a family member[d]	9 (64.3%)	4 (28.6%)	1 (7.1%)	0	0	14
Disobedience to a family member[e]	2 (28.6%)	5 (71.4%)	0	0	0	7
Ill language to a family member	2 (40.0%)	3 (60.0%)	0	0	0	5
Neglecting family worship	4 (80.0%)	1 (20.0%)	0	0	0	5
Breaking Marriage Engagement	2 (100%)	0	0	0	0	2
Total	168 (29.6%)	184 (32.6%)	103 (18.1%)	87 (15.4%)	25 (4.4%)	567

Sources: See sources for Table A.3.

Note: This table takes a closer look at charges concerning families and households. To do so, it breaks apart some previously used categories and creates new categories.

[a] Includes accusations of allowing children to go to dancing school or balls; not exercising authority over children; and allowing them to be baptized as infants.
[b] Includes charges of mistreatment that do not explicitly include physical assault, including ill treatment of spouse; mistreating father; lying to mother; being jealous of husband; and unbecoming conduct to spouse.
[c] Includes charges of marrying a close relative (brother's widow, half sister's son, uncle's wife); marrying too quickly (eight days after meeting); and marrying without notifying husband of pregnancy. It does not include bigamy, which is listed separately.
[d] Includes abusing one's children or children bound to one; abusing daughter-in-law; striking father-in-law; and attempting to kill wife and children. It does not include spousal abuse, which is listed separately.
[e] Includes disobedience to parents; disobedience to father; and rejecting husband's authority. Five of the six cases regarding women concerned their relationships to their husbands.

TABLE A.9. Charges between Whites and Blacks

Charge	White Men	White Women	Slave Men	Slave Women	Total
Conflict with church relating to slavery[a]	27 (46.6%)	19 (32.8%)	8 (13.8%)	4 (6.9%)	58
Running away	0	0	28 (71.8%)	11 (28.2%)	39
Disobedience[b]	0	0	26 (78.8%)	7 (21.2%)	33
General disorderly conduct to whites or blacks[c]	4 (14.8%)	5 (18.5%)	10 (37.0%)	8 (29.6%)	27
Mistreatment of whites or blacks[d]	6 (50.0%)	4 (33.3%)	1 (8.3%)	1 (8.3%)	12
Ill language or insolence to whites or blacks	1 (14.3%)	0	2 (28.6%)	4 (57.1%)	7
Interracial sex	5 (71.4%)	0	0	2 (28.6%)	7
Physical assault[e]	3 (60.0%)	0	2 (40.0%)	0	5
Illicit trading with whites or blacks	2 (50.0%)	2 (50.0%)	0	0	4
Lying to whites or blacks	0	1 (33.3%)	0	2 (66.7%)	3
Neglects work or laziness	0	0	1 (33.3%)	2 (66.7%)	3
Not taking gospel steps[f]	1 (50.0%)	1 (50.0%)	0	0	2
False accusation of whites or blacks	0	0	0	2 (100%)	2
Harboring a slave	1 (100%)	0	0	0	1
Wants to sit in church with whites or blacks	1 (100%)	0	0	0	1
Total	51 (25.0%)	32 (15.7%)	78 (38.2%)	43 (21.1%)	204

Sources: See sources for Table A.3

Note: This table examines how churches judged (or did not judge) the behavior of slaves and owners to one another in cases where race was explicitly mentioned. To do so, it breaks apart some previously used categories and creates new categories. There may be, and no doubt are, additional charges that concern master-slave relationships but were not designated as such in the churchbooks (e.g., thirty-five slaves were accused of ill language or swearing, but only four of those cases indicated it was to or about a white person). Also, this table does not include all of the discipline leveled against slaves or slave owners.

[a] Includes charges of challenging a decision of the church (regarding the preaching of emancipation or slave titles); withdrawing from the church over slavery; and supporting the black members in schism. In the conflicts of 1805-1808, a few churches (such as South Fork) identified members as withdrawn but did not indicate subsequent discipline; those cases are not included here.
[b] Whites were occasionally charged with disobedience. Some white women were accused of disobedience to a particular person or persons (parents or husbands), and both white men and white women were charged with "disobedience," presumably referring to the church in regard to some other disciplinary matter. For this category, I have assumed that all disobedience charges leveled against slaves referred to owners or overseers, unless explicitly designated otherwise.
[c] Includes charges of being disorderly; quarreling; being willing to leave for old master; and allowing roguery.
[d] Includes charges of mistreatment outside of explicit mention of physical assault, such as denying contact with child; selling husband from wife; and churchbooks' own designation of "mistreatment."
[e] Includes only charges that specify physical assault, such as burning, whipping, and fighting.
[f] All members were required to use the gospel method of discipline, which required the intervention and mediation of the church.

Notes

ABBREVIATIONS

ABQ	*American Baptist Quarterly*
AHR	*American Historical Review*
HMPEC	*Historical Magazine of the Protestant Episcopal Church*
JAH	*Journal of American History*
JER	*Journal of the Early Republic*
JSH	*Journal of Southern History*
KHS	Kentucky Historical Society Library, Frankfort
LC	Rare Book Room, Library of Congress, Washington, D.C.
LVA	Archives, Library of Virginia, Richmond
NCBHC	North Carolina Baptist Historical Collection, Z. Smith Reynolds Library, Wake Forest University, Winston-Salem
NCLA	North Carolina State Library and Archives, Raleigh
SBHLA	Southern Baptist Historical Library and Archives, Nashville, Tennessee
SBTS	Archives and Special Collections, James P. Boyce Centennial Library, Southern Baptist Theological Seminary, Louisville, Kentucky
SHSW	State Historical Society of Wisconsin, Madison
TSLA	Tennessee State Library and Archives, Nashville
UK	Special Collections and Archives, Margaret I. King Library, University of Kentucky, Lexington
VBHS	Virginia Baptist Historical Society, University of Virginia, Richmond
VHS	Virginia Historical Society, Richmond

WL Wilson Library (Manuscripts), University of North Carolina, Chapel Hill
WMQ *William and Mary Quarterly*

INTRODUCTION

1. Paul Leicester Ford, ed., *The Works of Thomas Jefferson*, 12 vols. (New York: Putnam's, 1904–1905), 1:62.

2. One of the best comprehensive works in this body of literature is Thomas J. Curry's *The First Freedoms: Church and State in America to the Passage of the First Amendment* (New York: Oxford University Press, 1986). There has also been some innovative work reconceptualizing this topic; see particularly Jonathan D. Sassi, *A Republic of Righteousness: The Public Christianity of the Post-Revolutionary New England Clergy* (New York: Oxford University Press, 2001); Mark Douglas McGarvie, *One Nation Under Law: America's Early National Struggles to Separate Church and State* (Northern Illinois University Press, 2005); and Nancy Isenberg, "'Pillars in the Same Temple and Priests of the Same Worship': Woman's Rights and the Politics of Church and State in Antebellum America," *JAH* 85 (June 1998): 98–128. The history of disestablishment in Virginia and the passage of Jefferson's Act for Establishing Religious Freedom have come under extensive scrutiny, and Virginia was indeed the site of the most dramatic and rapid cases of revolutionary era transformations. Only a few years before the Revolution, authorities sought to protect the religious establishment by imprisoning some of the troubling dissenting ministers. But during the following fifteen years, not only was the church establishment dismantled, but it was replaced with the "establishment" of religious freedom. Moreover, the participation of such leaders as Thomas Jefferson and James Madison elevated the Virginia struggle from a local conflict to a precursor to the national debate over religion's role in government and government's role in religion. Good treatments of Virginia's disestablishment include Thomas E. Buckley, *Church and State in Revolutionary Virginia, 1776–1787* (Charlottesville: University of Virginia Press, 1977); and Merrill D. Peterson and Robert C. Vaughan, eds., *The Virginia Statute for Religious Freedom: Its Evolution and Consequences in American History* (Cambridge: Cambridge University Press, 1988).

For discussions specifically concerning the Baptists' involvement in the Virginia debates, see Garnett Ryland, *The Baptists of Virginia, 1699–1926* (Richmond: Virginia Baptist Board of Missions and Education, 1955), chaps. 4–7; Joe L. Coker, "Sweet Harmony vs. Strict Separation: Recognizing the Distinctions between Isaac Backus and John Leland," *ABQ* 16(3) (1997): 241–250; and Andrew M. Manis, "Regionalism and a Baptist Perspective on Separation of Church and State," *ABQ* 2(3) (1983): 213–227.

3. R. Laurence Moore, *Selling God: American Religion in the Marketplace of Culture* (New York: Oxford University Press, 1994), 7–8.

4. Rhys Isaac, *The Transformation of Virginia, 1740–1790* (Chapel Hill: University of North Carolina Press, 1982); and Donald G. Mathews, *Religion in the Old South*

(Chicago: University of Chicago Press, 1977). See also Cynthia Lynn Lyerly, *Methodism and the Southern Mind, 1770–1810* (New York: Oxford University Press, 1998); Nathan O. Hatch, *The Democratization of American Christianity* (New Haven, Conn.: Yale University Press, 1989); Patricia U. Bonomi, *Under the Cope of Heaven: Religion, Society, and Politics in Colonial America* (New York: Oxford University Press, 1986); and Albert J. Raboteau, *Slave Religion: The "Invisible Institution" in the Antebellum South* (New York: Oxford University Press, 1978). In *On Jordan's Stormy Banks: Evangelicalism in Mississippi, 1773–1876* (Athens: University of Georgia Press, 1994), Randy J. Sparks found a continuation of some of these early national patterns in frontier Mississippi. In contrast, see Christine Leigh Heyrman, in *Southern Cross: The Beginnings of the Bible Belt* (Chapel Hill: University of North Carolina Press, 1997). For other works that argue against the revolutionary nature of evangelical churches, see Jon Butler, *Awash in a Sea of Faith: Christianizing the American People* (Cambridge, Mass.: Harvard University Press, 1990); and Sylvia R. Frey, *Water from the Rock: Black Resistance in a Revolutionary Age* (Princeton, N.J.: Princeton University Press, 1991), particularly chap. 8.

5. This was in stark contrast to Anglicanism, in which the sacred space of a church building was a central element of the religious culture. See Dell Upton, *Holy Things and Profane: Anglican Parish Churches in Colonial Virginia* (New York: Architectural History Foundation; Cambridge, Mass.: MIT Press, 1986), chap. 8. See also Isaac, *Transformation of Virginia*, 58–70.

6. See Stephanie McCurry, *Masters of Small Worlds: Yeoman Households, Gender Relations, and the Political Culture of the Antebellum South Carolina Low Country* (New York: Oxford University Press, 1995), particularly chap. 1.

7. There is a vast literature on this subject for New England which includes such important works as Edmund S. Morgan, *The Puritan Family: Religion and Domestic Relations in Seventeenth-Century New England* (1944; reprint, New York: Harper & Row, 1966); Richard L. Bushman, *From Puritan to Yankee: Character and the Social Order in Connecticut, 1690–1765* (New York: Norton, 1967); David D. Hall, *Worlds of Wonder, Days of Judgment: Popular Religious Belief in Early New England* (New York: Knopf, 1989); and Christine Leigh Heyrman, *Commerce and Culture: The Maritime Communities of Colonial Massachusetts, 1690–1750* (New York: Norton, 1984). The literature on religion and colonization in the Mid-Atlantic region has been growing steadily since the late twentieth century. See, for instance, Bonomi's comprehensive study of religion in the British colonies, *Under the Cope of Heaven*; Sally Schwartz, *"A Mixed Multitude": The Struggle for Toleration in Colonial Pennsylvania* (New York: New York University Press, 1987); and Aaron Spencer Fogleman, "Jesus Is Female: The Moravian Challenge in the German Communities of British North America," *WMQ* 3d ser., 60 (2003): 295–332. For the northern Spanish frontier, see Ramón A. Gutiérrez, *When Jesus Came, the Corn Mothers Went Away: Marriage, Sexuality, and Power in New Mexico, 1500–1846* (Stanford, Calif.: Stanford University Press, 1991).

8. For an introduction to the ideologies of spheres and gender, see Linda K. Kerber, "Separate Spheres, Female Worlds, Woman's Place: The Rhetoric of Women's

History," *JAH* 75 (June 1988): 9–39; and Linda K. Kerber, Nancy F. Cott, et al., "Beyond Roles, Beyond Spheres: Thinking about Gender in the Early Republic," *WMQ* 3d ser., 46 (July 1989): 565–585. For the impact of spheres ideology on the language of labor, see Jeanne Boydston, *Home and Work: Housework, Wages, and the Ideology of Labor in the Early Republic* (New York: Oxford University Press, 1990). For architectural expressions of the increasing desire to divide private from public, see Isaac, *Transformation of Virginia*, 70–74, 302–305; and Jack Larkin, *The Reshaping of Everyday Life, 1790–1840* (New York: Harper & Row, 1988), chap. 3, particularly 116–127.

Jürgen Habermas offers another model of these spheres in *The Structural Transformation of the Public Sphere: An Inquiry into a Category of Bourgeois Society*, translated by Thomas Burger in association with Frederick Lawrence (Cambridge, Mass.: MIT Press, 1989). In an argument that has been profoundly influential as well as consistently critiqued, Habermas posited the creation of an eighteenth-century bourgeois public sphere that was a locus of politics and civic discourse, an arena apart from a private sphere of family, domesticity, and economic life. Habermas argued that this public sphere consisted of the institutions and structures that allowed men the spaces to critique, challenge, and negotiate with the state. For Habermas, then, the eighteenth-century public and private spheres represented different interests and spaces, but were not in a dualistic relationship, since the public sphere stood between, and mediated, the private sphere and the state.

CHAPTER I

1. William Waller Hening, ed., *The Statutes at Large: Being a Collection of All the Laws of Virginia, from the First Session of the Legislature in the Year 1619*, 13 vols. (New York, 1819–1823), 1:67–75; H. J. Eckenrode, *Separation of Church and State in Virginia: A Study in the Development of the Revolution* (1910; reprint, New York: Da Capo, 1971), 5–7, 7–13. For more, see Dell Upton, *Holy Things and Profane: Anglican Parish Churches in Colonial Virginia* (New York: Architectural History Foundation; Cambridge, Mass.: MIT Press, 1986), chap. 1; and William H. Seiler, "The Anglican Church: A Basic Institution of Local Government in Colonial Virginia," in Bruce C. Daniels, ed., *Town and County: Essays on the Structure of Local Government in the American Colonies* (Middletown, Conn.: Wesleyan University Press, 1978).

2. Hugh Talmage Lefler, "The Anglican Church in North Carolina: The Proprietary Period," in Lawrence Foushee London and Sarah McCulloh Lemmon, eds., *The Episcopal Church in North Carolina, 1701–1959* (Raleigh: Episcopal Diocese of North Carolina, 1987); and Hugh Talmage Lefler, "The Anglican Church in North Carolina: The Royal Period," in London and Lemmon, eds., *The Episcopal Church in North Carolina*. See also Gary Freeze, "Like a House Built upon Sand: The Anglican Church and Establishment in North Carolina, 1765–1776," *HMPEC* 48 (1979): 405–432.

3. George MacLaren Brydon, *Virginia's Mother Church and the Political Conditions under Which It Grew*, 2 vols. (Richmond, Va., 1947), 1:396.

4. Robert W. Prichard, *A History of the Episcopal Church* (Harrisburg, Pa.: Morehouse, 1991), 34, 29–36; and Frederick V. Mills, *Bishops by Ballot: An Eighteenth-Century Ecclesiastical Revolution* (New York: Oxford University Press, 1978), 6. For a good overview, see Prichard, *A History of the Episcopal Church*, chap. 2.

5. Richard R. Beeman, *The Evolution of the Southern Backcountry: A Case Study of Lunenburg County, Virginia, 1746–1832* (Philadelphia: University of Pennsylvania Press, 1984).

6. Upton, *Holy Things and Profane*, 199–200, 175–198. See also Rhys Isaac, *The Transformation of Virginia, 1740–1790* (Chapel Hill: University of North Carolina Press, 1982), 58–70; and Upton, *Holy Things and Profane*, chap. 10.

7. Carl Bridenbaugh, *Myths and Realities: Societies of the Colonial South* (Baton Rouge: Louisiana State University Press, 1952), 3.

8. W. Stitt Robinson, *The Southern Colonial Frontier, 1607–1763* (Albuquerque: University of New Mexico Press, 1979), 107–110, 121–161, 176–180. Jack P. Greene explores the different socioeconomic regions within the southern backcountry in "Independence, Improvement, and Authority: Toward a Framework for Understanding the Histories of the Southern Backcountry during the Era of the American Revolution," in Ronald Hoffman, Thad W. Tate, and Peter J. Albert, eds., *An Uncivil War: The Southern Backcountry during the American Revolution* (Charlottesville: Published for the U.S. Capitol Historical Society by the University of Virginia Press, 1985).

9. Robinson, *Southern Colonial Frontier*, 179–180; John B. Boles, *The South through Time: A History of an American Region* (Englewood Cliffs, N.J.: Prentice-Hall, 1995), 53–56. For an excellent study of the development of a western county, see Beeman, *Evolution of the Southern Backcountry*. See also Bridenbaugh, *Myths and Realities*, 121–144.

10. See Jack P. Greene, *Pursuits of Happiness: The Social Development of Early Modern British Colonies and the Formation of American Culture* (Chapel Hill: University of North Carolina Press, 1988), chap. 4. Quote on p. 85.

11. Ibid., 82.

12. Upton, *Holy Things and Profane*, 11–17, 19–22. For an example of conflicts between ministers and clergy, see William L. Saunders, ed., *The Colonial Records of North Carolina*, 10 vols. (Raleigh, N.C., 1886–1890), 4:254.

13. Maryland Clergy to the Lord Bishop of London, Maryland, Port Annapolis, May 18, 1696, in William Stevens Perry, D.D., ed., *Historical Collections Relating to the American Colonial Church*, 5 vols. (Hartford, Conn., 1870–1878), 4:10; Mr. Forbes' Account of the State of the Church in Virginia, July 21, 1724, in Perry, ed., *Historical Collections*, 1:326; and John Boyd to [Bishop of London], North West Parish, No. Carolina, April 12, 1735, in Saunders, ed., *Colonial Records*, 4:7. There was also a human cost to these travels. Studies of Methodist itinerants suggest they died younger than the norm after years of traveling through inclement weather, uncertain lodgings, a demanding schedule, and the hazards of horseback riding. But whereas most Methodist itinerants began their careers as young men who willingly chose their path, Anglican ministers did not expect to be itinerants. They

reported frequent illnesses and infirmities. Indeed, a missionary's frequent and varied complaints to his superiors could be so incessant that he appeared to be whining, until a subsequent letter announced the minister's untimely death.

14. Even in Edenton (which offered a better living than many of the surrounding areas), the church was unfinished in 1745, and the community lacked a Bible and a Book of Common Prayer. As late as 1767, seven of the thirty North Carolina counties claimed they were unable to support a minister, and only ten had ministers. Stories of the dire conditions in North Carolina filled the correspondence to the SPG leadership in London. Clement Hall to the Secretary, North Carolina, Perquimons, Feb. 27, 1744/45, in Saunders, ed., *Colonial Records*, 4:752–53; Return of the Names of the Counties and Parishes, Estimate of 1767..., in Saunders, ed., *Colonial Records*, 7:541.

15. Mr. Adams to the Bishop of London (Extract), Stephney Parish, Somerset County, Maryland, 2d July 1711, in Perry, ed., *Historical Collections*, 4:63.

16. Letter from Governor Tyron to the Society for the Propagation of the Gospel in Foreign Parts, Brunswick, 31 July 1765, in Saunders, ed., *Colonial Records*, 7:103.

17. Mr. Lang to the Bishop of London, Virginia, February, 7th, 1725/26, in Perry, ed., *Historical Collections*, 1:346; Rev. Giles Ransford to [Bishop of London], Chowan, North Carolina, 1712, July 25, in Robert J. Cain, ed., *The Colonial Records of North Carolina*, Second Series, vol. 10: *The Church of England in North Carolina: Documents, 1699–1741* (Raleigh: Department of Archives and History, 1999), 145; M^r. Nicholas Moreau, to the Right Honorable the Lord Bishop of Lichfield and Coventry, His Majesty's High Almoner, Virginia, 12th April, 1697, in Perry, ed., *Historical Collections*, 1:30.

18. Philip Vickers Fithian, *Journal and Letters of Philip Vickers Fithian, 1773–1774: A Plantation Tutor of the Old Dominion* (Charlottesville: University of Virginia Press, 1957), 137; Rev. John Urmston to Bishop of London, Jan. 21, 1711/12, in Cain, ed., *Colonial Records*, 10:135. Italics mine; Richard J. Hooker, ed., *The Carolina Backcountry on the Eve of the Revolution: The Journal and Other Writings of Charles Woodmason, Anglican Itinerant* (Chapel Hill: University of North Carolina Press, 1953), 103–104; Rev. Mr. Skippon to the Right Revd Lord Bishop of London, Annapolis, Jan. 19th, 1714/15, in Perry, ed., *Historical Collections*, 4:73; Mr Barnett to the Secretary, Brunswick 22 Aug 1767, in Saunders, ed., *Colonial Records*, 7:515; Reverend John Alexander, Will, 4, April 1795, Drane Collection, Robert Brent Drane Papers, #2987, folder 2, WL. Historians have debated the religiosity of the Anglican South, at times disagreeing as passionately as the colonists themselves. The early historiography of the Church of England depicted the southern colonial church (particularly that of Virginia) as an institution more worldly than divine, concerned primarily with serving civil needs and beset with a greedy, immoral clergy remarkable more for their antics than for their piety. Ironically, these depictions began in nineteenth-century denominational studies by Episcopalians. Influenced by the evangelical wing of Episcopalianism, Bishop William Meade in *Old Churches, Ministers, and Families of Virginia* (Philadelphia: Lippincott, 1861) portrayed the colonial church as suffering in a dark era out of which emerged a better and purer church.

Later histories often repeat this view of a worldly and ineffectual church. Richard Middleton presents a typical view when he states, "in the South [the Anglican Church] tended to remain the religion of the planter class, who seemingly adopted it for reasons of social snobbery rather than conviction." Richard Middleton, *Colonial America: A History, 1607–1760* (Cambridge, Mass.: Blackwell, 1992), 251. See also Bridenbaugh, *Myths and Realities*, 30–32. Other historians have challenged these portrayals of a troubled Church of England and a worldly lay population. See Patricia U. Bonomi, *Under the Cope of Heaven: Religion, Society, and Politics in Colonial America* (New York: Oxford University Press, 1986); and Joan R. Gundersen, "Evangelical Captives: Historians and Religion in Early America," paper delivered at the Institute for Early American History and Culture Conference, Ann Arbor, Mich., 1995. See also George MacLaren Brydon, "New Light upon the History of the Church in Colonial Virginia," *HMPEC* 10 (June 1941): 69–103; and Joan R. Gundersen, *The Anglican Ministry in Virginia, 1723–1766: A Study of a Social Class* (New York: Garland, 1989).

The nature of this historiographic debate itself contributes to the difficulty of assessing the religious culture within the southern Church of England. Those who have studied the Anglican Church since the 1980s—and there are remarkably few—continue to direct their arguments to countering older assertions about the southern Anglican Church. Thus the literature often focuses on what the Anglican Church was *not* rather than what it *was* and pursues an agenda (for instance, the character of the ministers or the independence of the vestry) that was set in the nineteenth century. For notable exceptions, see Upton, *Holy Things and Profane*, and Nancy L. Rhoden, *Revolutionary Anglicanism: The Colonial Church of England Clergy during the American Revolution* (New York: New York University Press, 1999).

19. For reports of the sects present, see Saunders, ed., *Colonial Records*, 6:265, 7:241, 7:285–288, 7:705; quote from 4:604; Bridenbaugh, *Myths and Realities*, 185.

20. See Rodger M. Payne, "New Light in Hanover County: Evangelical Dissent in Piedmont Virginia, 1740–1755," *JSH* 61 (Nov. 1995): 665–694; and Wesley M. Gewehr, *The Great Awakening in Virginia, 1740–1790* (Durham, N.C.: Duke University Press, 1930).

21. It is very difficult to state with certainty what exactly were common religious beliefs of eighteenth-century slaves, because of a dearth of sources. Most historians who have studied this difficult topic approach the issue by first identifying patterns of belief in West Africa and use the more available sources from the nineteenth century to posit their version of survivals, "Africanisms," transplantations, and cultural synthesis. This method is suggestive for the eighteenth century, but connecting the dots between what was believed or practiced in Africa and what was believed and practiced in the British-American colonies is a platform from which few historians wish to leap without a documentary net beneath them. More work has been done to explore the religious worlds of nineteenth-century slaves, particularly in the antebellum period. Melville J. Herskovits in *The Myth of the Negro Past* (1941; reprint, Boston: Beacon, 1990) offered one of the earliest and most influential discussions

of survivals. Many scholars have developed and revised this model in a rich literature. See Albert J. Raboteau, *Slave Religion: The "Invisible Institution" in the Antebellum South* (New York: Oxford University Press, 1978), chaps. 1 and 2; Sylvia R. Frey and Betty Wood, *Come Shouting to Zion: African American Protestantism in the American South and British Caribbean to 1830* (Chapel Hill: University of North Carolina Press, 1998), chaps. 1 and 2; Eugene D. Genovese, *Roll, Jordan, Roll: The World the Slaves Made* (1974; reprint, New York: Vintage, 1976), 161–202; Mechal Sobel, *Trabelin' On: The Slave Journey to an Afro-Baptist Faith* (1979; reprint, Princeton, N.J.: Princeton University Press, 1988); and Marvin L. Michael Kay and Lorin Lee Cary, *Slavery in North Carolina, 1748–1775* (Chapel Hill: University of North Carolina Press, 1995), chap. 8. Lawrence W. Levine, while rejecting the term "survivals," traces the transformations of African beliefs and rituals in slave culture in *Black Culture and Black Consciousness: Afro-American Folk Thought from Slavery to Freedom* (New York: Oxford University Press, 1977), chap. 1. Jon Butler rejects the model of survivals, arguing that the brutality of slavery and the use of Christianity to extend masters' authority resulted in an "African spiritual holocaust" in *Awash in a Sea of Faith*, chap. 5.

22. William Waller Hening, ed., *The Statutes at Large: Being a Collection of All the Laws of Virginia, from the First Session of the Legislature in the Year 1619*, 13 vols. (New York, 1819–1823), 2:244; quoted in Brydon, *Virginia's Mother Church*, 1:392, 393.

23. For analyses of Congregational revivals and the evangelical sects that emerged from them, see Bonomi, *Under the Cope of Heaven*, 123–160; Barbara E. Lacey, "Women and the Great Awakening in Connecticut" (Ph.D. diss., Clark University, 1982); William L. Lumpkin, *Baptist Foundations in the South: Tracing through the Separates the Influence of the Great Awakening, 1754–1787* (Nashville, Tenn.: Broadman, 1961), reprinted in William L. Lumpkin and L. H. Butterfield, eds., *Colonial Baptists and Southern Revivals* (New York: Arno, 1980); Edwin S. Gaustad, *The Great Awakening in New England* (New York: Harper, 1957); and C. C. Goen, *Revivalism and Separatism in New England, 1740–1800* (New Haven, Conn.: Yale University Press, 1962). For works that analyze revivalism in a broader continental and transatlantic context, see particularly Frank Lambert, *Inventing the "Great Awakening"* (Princeton, N.J.: Princeton University Press, 1999); Michael J. Crawford, *Seasons of Grace: Colonial New England's Revival Tradition in Its British Context* (New York: Oxford University Press, 1991); and Leigh Eric Schmidt, *Holy Fairs: Scotland and the Making of American Revivalism* (Princeton, N.J.: Princeton University Press, 1989).

24. There have been many excellent works on the arrival and growth of the Separate Baptists in the Upper South and the subsequent development of the Baptist evangelical movement. For good general works on the topic, see Reuben Edward Alley, *A History of Baptists in Virginia* (Richmond: Virginia Baptist General Board, 1973); Gewehr, *The Great Awakening in Virginia*; Lumpkin, *Baptist Foundations*; and Garnett Ryland, *The Baptists of Virginia, 1699–1926* (Richmond: Virginia Baptist Board of Missions and Education, 1955).

In the 1980s, Rhys Isaac's path-breaking work, *The Transformation of Virginia*, revived historians' interest in the development of a Baptist evangelical movement and was followed by a host of studies that reexamined the growth of this sect in the late colonial and early national eras. See, for instance, Janet Moore Lindman, "A World of Baptists: Gender, Race, and Religious Community in Pennsylvania and Virginia, 1689–1825" (Ph.D. diss., University of Minnesota, 1994); and J. Stephen Kroll-Smith, "Transmitting a Revival Culture: The Organization Dynamic of the Baptist Movement in Colonial Virginia, 1760–1777," *JSH* 50 (Nov. 1984): 551–568.

25. Morgan Edwards, *Materials towards a History of the Baptists*, 2 vols. (Danielsville, Ga.: Heritage Papers, 1984), 2:92.

26. James B. Taylor, *Lives of Virginia Baptist Ministers*, 2nd ed. (Richmond, Va., 1838), 21, 11; Edwards, *Materials towards a History of the Baptists*, 2:45; Adelaide L. Fries, *Records of the Moravians in North Carolina*, 11 vols. (Raleigh, N.C.: Edwards & Broughton, 1922), 1:321; [Alexander] Stewart to the Secretary, Bath, N. Carolina, Oct. 10, 1760, in Saunders, ed., *Colonial Records*, 6:316; Rev. Mr. [Charles Edward] Taylor to the Secretary, St. George's Parish, Northhampton County, North Carolina, May 17th, 1774 [extract], in Saunders, ed., *Colonial Records*, 9:23.

27. As David Thomas explained in 1774, "the Gospel-Church, must signify a company of persons removed in compliance with some call. 'Tis customary indeed in some places, to call the house dedicated to divine service, 'the 'Church:' But this is not according to Scripture." Thomas, *The Virginian Baptist: or, A View and Defence of the Christian Religion, as It is Professed by the Baptists of Virginia* (Baltimore, Md., 1774), 23.

28. Robert B. Semple, *A History of the Rise and Progress of the Baptists in Virginia* (Richmond, 1810), 5, 8.

29. Taylor, *Lives*, 20.

30. Significantly, however, Isaac's evidence in *Transformation of Virginia* is drawn from both Separate and Particular (or "Regular") churches. For other depictions of the differences between Separate and Particular Baptists, see Sydney E. Ahlstrom, *A Religious History of the American People* (New Haven, Conn.: Yale University Press, 1972); and Lumpkin, *Baptist Foundations*. Janet Moore Lindman also challenges Isaac's characterization of the Separates in "A World of Baptists," chap. 2.

31. Robert G. Gardner conservatively estimated that the number of Particular Baptist congregations rose from (at most) one in 1750, to sixteen by 1760, and to twenty-seven by 1770. Separate Baptists experienced a similar increase, with the number of Separate churches rising from zero in 1750, to eight by 1760, and to twenty-five by 1770. The number of congregants in Particular and Separate churches underwent similar increases, with the number of Particular members rising from 0 in 1750, to 1,072 by 1760, and 2,935 by 1770, and the number of Separate members rising from (at most) 5 in 1750, to 509 by 1760, to 2,418 by 1770. Only the General Baptists declined (from 711 members to 175), primarily because they were evangelized and reorganized to conform to the Particular Baptist church structure. The overall number of members of General, Particular, and Separate churches rose from 711 in 1750, to 1,890 by 1760, and to 5,483 by 1770. Robert G.

Gardner, *Baptists of Early America: A Statistical History, 1639–1790* (Atlanta: Georgia Baptist Historical Society, 1983).

After the War for Independence, the differences that distinguished the Particular and Separate Baptists seemed less important and, throughout the southern states, they took steps to officially unite as one sect. The Virginia Baptists united in 1787, and the North Carolina Baptists quickly followed their lead.

32. David Benedict, *A General History of the Baptist Denomination in America, and Other Parts of the World*, 2 vols. (Boston, 1813), 2:29–34; Taylor, *Lives*, 70.

33. Ryland, *The Baptists of Virginia*, 55; Benedict, *A General History*, 2:31.

34. A theological strain of primitivism was part of a number of religious sects in the British colonies. For an excellent comparative view on primitivism, see Richard T. Hughes and C. Leonard Allen, *Illusions of Innocence: Protestant Primitivism in America, 1630–1875* (Chicago: University of Chicago Press, 1988).

CHAPTER 2

1. John Leland, *The Writings of the Late Elder John Leland Including Some Events in His Life Written by Himself*, ed. L. F. Greene (New York, 1845), 20.

2. As early as the 1770s, Morgan Edwards traveled throughout the colonies collecting information from local Baptists because he intended to write a twelve-volume history of the Baptists. While Edwards never finished his intended series, other Baptists followed in his footsteps, collecting information from the earliest converts to the faith. In the 1790s, southern Baptist associations began collecting biographies and recollections from their ministers in order to produce histories of their sect. These histories drew freely upon each other and often quoted individual ministers' writings extensively. These narratives reveal a picture of the first generation of southern Baptist evangelicals. Just as important, they were recollections and retellings, and thus they also display a conscious self-representation of the Baptists and their own portrayal of their immediate past. This chapter will consider these stories in both lights: for what information they do reveal about early Baptist experiences, and as constructed stories of a prior "heroic" era. For a description of Baptist efforts to collect materials from the early evangelical Baptists, see James B. Taylor, *Lives of Virginia Baptist Ministers*, 2nd ed. (Richmond, Va., 1838), 131.

3. There has been a wealth of studies that have examined how the evangelicals challenged social norms in the mid-eighteenth-century southern colonies, though most of these have focused on conflicts of rank. Rhys Isaac's *The Transformation of Virginia, 1740–1790* reconceptualized the meanings of the early evangelical movement by analyzing religious rituals, words, and spaces. Seeing the rise of the Baptist movement as a cultural revolution that challenged the values and activities of gentry life while heralding those of evangelical yeomen, Isaac revealed the implications of the rise of evangelicalism for southern class structures. While Isaac did not address the racial implications of this countercultural movement, a number of historians have analyzed its transformative elements as well as its failures. See Donald Mathews, *Religion in the Old South* (Chicago: University of Chicago Press, 1977); Larry M. James,

"Biracial Fellowship in Antebellum Baptist Churches," in John Boles, ed., *Masters and Slaves in the House of the Lord: Race and Religion in the American South, 1740–1870* (Lexington: University Press of Kentucky, 1988), 37–57; Sylvia Frey, *Water from the Rock: Black Resistance in a Revolutionary Age* (Princeton, N.J.: Princeton University Press, 1991); and Randolph Scully, "'Somewhat Liberated': Baptist Discourses of Race and Slavery in Nat Turner's Virginia, 1770–1840," *Explorations in Early American Culture* 5 (2001): 328–371.

4. Much of the literature on southern evangelical womanhood has focused on the antebellum era and has argued that churches helped to structure gender difference and gender inequality. In *Religion in the Old South*, Mathews argues that, while these churches valued women and elevated their status, they did so by defining women's spirituality as different, and in some ways superior, to men's. He found that by the 1830s, churches saw women's spiritual strength as rooted in the domestic sphere and their "natural" modesty and benevolence; see 109–124. Jean Friedman's *The Enclosed Garden: Women and Community in the Evangelical South, 1830–1900* (Chapel Hill: University of North Carolina Press, 1985) also finds that churches structured gender difference, though, unlike Mathews, she stresses the confining nature of this narrow prescription of womanhood. In contrast, Cynthia Lynn Lyerly's study *Methodism and the Southern Mind, 1770–1810* (New York: Oxford University Press, 1998) argues that Methodism lacked a strict prescriptive domesticity and instead offered laywomen a variety of roles that served to empower them in their churches; see chap. 5.

5. For a discussion of the Presbyterian Church's and the Society of Friends's relationships to the colonial authorities of Virginia, see H. J. Eckenrode, *Separation of Church and State in Virginia: A Study in the Development of the Revolution* (1910; reprint, New York: Da Capo, 1971), 31–34; Charles F. James, *Documentary History of the Struggle for Religious Liberty in Virginia* (1899; reprint, New York: Da Capo, 1971), 20–26; and Thomas E. Buckley, *Church and State in Revolutionary Virginia, 1776–1787* (Charlottesville: University of Virginia Press, 1977), 12–14. Many Particular Baptists complied with these regulations and sought and were granted the appropriate licenses. See David Benedict, *A General History of the Baptist Denomination in America, and Other Parts of the World*, 2 vols. (Boston, 1813), 2:31; James, *Documentary History*, 26; and Buckley, *Church and State in Revolutionary Virginia*, 14.

6. Eckenrode, *Separation of Church and State*, 36–38; Rhys Isaac, "'The Rage of Malice of the Old Serpent Devil': The Dissenters and the Making and Remaking of the Virginia Statute for Religious Freedom," in Merrill D. Peterson and Robert C. Vaughan, eds., *The Virginia Statute for Religious Freedom: Its Evolution and Consequences in American History* (Cambridge: Cambridge University Press, 1988), 139–169. In these early conflicts with colonial authorities, the Baptists had not yet fully developed or articulated a belief in the separation of church and state, but simply wanted a broad interpretation of the English Toleration Act which would grant them greater liberty to exercise their consciences as dissenters from the state-supported church. The development of their belief in the separation of church and state and their conflicts with the government are discussed in chapter 5.

7. John Williams, Journal, May 10, [1771], VBHS. This episode reveals the transmission of these stories. Williams did not observe the incident, but Brother Waller told of the experience two weeks later to a group of Baptists, including Williams. Morgan Edwards, one of the ministers who traveled through the colonies collecting information also heard and recorded the event in his 1772 notes on Virginia Baptists. Williams's and Edwards's accounts were very similar, though Edwards supplied greater details about the people involved in the attack. Edwards, *Materials towards a History of the Baptists*, 55–56.

8. Robert B. Semple, *A History of the Rise and Progress of the Baptists in Virginia* (Richmond, 1810), 17–18; Taylor, *Lives*, 119–120, quote on 119; Leland, *Writings*, 107. For a full account of the persecution of the Virginia Baptists, see Lewis P. Little, *Imprisoned Preachers and Religious Liberty in Virginia* (Lynchburg, Va.: Bell, 1938). Of North Carolina, Morgan Edwards stated, "The persecution against the baptists has not been so fierce in this province as in Virginia." North Carolina authorities did initiate some prosecution in the late 1760s, and "for that end the court summoned about 72 persons to appear against them; but in the course of examination the complaints of blasphemy, riots, heresy etc. appeared so ill-grounded that the court soon dismissed the whole matter." Edwards, *Materials*, 2:102. See also ibid., 2:88.

9. Taylor, *Lives*, 126.

10. Ibid., 49; Semple, *A History of the Rise and Progress of the Baptists*, 18; Edwards, *Materials*, 55; Taylor, *Lives*, 120; Semple, *A History of the Rise and Progress of the Baptists*, 19. See also Edwards, *Materials*, 60. Other authorities came to similar conclusions about the power of these scenes: those holding James Greenwood, the minister whose preaching made the multitudes weep, soon agreed to release him. Taylor, *Lives*, 126. See also Edwards, *Materials*, 55.

11. Philip Vickers Fithian, *Journal and Letters of Philip Vickers Fithian, 1773–1774: A Plantation Tutor of the Old Dominion* (Charlottesville: University of Virginia Press, 1957); Semple, *A History of the Rise and Progress of the Baptists*, 19; Edwards, *Materials*, 49; Taylor, *Lives*, 65; Edwards, *Materials*, 62.

12. Edwards, *Materials*, 38; Taylor, *Lives*, 43; Semple, *A History of the Rise and Progress of the Baptists*, 357; see also Little, *Imprisoned Preachers*, 461–464. For statistics concerning church membership during this era, see Chapter 1, n. 31; see also Tables A.1 and A.2.

13. Janet Moore Lindman studied the violence leveled against ministers and also suggests a conflict between competing definitions of white manhood. However, Lindman argues that evangelicals "co-opt[ed] traditional manly characteristics of contentiousness, combativeness, and martial language," though she acknowledges that men in these stories "tended to turn the other cheek." As argued here, combat did come, but it was not the ministers who waged it, either in word or deed; it was the vengeful hand of God that fought the opposition and transformed or punished opponents. She also suggests that this masculinity was marked by "stalwart spirituality, undaunted conviction, and Christian courage." A comparison of Baptist descriptions of idealized womanhood, though, demonstrates that these

characteristics apply as easily to women as to men and should therefore be thought of as a Christian code, rather than a specifically masculine one. Lindman, "Acting the Manly Christian: White Evangelical Masculinity in Revolutionary Virginia," *WMQ* 3d ser., 57 (April 2000): 397, 405, 406.

14. Isaac, *Transformation of Virginia*, 95, 119–120. See Edward L. Ayers, *Vengeance and Justice: Crime and Punishment in the Nineteenth-Century American South* (New York: Oxford University Press, 1984), chap. 1; Bertram Wyatt-Brown, *Southern Honor: Ethics and Behavior in the Old South* (New York: Oxford University Press, 1982); and Elliot J. Gorn, " 'Gouge and Bite, Pull Hair and Scratch': The Social Significance of Fighting in the Southern Backcountry," *AHR* 90 (Feb. 1985): 18–43; and A. Gregory Schneider, *The Way of the Cross Leads Home: The Domestication of American Methodism* (Bloomington: Indiana University Press, 1993), 4–7. Kathleen M. Brown argues that after Bacon's Rebellion, Virginia's elite men and yeomen united over a shared vision of manhood in *Good Wives, Nasty Wenches, and Anxious Patriarchs: Gender, Race, and Power in Colonial Virginia* (Chapel Hill: University of North Carolina Press, 1996), 137–140, 173–179. See also Gorn, " 'Gouge and Bite,' " 41. For the continuing contradictions between southern manhood and evangelical religion in the late nineteenth-century, see Ted Ownby, *Subduing Satan: Religion, Recreation, and Manhood in the Rural South, 1865–1920* (Chapel Hill: University of North Carolina Press, 1990).

15. A gander pull, like other community events, could become a fair-like atmosphere in which there was a plethora of ways for men to assert their prowess publicly. One North Carolina observer described spectators at a gander pull as including "buxome young lasses, who wish to see the weight and prowess of their sweethearts tried in open field." Even men who did not compete might publicly display their honor such as the

> overseers and enterprisers, [who] have an opportunity to recount their exploits in beating up negro-quarters on a patrol night, in gouging a champion who was stout-hearted enough to attack them, or in shouting, quizzing, or chuckling at a gentleman traveller on a tobacco rolling. They shall then be able to prove their alertness in beating the earth with the body of a wrestler, by lifting & tossing him with a crotch lock or a cross buttock.

In this telling, the overseers and "enterprisers" used language to assert their prowess by distinguishing themselves from the men below (slaves) and above (a gentleman traveler) them in the social strata. Thomas Henderson, "Letter-Book, 1810–1811," in Hugh Talmage Lefler, ed., *North Carolina History Told by Contemporaries* (Chapel Hill: University of North Carolina Press, 1970), 197.

16. For examples of Biblical comparisons, see Taylor, *Lives*, 48–49, 93, 97, 99–101. Ibid., 59 (emphasis in original); Leland, *Writings*, 27.

17. Edwards, *Materials*, 2:36.

18. The instrument of death was alternately described as a gun and a club. Taylor, *Lives*, 27; see also Edwards, *Materials*, 2:45–46.

19. Edwards, *Materials*, 2:41; Taylor, *Lives*, 59, see also 60.

20. Edwards, *Materials*, 2:38; Taylor, *Lives*, 120; Semple, *A History of the Rise and Progress of the Baptists*, 20.

21. For more on constructions of eighteenth-century southern womanhood, see Cynthia A. Kierner, *Beyond the Household: Women's Place in the Early South, 1700–1835* (Ithaca, N.Y.: Cornell University Press, 1998). See also Julia Cherry Spruill, *Women's Life and Work in the Southern Colonies* (1938; reprint, New York: Norton, 1972); Margaret Ripley Wolfe, *Daughters of Canaan: A Saga of Southern Women* (Lexington: University Press of Kentucky, 1995), chaps. 1 and 2; Arthur Frederick Ide, *Woman in the American Colonial South* (Mesquite, Tex.: Ide House, 1980); and Brown, *Good Wives, Nasty Wenches, and Anxious Patriarchs*, chaps. 8 and 9. More work has been done on southern women in the antebellum period. See Anne Firor Scott, *The Southern Lady: From Pedestal to Politics, 1830–1930* (Chicago: University of Chicago Press, 1970); Catherine Clinton, *The Plantation Mistress: Woman's World in the Old South* (New York: Pantheon, 1982); Elizabeth Fox-Genovese, *Within the Plantation Household: Black and White Women of the Old South* (Chapel Hill: University of North Carolina Press, 1988); and Friedman, *The Enclosed Garden*.

22. *Virginia Gazette* (Purdie), January 21, 1773; *Virginia Gazette* (Parks), May 20, 1737. For an excellent discussion of the connections among gender, the household, and the southern social order, see Stephanie McCurry, *Masters of Small Worlds: Yeoman Households, Gender Relations, and the Political Culture of the Antebellum South Carolina Low Country* (New York: Oxford University Press, 1995), especially 87–89.

23. William Hickman, "A Short Account of My Life and Travels: For More than Fifty Years, a Professed Servant of Jesus Christ" (1828), VHS, 15–16.

24. Apparently the first man's appetite proved more powerful than his outrage, since Leland noted he came around by dinner time. Leland, *Writings*, 20. Lemuel Burkitt and Jesse Read, *A Concise History of the Kehukee Baptist Association from Its Original Rise Down to Present Times* (Halifax, N.C., 1803), 55; Leland, *Writings*, 21.

Hannah Lee Corbin Hall, a convert to the Baptist faith in the early 1760s, found a similar solace in the face of hostility by her prominent Anglican family. She acknowledged the attacks against the Baptists as "Enthusiasts or Hypocrites" but responded, "the followers of the Lamb have been ever esteemed so; that is our comfort." Hannah Lee Corbin Hall, quoted in Ethel Armes, *Stratford Hall* (Richmond, Va.: Garrett and Massie, 1936), 205.

25. R. Laurence Moore has found similar tales in the northern evangelical literature of the early nineteenth century. Here too the stories often concluded happily with the husband's (or father's) conversion; see R. Laurence Moore, *Selling God: American Religion in the Marketplace of Culture* (New York: Oxford University Press, 1994), 133. Taylor, *Lives*, 59–60.

26. Leland, *Writings*, 21–22; Burkitt and Read, *A Concise History of the Kehukee Association*, 56.

27. Richard J. Hooker, ed., *The Carolina Backcountry on the Eve of the Revolution: The Journal and Other Writings of Charles Woodmason, Anglican Itinerant* (Chapel

Hill: Published for the Institute of Early American History and Culture at Williamsburg, Virginia, by the University of North Carolina Press, 1953), 103–104. While critics of Baptists often used adult immersion as evidence of sexual licentiousness, evangelicalism itself seemed to be the cause and immersion was the specific evidence leveled against Baptists. Cynthia Lynn Lyerly found similar charges against Methodist women (who would not be baptized by immersion), who were accused of "expos[ing] themselves," "excessive passions," and "immodesty." Lyerly, "Enthusiasm, Possession, and Madness: Gender and the Opposition to Methodism in the South," in Janet Coryell et al., eds., *Beyond Image and Convention* (Columbia: University of Missouri Press, 1998), 53–73.

28. Leland, *Writings*, 87–88.

29. Hickman, "A Short Account," 4; Taylor, *Lives*, 211, 266, 340–341. For another story of a wife converting her layman husband, see James B. Taylor, *A History of Ten Baptist Churches of Which the Author Had Been Alternately a Member*, 2nd ed. (New York, 1827), 73–74. Men often outnumbered women when a church was founded, but women soon came to be more numerous. See Tables A.2 and A.3.

30. Taylor, *Lives*, 24, 227, 20. For women initiating or hosting meetings, see Taylor, *Lives*, 212, 265, 340; Leland, *Writings*, 21, 27. For other wives assisting in the ministry of their husbands, see Leland, *Writings*, 41–45; Taylor, *Ten Baptist Churches*, 47; and Taylor, *Lives*, 330.

31. The historiography for northern colonial communities has been well established for decades. However, because they relied on towns as the communal model, these studies gained few southern counterparts, since colonial southern settlements rarely had towns at their center either geographically or socially. In 1984, two studies proposed that counties provided a distinctly southern model of community: Richard R. Beeman, *The Evolution of the Southern Backcountry: A Case Study of Lunenburg County, Virginia, 1746–1832* (Philadelphia: University of Pennsylvania Press, 1984); and Darrett B. Rutman and Anita H. Rutman, *A Place in Time: Middlesex County, Virginia, 1650–1750* (New York: Norton, 1984). These studies spawned further consideration of the county as a southern communal unit. Historians have added new axes of analysis to studies of individual communities, creating works that go beyond the traditional model of a community study. See, for instance, Jean B. Lee, *The Price of Nationhood: The American Revolution in Charles County* (New York: Norton, 1994); and Daniel P. Thorp, *The Moravian Community in Colonial North Carolina: Pluralism on the Southern Frontier* (Knoxville: University of Tennessee Press, 1989).

32. Isaac examines the social meanings of church and court in eighteenth-century Virginia in *Transformation of Virginia*, 58–61 and 88–90. See also A. G. Roeber, *Faithful Magistrates and Republican Lawyers: Creators of Virginia Legal Culture, 1680–1810* (Chapel Hill: University of North Carolina Press, 1981); and E. Lee Shepard, "'This Being Court Day': Courthouses and Community Life in Rural Virginia," *Virginia Magazine of History and Biography* 103 (Oct. 1995): 459–470.

33. Matrimony Creek Baptist Church Book, North Carolina, Covenant (1776), WL.

34. Ibid.; Morattico Baptist Church Records, Virginia, [1764] 1778–1844, Covenant (1778), LVA; Mill Creek Baptist Church Book, Frederick and Berkeley County, Virginia, Covenant (1761), LVA; High Hills Baptist Church Book, Virginia, Covenant (1787), LVA.

35. Brock's Gap Baptist Church Records, Rockingham County, Virginia, 1756–1844, Covenant, 1756, LVA; Leigh Eric Schmidt, "'A Church-Going People Are a Dress-Loving People': Clothes, Communication, and Religious Culture in Early America," *Church History* 58 (1989): 36–51; Leland, *Writings*, 117. Leland noted, however, that with the Revolution these differences between the Baptists and other southerners diminished as southerners adopted a more austere dress and style. In using this form of communication, the early southern Baptists resembled sects such as the Quakers and Moravians, who also used dress, speech, and intense church discipline to mark themselves apart from worldly society.

36. Hickman, "A Short Account," 20. Heyrman argues that, in creating a spiritual family, the southern evangelicals challenged the southern family ideal and positioned themselves as outsiders. However, eighteenth-century southern families commonly reconstituted themselves, integrating distant kin or non-kin into their family units. Christine Heyrman in *Southern Cross: The Beginnings of the Bible Belt* (New York: Knopf, 1997), 128–141.

37. Studying Zambian rites of passage, Turner argues that communitas emerges out of liminal spaces and times or at the margins of society. He notes, "It is almost everywhere held to be sacred or 'holy,' possibly because it transgresses or dissolves the norms that govern structured and institutionalized relationships and is accompanied by experiences of unprecedented potency," and it thus exists within as well as outside of secular society. It is normative in that it is a recurring phenomenon, yet it is a moment in which social norms are willfully dissolved. Victor Turner, *The Ritual Process: Structure and Anti-Structure* (Chicago: Aldine, 1969). This model has been applied to the Baptists most notably in Susan Juster's *Disorderly Women: Sexual Politics and Evangelicalism in Revolutionary New England* (Ithaca, N.Y.: Cornell University Press, 1994). Turner's model has been questioned by feminist scholars such as Caroline Walker Bynum. Bynum argues that the model of liminality illuminates more about men's rituals and symbols than about women's; see "Women's Stories, Women's Symbols: A Critique of Victor Turner's Theory of Liminality," in Robert L. Moore and Frank E. Reynolds, eds., *Anthropology and the Study of Religion* (Chicago: Center for the Scientific Study of Religion, 1984), 105–125.

38. *Minutes of the Elkhorn Association of Babtists [sic] Held at Bryan's, Fayette County, State of Kentucky, August 9th, 10th, 11th, 1800* (Lexington, Ky., 1800), 3; *Minutes of Two Sessions of the Baptist Middle-District Association, Holden at Salem and Spring Creek Meeting-House, in Chesterfield County* (Richmond, Va., 1814), 12 (emphasis in original); *Minutes of the Ketocton Baptist Association, Held at Happy Creek Meeting-House, in Frederick County, Virginia, August, 1801* (Winchester, Va., 1801), 5. See also Taylor, *Ten Baptist Churches*, 90, 159.

39. Brock's Gap Baptist Church, Covenant, 1756; Sandy Run Church Book, Mooresboro, Articles of Faith, NCBHC; Edwards, *Materials*, 46, 50, 51, 54. Ac-

knowledging women alongside men was not a common rhetorical choice in the revolutionary and early national eras. But it was not unusual for Baptists to make that choice, again indicating their belief in the importance of all members in building a holy church. John Taylor provided another typical example when he noted that, after preaching, "a number of old professors rose up, male and female and in a flood of tears, desired prayers" to be made for them. Taylor, *Ten Baptist Churches*, 86; see also 20, 94.

40. Hartwood Church Book, Membership List (1771), VBHS. See also Buck Mountain [Albemarle] Baptist Church Minute Book, 1773–1779, 1792–1811, Membership List (1773), LVA; Records of Chesterfield Church, Membership List (1773), LVA; Jersey Baptist Church Record Book (1784), SHSW; Records of the Chappawamsic Baptist Church Minute Book, 1766–1832, Membership List (1766), LVA; and Red Banks Church Minute Book, 1791–1882, Membership List (1791), NCBHC. Membership lists created after 1800 tended to divide members by both sex and race. So too in the early decades of the nineteenth century, churches came to designate specific seating for African Americans. W. Harrison Daniel found that the first documentary evidence of racial segregation in church seating occurred in 1811 in Alexandria. W. Harrison Daniel, "Virginia Baptists and the Negro in the Early Republic," *Virginia Magazine of History and Biography* 80 (January 1972): 60.

41. Despite southern evangelicals' commitment to churching slaves, southern Baptists attempted very little missionary work among Native Americans before 1815 (though Daniel Marshall first moved south from New England to do missionary work among the Mohawk near the head of the Susquehanna River). Therefore, southern Baptists claimed very few Native American members before the mid-nineteenth century.

42. Robert G. Gardner, *Baptists of Early America: A Statistical History, 1639–1790* (Atlanta: Georgia Baptist Historical Society, 1983). For patterns across the Upper South, see Tables A.1 and A.2 and Gardner, 101–110 and 120–124.

43. The historiography of southern evangelicalism has often downplayed or even ignored the extent to which these churches functioned as biracial religious communities, dividing slave Christianity from white. Path-breaking works by Eugene Genovese and Albert J. Raboteau have explored central elements of black evangelicalism, particularly as it existed in the antebellum era. Christian spirituals, emotional styles of worship, and messages of freedom and redemption—all shaped by African religious practices and styles—galvanized enslaved African Americans as Christianity never had before and became vital elements of slave spiritual life. Eugene D. Genovese, *Roll, Jordan, Roll: The World the Slaves Made* (1974; reprint, New York: Vintage, 1976); and Albert J. Raboteau, *Slave Religion: The "Invisible Institution" in the Antebellum South* (New York: Oxford University Press, 1978). See also Mechal Sobel, *Trabelin' On: The Slave Journey to an Afro-Baptist Faith* (1979; reprint, Princeton, N.J.: Princeton University Press, 1988); Sylvia R. Frey and Betty Wood, *Come Shouting to Zion: African American Protestantism in the American South and British Caribbean to 1830* (Chapel Hill: University of North Carolina Press, 1998); Marvin L. Michael Kay and Lorin Lee Cary, *Slavery in North Carolina, 1748–1775*

(Chapel Hill: University of North Carolina Press, 1995), chap. 8. The power of these elements within antebellum slave communities, however, has led historians to describe white and black evangelicalism as discrete entities, a characterization particularly misleading when applied to the revolutionary and early national eras.

Some historians have argued that late eighteenth- and early nineteenth-century evangelical churches were primarily a white arena, contending that European Americans dominated membership rolls and leadership positions, and African Americans received few of the rights and privileges of membership. Christine Heyrman in *Southern Cross: The Beginnings of the Bible Belt* has argued that white evangelicals sacrificed egalitarian elements of their theology in order to secure a status of "respectability" within southern society, a concession that left African-American congregants subject to the arbitrary power of their white brethren. See also Ellen Eslinger, "The Beginnings of Afro-American Christianity among Kentucky Baptists," in Craig Thompson Friend, ed., *The Buzzel about Kentuck: Settling the Promised Land* (Lexington: University Press of Kentucky, 1999), 197–215; and Jewel Spangler, "Salvation Was Not Liberty: Baptists and Slavery in Revolutionary Virginia," *ABQ* 13 (1994): 221–236.

44. Henry Toler, Diary, 9, VBHS; John Leland, *The Virginia Chronicle: with Judicious and Critical Remarks, under XXIV Heads* (Fredericksburg, Va., 1790), 13.

45. Brock's Gap Baptist Church, Covenant, 1756.

46. Edwards, *Materials*, 46, 50, 51, 54, 56, 59, 60, 61, 91, 95, 96; John Smyth, *Principles and Inferences* (1607), reprinted in Leon H. McBeth, *Sourcebook for Baptist Heritage* (Nashville, Tenn.: Broadman, 1990), 55. English deacons, in contrast to the deaconesses, were responsible for the collection and distribution of the church's treasury. See also Roger Hayden, ed., *The Records of a Church of Christ in Bristol* ([Bristol, U.K.]: Bristol Record Society, 1974), 208–209.

47. Mathews, *Religion in the Old South*, 25–26; Leon McBeth, *Women in Baptist Life* (Nashville, Tenn.: Broadman, 1979), chap. 1; and William L. Lumpkin, *Baptist Foundations in the South: Tracing through the Separates the Influence of the Great Awakening* (Nashville, Tenn.: Broadman, 1961), reprinted in William L. Lumpkin and L. H. Butterfield, eds., *Colonial Baptists and Southern Revivals* (New York: Arno, 1980). Other historians who argue for a "radical moment" in the early Baptist evangelical movement include Rhys Isaac, *Transformation of Virginia*; and Mechal Sobel, *Trabelin' On*. These historians stress the differences between the Separate Baptists and the Particular Baptists, and locate the radical practices exclusively within the Separates. As I argued in chapter 1, these two strains quickly influenced each other and were more similar than dissimilar. The historians who stress the early evangelical challenges to gender, racial, and cultural norms are part of a larger literature that has connected eighteenth-century evangelicalism with emerging social movements; see Richard Bushman, *From Puritan to Yankee: Character and the Social Order in Connecticut, 1690–1765* (New York: Norton, 1967); Barbara Lacey, "Women and the Great Awakening in Connecticut" (Ph.D. diss., Clark University, 1982); and Juster, *Disorderly Women*.

48. Flatty Creek Baptist Church Book, North Carolina, January 9, 1812, NCBHC.

49. Taylor, *Ten Baptist Churches*, 20, 96, 95; Flat Rock Baptist Church Records, August 1787, NCBHC; Taylor, *Ten Baptist Churches*, 204–205. For other examples of women exhorting, see Taylor, *Lives*, 20; Taylor, *Ten Baptist Churches*, 208–209, 95; and Toler, *Diary*, 20. Catherine A. Brekus, in *Strangers and Pilgrims: Female Preaching in America, 1740–1845* (Chapel Hill: University of North Carolina Press, 1998), has written the most comprehensive study of women preachers and exhorters in the eighteenth and early nineteenth centuries; for female Baptist exhorters in the context of the Separates and revivalism, see particularly 44–67. Brekus suggests that Baptist ministers quickly sought to erase the work of these women (66–67). However, that was the work of subsequent historians in the late nineteenth and twentieth centuries. The earliest Baptist historians (such as Morgan Edwards in the 1770s, Robert Semple in 1810, David Benedict in 1813, John Taylor in 1823) all noted women's roles as exhorters and teachers.

50. Taylor, *Lives*, 98; Taylor, *Ten Baptist Churches*, 157. For other examples, see Taylor, *Ten Baptist Churches*, 99–100, 105; Semple, *History of the Rise and Progress of the Baptists in Virginia*, 5; David Benedict, *Fifty Years Among the Baptists* (New York, 1860), 419–421; and William L. Lumpkin, "The Role of Women in Eighteenth Century Virginia Baptist Life," *Baptist History and Heritage* 8 (1973): 164–165.

51. Providence Baptist Church First Record Book, Clark County, Kentucky, transcribed by George F. Doyle [1924], March 14, 1787, 8, UK; Waterlick Baptist Church Minutes, 1787–1817, Shenandoah County, Virginia, May 19, 1787, June 16, 1787, February 27, 1808, VBHS; see also December 26, 1807. For women voting on the choice of a minister, see Taylor, *Ten Baptist Churches*, 56. Because of the power they invested in speech, evangelicals also recognized its potential threat to religious and communal order. Just as the unfettered tongue could be the tool of God, it could also be the instrument of the devil, and Baptists went to great lengths to supervise the speech of their congregants. Within their churches, common speech crimes included gossip, slander, swearing, speaking out of the way, hard words, unbecoming talk, and quarreling—terms which certainly overlapped but also indicated a determined commitment to monitor speech. And, just as women were part of the godly speaking public, they also found a place among those who spoke with un-Christian tongues, engaging in speech crimes that were quite similar to men's. Both men and women were accused of the most common types of speech crimes: lying, ill language, swearing, and slander. (See Table A.4.) In these cases, the majority of the accusations were leveled against men, but women were subject to the same types of accusations. Women made up 42.9 percent of those accused of lying, and men were accused of lying in 54.8 percent of the cases (with 2.4 percent unknown). Charges of ill or "unbecoming" language were directed more heavily against men (67.4 percent). While disorderly speaking was not associated with either men or women exclusively, there were some specific charges within that general category that were more likely to be associated with women, in particular that of gossiping or "backbiting." In the Baptist congregations used in this study, white

women made up 86% percent of those who were accused of gossiping or backbiting. This might suggest that disorderly speaking was, in fact, gendered—that southerners in the eighteenth century perceived men and women to be engaged in different types of speaking, and when faced with women who spoke in disruptive ways, they defined it differently than for men. However, there were only seven such charges. The vast majority of accusations of disorderly speech used the same kind of language for men and for women.

52. High Hills Church Book, 1787–1845, Covenant and Decorum (1787), LVA; Roanoke District Baptist Association Minute Book, 1789–1831, October 1799; see also October 1798, LVA.

53. The key passage reads:

Moreover if thy brother shall trespass against thee, go and tell him his fault between thee and him alone: if he shall hear thee, thou hast gained thy brother. But if he will not hear thee, then take with thee one or two more, that in the mouth of two or three witnesses every word may be established. And if he shall neglect to hear them, tell it unto the church: but if he neglect to hear the church, let him be unto thee as an heathen man and a publican. Verily I say unto you, Whatsoever ye shall bind on earth shall be bound in heaven: and whatsoever ye shall loose on earth shall be loosed in heaven. (Matthew 18:15–18)

54. Flat Rock Baptist Church, January 1793; Cove Creek Baptist Church, Sherwood, North Carolina, 1799–1838, April 1815, SBHLA; Buck Mountain [Albemarle] Baptist Church, May 18, 1777.

55. Sandra K. Gorin, comp., *Mt. Tabor Church Minutes, Barren County, Kentucky. Vol. 1: November 5, 1798–December 1829* (Glasgow, Ky.: Gorin Genealogical, 1994), July, Third Saturday, 1803, August, Third Saturday, 1803; Mill Creek Baptist Church Records, Berkeley County, Virginia, March 1805, May 1805, LVA; Abbott's Baptist Church Minute Book, 1783–1874, December, First Saturday, 1806, NCBHC. Based on the women's reports, the accused were excommunicated for fornication. See January, First Saturday, 1807. Women, then, engaged in a wide range of speech in evangelical churches and communities, having access to some of the official speaking roles (with the notable exception of preaching) and engaging in similar types of disorderly language as men. Their broad participation in the dialogues of their churches reveals women's centrality to early Baptist communities, but it also highlights broader issues about women's place in the eighteenth- and early nineteenth-century South. Historians have sought to identify to what degree women had access to the public realm (if at all) or, conversely, to what degree women's experiences were limited or defined by the private or domestic realm—inquiries complicated by close examinations of such significant factors as race, class, status, and emerging changes in the revolutionary age. Women's roles in exhorting and in church discipline further complicate this question. The spoken word defies easy categorization into public or private. Its designation as either public or private depends on the content, audience, and reception. For instance, an accusation that a neighbor had

stolen some corn might be called gossip in some settings or might be called slander. Churches too challenge easy divisions of public and private. Piety is often defined as individual and personal, while churches—as communal organizations—suggest a public arena. Meetings concerned personal beliefs and individual reflection, but also business disputes, land conflicts, and behavior in such spaces as courthouses and taverns. These complications remind us that the categories of public and private are too stark and inflexible to illuminate the late eighteenth-century world.

CHAPTER 3

1. Meherrin Baptist Church Minute Book, 1771–1837, September, Second Saturday, 1775, September 22, 1775, LVA.

2. It is not clear from the churchbook what happened to Brother Walton. The church apparently believed the child was not his but was not prepared to acquit him altogether. The members declared even when they were close to clearing him of the charge that "they think [him] not restord in Gospel order from his great Misfortune & sin." Meherrin Baptist Church, September 22, 1775. A Copy of the First Minutes of Bryan Station Church, Fayette County, Kentucky, 1786–1895, June, First Saturday, 1792, UK.

3. Nancy F. Cott, *Public Vows: A History of Marriage and the Nation* (Cambridge, Mass.: Harvard University Press, 2000).

4. Spaces within the home also became more privatized as sleeping quarters were secluded whenever possible, giving the marital bed new privacy, and individuals were more likely to have separate beds. These trends can also be seen in eating customs, hygiene, and decorative choices. Historians have associated these changes with an increasing attention to "refinement" and with broader consumption patterns. See Rhys Isaac, *The Transformation of Virginia, 1740–1790* (Chapel Hill: University of North Carolina Press, 1982), 302–305; and Jack Larkin, *The Reshaping of Everyday Life, 1790–1840* (New York: Harper & Row, 1988), chap. 3, particularly 116–127.

5. Stephanie McCurry, *Masters of Small Worlds: Yeoman Households, Gender Relations, and the Political Culture of the Antebellum South Carolina Low Country* (New York: Oxford University Press, 1995), especially chaps. 1 and 2. See also Kathleen M. Brown, *Good Wives, Nasty Wenches, and Anxious Patriarchs: Gender, Race, and Power in Colonial Virginia* (Chapel Hill: University of North Carolina Press, 1996); and Bertram Wyatt-Brown, *Southern Honor: Ethics and Behavior in the Old South* (New York: Oxford University Press, 1982).

6. Gregory A. Wills, *Democratic Religion: Freedom, Authority, and Church Discipline in the Baptist South, 1785–1900* (New York: Oxford University Press, 1997), 8. Wills provides a wealth of information on the procedures and religious meanings of church discipline. For another excellent discussion of the purpose and patterns of discipline in nineteenth-century churches, see Randy J. Sparks, *On Jordan's Stormy Banks: Evangelicalism in Mississippi, 1773–1876* (Athens: University of Georgia Press, 1994), chap. 9.

7. Glen's Creek Baptist Church Minutes, Kentucky, 1801–1868, August 6, 1796, 14, KHS.

8. Isaac, *Transformation of Virginia*, 170.

9. For more on the rise of companionate marriage in the South, see Anya Jabour, *Marriage in the Early Republic: Elizabeth and William Wirt and the Companionate Ideal* (Baltimore, Md.: Johns Hopkins University Press, 1998). See also Melinda S. Buza, "'Pledges of Our Love': Friendship, Love, and Marriage among the Virginia Gentry, 1800–1825," in Edward L. Ayers and John C. Willis, eds., *The Edge of the South: Life in Nineteenth-Century Virginia* (Charlottesville: University of Virginia Press, 1991).

10. For some evangelicals, finding a partner who shared their religious convictions was of paramount importance. See Anya Jabour, "Resisting the Altar: A Case Study of Conversion and Courtship in the Antebellum South," *Maryland Historical Magazine* 96 (2001): 29–51.

11. Far from repenting, Rogers aggravated her situation by lying and then declaring that her conversion experience was not real. Meherrin Baptist Church, April 19, 1774, June 11 and 12, 1774; Newfound Baptist Church Minutes, Buncombe County, North Carolina, December 17, 1808, January 18, 1809, April 14, 1809, NCBHC.

12. Abbott's Baptist Church Minute Book, Davidson, North Carolina, 1783–1874, March, First Saturday, 1805, NCBHC.

13. In her study of evangelical churches during the antebellum era, Jean Freidman argues that there was a sexual double standard in which women were blamed for sexual misconduct in *The Enclosed Garden: Women and Community in the Evangelical South, 1830–1900* (Chapel Hill: University of North Carolina Press, 1985), 14–15, 77–78. See also Susan Juster, *Disorderly Women: Sexual Politics and Evangelicalism in Revolutionary New England* (Ithaca, N.Y.: Cornell University Press, 1994), 151; and Janet Moore Lindman, "Acting the Manly Christian: White Evangelical Masculinity in Revolutionary Virginia," *WMQ* 3d ser., 57 (April 2000): 410.

14. Hartwood Baptist Church Records, May 24, 1778, VBHS; Severn's Valley Baptist Church, Elizabethtown, Kentucky, 1788–1884, January 1793, March 1793. Some women tried to escape the condemnation of their church and community by moving away during their pregnancies, as did Sister Wallace when she moved "in a private manner & being with child with a Bastard." But churches made a point to track and monitor congregants when they were away from the church, so a number of these cases still became public. Meherrin Baptist Church, December, First Saturday and Sunday, 1776.

15. Hartwood Church Book, June 25, 1785; Antioch [Raccoon Swamp] Baptist Church Records, Virginia, May 1794, LVA; Tate's Creek Baptist Church Minutes, Kentucky, July, First Saturday, 1799, SBTS.

16. Eighteenth-century southern evangelicals, like eighteenth-century southerners more generally, did not produce extensive treatises on the nature of marriage and the roles of husbands and wives, as did their northern cousins, such as the Congregationalists. Perhaps their extensive church discipline in family matters made such proclamations unnecessary. Certainly the South, even as late as the revolutionary

era, did not support a large publishing economy, and a less-affluent sect like the Baptists would not be likely candidates to improve that trade. But Baptist associations did publish and distribute annual minutes, and these did include sermons or short essays on a variety of subjects.

17. Minutes of the Stockton Valley Association, Tennessee, September 1810, 40, SBHLA (emphasis mine); Concord Association Minutes, Tennessee, 1812, 9–10, SBHLA.

18. Stockton Valley Association, Tennessee, September 1810, 40; Concord Association Minutes, Tennessee, 1812, 9–10, SBHLA; Cott, *Public Vows*, 3.

19. Minutes of Dandridge Baptist Church, Jefferson County, Tennessee, June [1803], July [1803], December [1803], December 29 [1803], SBHLA; Mill Creek Baptist Church Minute Book, Shenandoah & Page County, Virginia, May 1802, June 1802, LVA; Minutes of the Goose Creek Baptist Church Minute Book, 1787–1821, April 1788, June 1788, June 1787, October 20, 1787, LVA; Bryan's Station Church, February 1804. With his acknowledgment of wrongdoing, the church admonished him and retained him as a member.

20. Jersey Baptist Church Records, October 5, 1799, October 17, 1799, SHSW.

21. Wheeley's Primitive Baptist Church Minutes, Pearson County, North Carolina, February, Second Saturday, 1814; March, Second Saturday, 1814, NCLA. Well's Chapel Baptist Church Minutes, Sampson County, 1793–1985, May 1799, May 21, 1814, NCBHC. Newton was expelled from the church.

22. Sandy Run Baptist Church Record Book, Franklin County, North Carolina, April 26, 1777, SHSW. Yeopim Baptist Church Record Book, Chowan County, North Carolina, May 1792, SHSW; see also ibid., March 1792.

23. Virginia Portsmouth Baptist Association Minutes, May 24, 1800, VBHS.

24. Chappawamsic Baptist Church, July 1802, 42; Meherrin Baptist Church, February 1785, March 1785. See also Goose Creek Baptist Church, July 1792; and Table A.8.

25. Forks of Elkhorn Baptist Church Minutes, Kentucky, 1788–1831, May 1807, June 1807, SBTS; Rules, Salt River Minutes in Fox Creek Church of Particular Baptists Record Book, KHS. Likewise, in 1810, Upper King and Queen Church requested that its members restrain their children from attending the feasts and parties of unbelievers. Upper King and Queen Baptist Church Minute Book, 1774–1816, December 1810, LVA.

26. Bryan Station Church, February 1795; Tate's Creek Baptist Church Minutes, Kentucky, January 1800, February 1800, SBTS. Tolbert eventually repented and was received back into the church in 1805; ibid., March 1805.

27. Dandridge Baptist Church, April 1811, May 1811; Providence Baptist Church First Record Book, Clark County, Kentucky, transcribed by George F. Doyle [1924], November 12, 1796, July 11, 1801, August 8, 1801, UK.

28. Meherrin Baptist Church, January 4, 1772; Mill Creek Baptist Church Minute Book, Shenandoah and Page, County, Virginia, 1798–1824, March 1800, LVA; Forks of Elkhorn Baptist Church, February 1796, March 1796; Burks Branch Church Minute Book, Kentucky, June 1805, August 1805, SBTS. Some scholars have

emphasized churches' leniency to white men. Lindman argues that Baptists were mostly interested in the "public" behavior of white men. Certainly, drinking and fighting were the two most frequent accusations leveled against white men, and many of these incidents would likely have been committed in public spaces. Lindman, "Acting the Manly Christian," 410. However, mistreating a family member or spouse was the fifth most common charge among specific charges, and white men made up a disproportionately large number of the accused (40.6 percent). Indeed, many of the frequent charges against white men cannot be labeled "public" (including lying, ill language, allowing bad company in the home, and sexual misconduct). See Table A.4. Wills in *Democratic Religion* (54–56) also argues that churches were more lenient to white men and held women to a stricter standard of behavior. He bases this contention on excommunication rates where white men had a lower exclusion rate than white women. However, white men were far more likely to face accusations; indeed they faced accusations at more than three times the rate of white women, even though they made up a smaller proportion of the membership overall. For accusation rates, see Tables A.3 and A.5; for membership numbers, see Tables A.1 and A.2 and Lindman, "A World of Baptists," 115–119.

29. Broad Run Baptist Church Book, Virginia, 1762–1872, June 1785, VBHS.

30. Burks Branch Church, February 1811, March 1811; Sandra K. Gorin, comp., *Mt. Tabor Church Minutes, Barren County, Kentucky. Vol. 1: November 5, 1798–December 1829* (Glasgow, Ky.: Gorin Genealogical, 1994), February 1802, 15. At best, the church could prevent Hall from being admitted to any other Baptist church until he renounced his behavior and demonstrated remorse. In his study of antebellum evangelical churches in Mississippi, Randy Sparks finds a continuation of this pattern in which the activities of churches "helped create a climate hostile to such abuses [of wives]." Sparks, *On Jordan's Stormy Banks*, 157.

31. Flat Rock Baptist Church Records, July 1797, NCBHC. However, none of these charges were numerous, and some were quite rare. For instance, there were only three cases of women being accused of disobedience to their husbands in nearly eighty churches over forty-five years. There were also other ways that churches maintained social hierarchy among their members, offering full membership only to white men. White women and slaves were less able to participate in many arenas of fellowship (see chapters 2 and 6).

32. The law of coverture, inherited from English common law, remained powerful in the United States in the early nineteenth century, though some fissures were visible. The use of separate estates as a tool to protect family property from the grasp of creditors in a volatile economy allowed some women to legally retain some property after marriage. For more on coverture in the South, see Cynthia A. Kierner, *Beyond the Household: Women's Place in the Early South, 1700–1835* (Ithaca, N.Y.: Cornell University Press, 1998), 23–24, 125–128.

33. There is no indication that Spoolman returned to her husband as a condition of her readmission, information that would almost certainly have been included in the churchbook. Abbott's Baptist Church, August, First Saturday, 1794; October, First Saturday, 1797; September 1812; June, First Saturday, 1812.

34. Providence Baptist Church, August 14th [1813], September 11th [1813], March 12th [1814], April 9th [1814], November 8th [1817].

35. In the 1770s, dissenters began petitioning the colonial legislatures for the right to perform marriages among their members and for recognition of the marriages that they had solemnized. Dissenting ministers' willingness to perform such ceremonies benefited western settlements where there often was no Anglican minister to do so. For information on slave marriage rites in the antebellum era, see Eugene D. Genovese, *Roll, Jordan, Roll: The World the Slaves Made* (1974; reprint, New York: Vintage, 1976), 475–481.

36. The Records of the Strawberry Baptist Association, 1787–1822, May 1793, 58, LVA; Gorin, comp., *Mt. Tabor Church*, July 1814, 59; March 1815, 62–63.

37. Minutes of the Tennessee Baptist Association, Holston, 1786–1850, October 1792, August 1793, SBHLA; Minutes of the Tennessee Baptist Association, 1802–1932, October 1810, 48, SBHLA (emphasis in original). See also ibid., October 1808, 37.

38. Upper King and Queen Baptist Church, December 18, 1797.

39. Forks of Elkhorn Baptist Church, August 1799.

CHAPTER 4

1. Lower Banister Baptist Church Book, 1798–1845, Pittsylvania, Virginia, July 1803, VBHS.

2. By "civil functions," I mean those activities that affected the secular community; I do not mean the *legal* division between civil and criminal cases. Baptist churches involved themselves in both types of court cases, and in acting on both types, they ultimately served the civil society.

3. Scholarship has tended to examine the ways in which Baptists challenged and disrupted southern society. Works such as Donald G. Mathews's *Religion in the Old South* and Albert J. Raboteau's *Slave Religion* argue that Baptist churches were part of an evangelical movement that offered a brief but significant challenge to the institution of slavery and racial hierarchies in the South. Likewise, even though Rhys Isaac's *Transformation of Virginia* examines the Baptists' preoccupation with notions of order, it emphasizes the ways that their belief in an orderly morality challenged cultural norms. In *Southern Cross: The Beginnings of the Bible Belt*, Christine Heyrman also emphasizes the disruptive nature of the evangelicals to southern society. Heyrman finds evidence as late as the 1820s of evangelicals disrupting families, gender norms, and authority, all of which left evangelicalism on the margins of southern society well into the nineteenth century. This sect, then, has been identified as a force of disorder: the disorder of young southern evangelicalism, the disorder of itinerants and exhorters, the disorder of the backcountry. However, this historiographic emphasis on disruption has obscured the Baptists' ongoing participation in the ordering of southern communities through the mundane business of their churches. For a compelling analysis of this historiographic debate, see Randy J. Sparks, *On Jordan's Stormy Banks: Evangelicalism in Mississippi, 1773–1876* (Athens: University of

Georgia Press, 1994), 148–150. Sparks concludes that discipline had ramifications beyond the membership. See also Rhys Isaac, "Evangelical Revolt: The Nature of the Baptists' Challenge to the Traditional Order in Virginia, 1765–1775," *WMQ* 3d ser., 31 (1974): 345–368; Larry M. James, "Biracial Fellowship in Antebellum Baptist Churches," in John Boles, ed., *Masters and Slaves in the House of the Lord: Race and Religion in American Society, 1740–1870* (Lexington: University Press of Kentucky, 1988); Mechal Sobel, *Trabelin' On: The Slave Journey to an Afro-Baptist Faith* (1979; reprint, Princeton, N.J.: Princeton University Press, 1988); and Nathan Hatch, *The Democratization of American Christianity* (New Haven, Conn.: Yale University Press, 1989).

4. Walter Clark, ed., *The State Records of North Carolina* (Winston and Goldsboro: State of North Carolina, 1895–1906), 23:288–289, 617–618; 25:476. See also Alan D. Watson, "The Anglican Parish in Royal North Carolina, 1729–1775," *HMPEC* 48 (Sept. 1979): 303–319.

5. William H. Seiler, "The Anglican Church: A Basic Institution of Local Government in Colonial Virginia," in Bruce C. Daniels, ed., *Town and County: Essays on the Structure of Local Government in the American Colonies* (Middletown, Conn.: Wesleyan University Press, 1978). See also Watson, "The Anglican Parish."

6. Upper King and Queen Baptist Church Minute Book, King and Queen County, Virginia, August 18, 1792, LVA; Tomahawk Baptist Church Records, Chesterfield County, Virginia, April 2, 1803, LVA; Wilson Creek Primitive Baptist Church Records, Williamson County, Tennessee, Covenant, 1804, TSLA. Brother Thomas told his congregation that the church should "Support their own poor Independent of the Civil Government," and since it failed to do that for an indigent sister, he took the woman into his home and declared nonfellowship with the church. The church responded that it needed the assistance of the government, but if he would "give her up they w[ould] afford her a comfortable Support in that way they think Eligible... [and] that if he [wa]s resolvd to keep her rather than Give her up to the Church they w[ould] contribute to her Support what they conveniently c[ould]." Ketoctin Baptist Church Minute Book, Loudoun County, Virginia, 1776–1890, June 1795, LVA.

7. Red Banks Church Minute Book, 1791–1882, April 1794, NCBHC; Forks of Elkhorn Baptist Church Minutes, Kentucky, 1788–1831, March 1795, December 1798, SBTS; A Copy of the First Minutes of Bryan Station Church, Fayette County, Kentucky, 1786–1895, December 1805, UK; Red Banks Church, 1792, 4. Red Banks Church, for instance "agree'd To Employ the Doctor to cure" a female member's child and paid the bill of over £8. See ibid., May 26, 1792, August 25, 1792, October 6, 1792; and Morattico Baptist Church Records, Virginia, [1764] 1778–1844, June 1779, LVA. The repeated church directives to deacons to supply the needs of the poor and the assignment of cash and foodstuffs to deacons for distribution to poor members indicate that assistance was an ongoing concern. These directives and collections occurred even when no individual names were recorded.

8. Virginia Portsmouth Baptist Association Minutes, May 1810, VBHS. Their pairing of a rich man's kitchen and "negro huts" seems discordant; they may have accepted a paternalistic vision of slavery in which it was assumed that provisions were readily available to slaves.

9. Marble Creek Baptist Church Records, Kentucky, 1787–1842, July 4, 1795, UK. For examples, see Berryville [Buck Marsh] Baptist Church Records, Frederick County, Virginia, 1785–1803, 1803–1841, December 1787, LVA; Records of the Chappawamsic Baptist Church Minute Book, 1766–1832, August 1805, LVA; Ketoctin Baptist Church, June 1795; and Forks of Elkhorn Baptist Church, November 1795.

10. Sandy Run Church Book, Mooresboro, October [1782], November [1782], [December 1782], February [1786], NCBHC.

11. For more, see John R. Finger, *Tennessee Frontiers: Three Regions in Transition* (Bloomington: Indiana University Press, 2001); and Walter T. Durham, *Before Tennessee, the Southwest Territory, 1790–1796: A Narrative History of the Territory of the United States South of the River Ohio* (Piney Flats, Tenn.: Rocky Mount Historical Association, 1990).

12. For conflicts between westerners and eastern authorities, see A. Roger Ekirch, *"Poor Carolina": Politics and Society in Colonial North Carolina, 1729–1776* (Chapel Hill: University of North Carolina Press, 1981).

13. Quoted in Lowell H. Harrison and James C. Klotter, *A New History of Kentucky* (Lexington: University Press of Kentucky, 1997), 48; Daniel Drake, *Pioneer Life in Kentucky, 1785–1800*, ed. Emmet Field Horine, M.D. (New York: Schuman, 1948), 43–44.

14. Morgan Edwards, *Materials towards a History of the Baptists* (Danielsville, Ga.: Heritage Papers, 1984), 2:91. Edwards found that other churches suffered similar losses during this era; Little River, for example, went from 500 congregants to "a handful." Ibid., 94; see also 88. Broad Run Baptist Church Book, Virginia, 1761–1872, passim, VBHS.

15. Providence Baptist Church First Record Book, Clark County, Kentucky, transcribed by George F. Doyle [1924], 1–2, UK. See also George W. Ranck, *The Traveling Church: An Account of the Baptist Exodus from Virginia to Kentucky in 1781 under the Leadership of Rev. Lewis Craig and Capt. William Ellis* (Louisville: Baptist Book Concern, 1891).

16. North Fork Primitive Baptist Church Records, 2, LVA; Cherokee Creek Baptist Church Minutes, Washington County, Tennessee, 2, TSLA.

17. Mill Swamp Baptist Church, Isle of Wight County, Records, 1774–1790, March 1778, LVA; The Records of the Strawberry Baptist Association, 1787–1822, October 1796, LVA; Roanoke District Association Minute Book, October 22–24, 1796, 141–142, LVA; Forks of Elkhorn Baptist Church Minutes, Kentucky, 1788–1831, August 1796, SBTS; Meherrin Baptist Church Minute Book, 1771–1837, July 1794, LVA.

18. The association asked:

> Is the market price in commerce the privilege of Church members? Answer. as the price of commodities are Very uncertain; and money itself is not always of the same value: we conclude that it is not in our power, to regulate commerce, therefore we agree that each one may act agreeable to the dictates of his own conscience; so that he does Not go beyond the common market price—nevertheless we Advise all in connection with us to

act in this matter with Caution. (Roanoke District Association, October 1796, 141–142)

For examples of particular professions being the source of debate or discipline, see Brier Creek Baptist Church, North Carolina, Minutes, 1783–1860, September 24, [1796]; Yeopim Baptist Church, Chowan County, North Carolina, 1781–1882, July 23, 1808, SHSW; and Benedict, *A General History*, 2:202.

19. Strawberry Baptist Association, May 1805; Kanawha Baptist Church Minutes, November 15, 1800 in C. P. Cawthorn and N. L. Warnell, *Pioneer Baptist Church Records of South-Central Kentucky and the Upper Cumberland of Tennessee, 1799–1899* (Galatin, Tenn.: Church History Research and Archives, 1985); Matrimony Creek Baptist Church Minutes, June 21, 1788, April 1784, WL.

20. Robert Wheeler, "The County Court in Colonial Virginia," in Bruce C. Daniels, ed., *Town and County: Essays on the Structure of Local Government in the American Colonies* (Middletown, Conn.: Wesleyan University Press, 1978), 116, 118–121.

21. Richard R. Beeman, *Evolution of the Southern Backcountry: A Case Study of Lunenburg County, Virginia, 1746–1832* (Philadelphia: University of Pennsylvania Press, 1984), chap. 4.

22. Ibid.; A. Roger Ekirch, *"Poor Carolina": Politics and Society in Colonial North Carolina, 1729–1776* (Chapel Hill: University of North Carolina Press, 1981). See also Wheeler, "The County Court in Colonial Virginia."

23. Wheeley's Primitive Baptist Church Minutes, Pearson County, North Carolina, August, Third Saturday, 1791, NCLA; Paw Paw Hollow [Formerly Fork of French Broad & Holston] Baptist Church Minutes, Sevier County, Tennessee, 1803–1880, May 1802, SHSW; Waller's Baptist Church Records, Virginia, 1799–1801, August 1, 1801, October 4, 1801, VBHS.

24. Meherrin Baptist Church, July 29, 1793, July 1797.

25. Berryville [Buck Marsh] Baptist Church Minute Book, March 1805, LVA. Even charges as serious as adultery were held to legal standards of evidence, as John Alderman found when he admitted to being "Acused with being Concernd with Lewd Women which Charge he denied and [when] *no other person Come forward to Accuse him* was Continued in fellowship" (italics mine). Well's Chapel Baptist Church, July, Saturday before Second Sunday, 1812. African-American members, while never equal to white members, were to be tried by these same rules of evidence and law. When Brother Jo of Kentucky was found in possession of some stolen flax seed, he was accused by another slave as being involved in the theft. The church ruled that "as neither Proof nor Circumstance has Appeared Against Jo to find him Guilty, the Church Agreed to Reprove him" only for trading in goods that slaves were unlikely to have come by honestly. Marble Creek Church, June 13, 1801.

26. Marble Creek Church, for instance, assigned three men "to procure Testamony, which may be Received as Evidence." Marble Creek Church, December 4, 1790.

27. Berryville [Buck Marsh] Baptist Church Minute Book, March 1794.

28. Waterlick Church, February 23, 1788, March 22, 1788, April 26, 1788, September 27, 1788, December 27, 1788.

29. Burks Branch Baptist Church Minute Book, Kentucky, 1801–1872, June 1809, October 1811, SBTS; Upper King and Queen Baptist Church, May 17, 1794.

30. Garrison Fork Baptist Church Minutes, Beech Grove, Tennessee, October 22, 1815, February 24, 1816, SBHLA; Minutes of the Tennessee Baptist Association, 1802–1932, 1805, SBHLA. See also Bethel Hill Baptist Church Minute and Roll Book, North Carolina, May 3, 1810, NCBHC. For an example of members bringing charges on behalf of family members, see Gorin, comp., *Mt. Tabor Church Minutes*, June 1809, 36–37.

31. Ibid., September 1802, 16–17.

32. Bethel Hill Baptist Church, January 5, 1814, March 18, 1814; Cornelia Hughes Dayton, "Turning Points and the Relevance of Colonial Legal History," *WMQ* 3d ser., 50 (Jan. 1993): 7–17; Cornelia Hughes Dayton, *Women before the Bar: Gender, Law, and Society in Connecticut* (Chapel Hill: University of North Carolina Press, 1995). See also Mary Beth Norton, "Gender, Crime, and Community in Seventeenth-Century Maryland," in James A. Henretta, Michael Kammen, and Stanley N. Katz, eds., *The Transformation of Early American History: Society, Authority and Ideology* (New York: Knopf, 1991).

33. Meherrin Church, February 8 and 9, 1772; Marble Creek Church, April 11, 1801, April 18, 1801, May 9, 1801.

34. Sweet argued that, in addition to Baptist churches, the Presbyterian and Methodist churches also acted as moral courts. Most of his evidence, however, is drawn from Baptist churches. His evidence from the Methodist Church primarily reveals that many of the ministers were for temperance. Discipline in the Presbyterian Church, he notes, was less stern and less frequent than in Baptist churches. William W. Sweet, "The Churches as Moral Courts of the Frontier," *Church History* 2 (Mar. 1933): 3–21; Beeman, *Evolution of the Southern Backcountry*, 108–109, 112.

35. Waller's Baptist Church, February 3, 1805; Chappawamsic Baptist Church, January 1803; Bethel Hill Baptist Church, July 13, 1805. For more on the role of the elite and the courts in maintaining the social order in eighteenth-century Virginia, see Isaac, *Transformation of Virginia*, particularly chaps. 5 and 6; and Beeman, *Evolution of the Southern Backcountry*.

36. Tate's Creek Baptist Church Minutes, Kentucky, May 1804, June 1804, July 1804, September 1804, October 1804, SBTS; Forks of Elkhorn Church, April 1812, June 1812.

37. Berryville [Buck Marsh] Baptist Church, May 1792, June 1792.

38. Ibid., August 1799, February 1801. It was over a year before the church reported that the matter had been settled and the two men were reconciled.

39. Bryan Station Church, July 1805, September 1805, October 1805.

40. Carroll Smith-Rosenberg, "Dis-Covering the Subject of the 'Great Constitutional Discussion,' 1786–1789," *JAH* 79 (1992): 841–873. See also Linda K. Kerber, "'I Have Don... Much to Carrey on the Warr': Women and the Shaping of Republican Ideology after the American Revolution," *Journal of Women's History* 1

(1990): 231–243; and Joan R. Gundersen, "Independence, Citizenship, and the American Revolution," *Signs* 13 (1987): 59–77.

41. The right of all members, including African Americans, to bring charges and to testify was in stark contrast to the policy of civil courts. The burgesses of Virginia restricted blacks from testifying except in capital cases against other blacks, decreeing, "they are people of such base and corrupt natures, that the credit of their testimony cannot be certainly depended upon." In later years, the burgesses agreed to allow blacks to testify against other blacks in both civil and criminal cases, but continued to prohibit their testifying against whites, again warning against "the corrupt and precarious evidence of negroes, mulattoes, and indians." Hening, ed., *Statutes at Large*, 4:325–327, 6:107.

In parts of the South, even free blacks were denied the right to testify in courts, which, as three free black petitioners noted in 1791, allowed some lawbreakers to escape punishment and ensured that free blacks could not give "Testimony in recovering Debts due to them, . . . whereby they are subject to great Losses and repeated Injuries without any means of redress." Tomas Cole, Peter Bassnett Mathews, and Matthew Webb, Petition to the South Carolina Senate, January 1, 1791, in John P. Kaminski, ed., *A Necessary Evil? Slavery and the Debate over the Constitution* (Madison, Wis.: Madison House, 1995), 230–231. There were no such restrictions against the testimony of African Americans in Baptist churches. Indeed, I have found no records that suggest that the question of their right to bring charges or testify against whites was ever raised in the years covered by this book. I am grateful to John Kaminski for bringing this document to my attention.

42. Julia Cherry Spruill found some spousal abuse prosecutions in colonial southern courts, including some from the late colonial period. Spruill, *Women's Life and Work in the Southern Colonies* (1938; reprint, New York: Norton, 1972), 340–344.

43. Tate's Creek Baptist Church, August 1803; Berryville [Buck Marsh] Baptist Church, January 1808, March 1808; Meherrin Baptist Church, May 30 and 31, 1772; June, Second Saturday and Sunday, 1772. These protections also extended to free blacks. For instance, in 1804, a white man was charged with striking a free black while acting as a patroller. Red Banks Church, July 8, 1804, August 8, 1804. See also Bethel Hill Baptist Church, October 6, 1804.

44. McCroys Creek Baptist Church Records, Davidson County, Tennessee, 1811–1816, January 23, 1813, SBHLA. See also Mill Swamp Baptist Church, March 1787.

45. Gorin, comp., *Mt. Tabor Church Minutes*, May 1813, June 1813, 56.

46. Forks of Elkhorn Baptist Church, January 1806, April 1806, May 1806.

47. See also Janet Moore Lindman, "A World of Baptists: Gender, Race, and Religious Community in Pennsylvania and Virginia, 1689–1825" (Ph.D. diss., University of Minnesota, 1994), 115–119.

CHAPTER 5

1. "Address of the Danbury Baptist Association, in the State of Connecticut, assembled October 7th, AD 1801" in Daniel L. Dreisbach, *Thomas Jefferson and*

the Wall of Separation between Church and State (New York: New York University Press, 2002), 143; Thomas Jefferson to Messrs. Nehemiah Dodge, Ephraim Robbins, and Stephen S. Nelson, A Committee of the Danbury Baptist Association in the State of Connecticut in ibid., 148. Many other printed versions of this letter have typographical errors.

 2. For an excellent discussion of this metaphor, see Dreisbach, *Thomas Jefferson and the Wall of Separation*. A number of scholars also analyzed the use and meanings of this metaphor in a 1999 forum; see particularly James H. Hutson and Thomas Jefferson, "Thomas Jefferson's Letter to the Danbury Baptists: A Controversy Rejoined," *WMQ* 3d ser., 56 (Oct. 1999): 775–790; Thomas E. Buckley, S.J., "Reflections on a Wall," *WMQ* 3d ser., 56 (Oct. 1999): 795–800; and Edwin S. Gaustad, "Thomas Jefferson, Danbury Baptists, and 'Eternal Hostility,'" *WMQ* 3d ser., 56 (Oct. 1999): 801–804.

 3. Good treatments of Virginia's disestablishment include Thomas E. Buckley, *Church and State in Revolutionary Virginia, 1776–1787* (Charlottesville: University of Virginia Press, 1977); and Charles F. James, *Documentary History of the Struggle for Religious Liberty in Virginia* (1899; reprint, New York: Da Capo, 1971). See also the collection of articles in Merrill D. Peterson and Robert C. Vaughan, eds., *The Virginia Statute for Religious Freedom: Its Evolution and Consequences in American History* (Cambridge: Cambridge University Press, 1988). For discussions specifically concerning the Baptist involvement in these Virginia debates, see Garnett Ryland, *The Baptists of Virginia, 1699–1926* (Richmond: Virginia Baptist Board of Missions and Education, 1955), chaps. 4–7; Joe L. Coker, "Sweet Harmony vs. Strict Separation: Recognizing the Distinctions between Isaac Backus and John Leland," *ABQ* 16(3) (1997): 241–250; and Andrew M. Manis, "Regionalism and a Baptist Perspective on Separation of Church and State," *ABQ* 2(3) (1983): 213–227.

 4. William L. Saunders, ed., *The Colonial Records of North Carolina*, 10 vols. (Raleigh, N.C., 1886–1890), 7:43.

 5. See Ryland, *The Baptists of Virginia*, 92–93. The Methodists, in fact, submitted petitions to the assembly explaining that, while some may perceive them as dissenters, they wished to "declare they are a religious society in communion with the church of England" and strongly opposed any efforts to disestablish the Anglican Church. *Journal of the House of Delegates of Virginia, 1776* (Williamsburg, Va., 1776), October 28, 1776, 40.

 6. *Journals of the House of Burgesses* (Williamsburg, Va., 1772), February 12, 1772, 11. See also *Journals of the House of Burgesses*, February 22, 1772, 32.

 7. *Journals of the House of Burgesses*, February 24, 1772, 35. As this petition from Baptists in the county of Amelia suggests, the legal issues were not altogether straightforward. With their petition campaign, the Baptists entered a debate in Virginia about the applicability of the Act of Toleration to the dissenters within the colony. The 1689 statute served as the cornerstone of legislation regarding dissenters in England, yet some colonial authorities argued that it never applied to the colonies because it had not been formally incorporated into the Virginia legal code. Others argued that it did extend to Virginia, offering colonial dissenters all of the

protections afforded to English dissenters. It was a long-standing dispute that had erupted periodically in the early eighteenth century but had never been permanently settled, and the Baptist petition campaign again asked Virginia lawmakers to clarify the legal scaffolding for dissenters' rights. For more on these debates, see H. J. Eckenrode, *Separation of Church and State in Virginia: A Study in the Development of the Revolution* (1910; reprint, New York: Da Capo, 1971), 33–34.

8. There is a voluminous literature that debates the facets and evolution of Henry's, Jefferson's, and Madison's views on church and state; see, for instance, Buckley, *Church and State in Revolutionary Virginia*; Edwin S. Gaustad, *Sworn on the Altar of God: A Religious Biography of Thomas Jefferson* (Grand Rapids, Mich.: Eerdmans, 1996); Frank Lambert, *The Founding Fathers and the Place of Religion in America* (Princeton, N.J.: Princeton University Press, 2003), particularly chaps. 7–9; Merrill D. Peterson and Robert C. Vaughan, eds., *The Virginia Statute for Religious Freedom* (Cambridge: Cambridge University Press, 1988); Lenni Brenner, *Jefferson and Madison on Separation of Church and State: Writings on Religion and Secularism* (Fort Lee, N.J.: Barricade, 2004); Irving Brant, "Madison on the Separation of Church and State," *WMQ* 3d ser., 8 (1951): 3–24; Donald Drakeman, "Religion and the Republic: James Madison and the First Amendment," *Journal of Church and State* 25(3) (1984): 31–54; James H. Hutson et al., "Forum," *WMQ* 3d ser., 56 (Oct. 1999): 775–824; and Dreisbach, *Thomas Jefferson and the Wall of Separation*.

9. Nancy L. Rhoden, *Revolutionary Anglicanism: The Colonial Church of England Clergy during the American Revolution* (New York: New York University Press, 1999), 88–89, 107–109, 96–103, 110–111. Like Virginia, North Carolina also had more patriot ministers than loyalist, but these states were distinctive; in most other states, loyalist ministers either outnumbered or fairly evenly matched patriot ministers. Ibid., 88–89. External pressure on Anglican clergy was substantial. In addition to watchful Whig congregants, vigilant Committees of Safety scrutinized their words and actions for signs of disloyalty. The Virginia Convention also required that ministers alter their services and swear an oath of allegiance to the state. For more on the difficulties facing the Church of England due to the American Revolution, see Sarah McCulloh Lemmon, "The Decline of the Church, 1776–1816," in Lawrence Foushee London and Sarah McCulloh Lemmon, eds., *The Episcopal Church in North Carolina, 1701–1959* (Raleigh: Episcopal Diocese of North Carolina, 1987); and Rhoden, *Revolutionary Anglicanism*, particularly chaps. 4 and 5.

10. Italics mine. Monday, 27 May 1776, Fifth Virginia Convention (Proceedings of Eighteenth Day of Session), in William J. Van Schreeven and Robert L. Scribner, eds., *Revolutionary Virginia: The Road to Independence*, 7 vols. (Charlottesville: University of Virginia Press, 1973–1983), 7:272.

11. Wednesday, 12, June 1776, in Schreeven and Scribner, eds., *Revolutionary Virginia*, 7:456–457n33; 450.

12. Hening, ed., *Statutes at Large*, 9:164–167.

13. Religious Petitions Presented to the General Assembly of Virginia, 1774–1802, Occoquon Baptist Church, Prince William County, June 20, 1776, LVA.

14. Religious Petitions Presented to the General Assembly, Miscellaneous Petition ("Ten-Thousand Name"), October 16, 1776. Other dissenters besides Baptists clearly signed the document and were involved in its circulation, but even other dissenters associated the massive document with the Baptists. Caleb Wallace, a Presbyterian leader, noted, "The Baptists circulated a Counter Petition [against the establishment], which was signed by above 10,000 Free-holders." Quoted in Ryland, *The Baptists of Virginia*, 100.

15. *The Proceedings of the Convention of Delegates . . . July, 1775* (Richmond, Va., 1775), August 16, 1775, 34–35; Religious Petitions Presented to the General Assembly, Miscellaneous Petition ("Ten-Thousand Name"), October 16, 1776, italics mine. For an example of a church asserting its right to take up arms in the war, see Hartwood Baptist Church Book, Stafford County, 1775–1861, September 16, 1775, VBHS. Minister John Leland reported that there was only one church in Virginia that did not allow its members to take up arms, which was a congregation mostly made up of Mennonite descendants. John Leland, *The Virginia Chronicle: with Judicious and Critical Remarks, under XXIV Heads* (Fredericksburg, Va., 1790), 20.

16. Paul Leicester Ford, ed., *The Works of Thomas Jefferson* (New York: Putnam's, 1904–1905), 1:62; Hening, ed., *Statutes at Large*, 9:164–167.

17. *Journal of the House of Delegates, 1776*, November 19, 1776, 85.

18. Rhys Isaac, " 'The Rage of Malice of the Old Serpent Devil': The Dissenters and the Making and Remaking of the Virginia Statute for Religious Freedom," in Merrill D. Peterson and Robert C. Vaughan, eds., *The Virginia Statute for Religious Freedom: Its Evolution and Consequences in American History* (Cambridge: Cambridge University Press, 1988), 146. For more on the assessment debate and the passage of Jefferson's bill, see Buckley, *Church and State in Revolutionary Virginia*; and Peterson and Vaughan, eds., *The Virginia Statute for Religious Freedom*.

19. *Minutes of the United Baptist Association, Formerly Called the Kehukee Association, Holden at Reedy-Creek Meeting-House, in Brunswick County, Virginia, May 1790* (Edenton, N.C., 1790), 5; Portsmouth Baptist Association Minutes, 1793, 5 (emphasis in original), VBHS; Thomas E. Buckley, "Evangelicals Triumphant: The Baptists' Assault the Virginia Glebes, 1786–1801," *WMQ* 3d ser., 45 (Jan. 1988): 33–69. During the 1790s, there were some disagreements among them on how to handle the issue of glebes. Some insisted on the immediate sale of the glebes, while others believed that compassion demanded that the incumbent ministers and their families be allowed to hold the land until the minister's death. The Roanoke Association, for instance, debated the Virginia General Committee's resolution to petition for the immediate sale of the glebes. The attending church representatives noted that, while they did not disagree with the spirit of the resolution, they believed "the feeling of lenity and Compassion *dictate* to us that only the vacant Glebes be sold." Occupied glebes, they believed, should be left in the hands of the occupants and their wives for their natural lives and sold only when vacant. Roanoke District Association Minute Book, 1789–1831, June 1790 (emphasis in original), LVA.

20. "Address of the *General Committee* representing the United Baptist Churches in Virginia, assembled in the City of Richmond, May 8th, 9th, 10th 1789," in

W. W. Abbot et al., eds., *The Papers of George Washington: Presidential Series* (Charlottesville: University of Virginia Press, 1987), 2:424–425n1 (emphasis in original).

21. Thomas J. Curry, *The First Freedoms: Church and State in America to the Passage of the First Amendment* (New York: Oxford University Press, 1986), 198–199; James Madison, Sr., to James Madison, Jr., January 30, 1788, in Robert A. Rutland et al., eds., *The Papers of James Madison*, 17 vols. (Charlottesville: University of Virginia Press, 1994–1999), 10:446; [Colonel] Joseph Spencer to James Madison, Jr., February 28, 1788 in Rutland et al., eds., *Papers of James Madison*, 10:541.

22. James Madison, Jr., to James Madison, Sr., July 1 [1788], in Rutland et al., eds., *Papers of James Madison*, 11:185; James Madison, Jr., to George Eve, January 2, 1789, in Rutland et al., eds., *Papers of James Madison*, 11:404; John Leland to James Madison, Jr., ca. February 15, 1789, in Rutland et al., eds., *Papers of James Madison*, 11:442–443; James Madison, Jr., to George Washington, November 20, 1789, in Rutland et al., eds., *Papers of James Madison*, 12:453.

23. Since the 1990s, historians have documented how different communities of people understood and developed their own vision of republicanism and the ways the common political discourses in the early national era could mask substantial divisions within the political culture. See, for instance, Drew McCoy, *The Elusive Republic: Political Economy in Jeffersonian America* (Chapel Hill: Published for the Institute of Early American History and Culture, Williamsburg, Va., by the University of North Carolina Press, 1980); Jay Fliegelman, *Prodigals and Pilgrims: The American Revolution against Patriarchal Authority, 1750–1800* (New York: Cambridge University Press, 1982); Sean Wilentz, *Chants Democratic: New York City and the Rise of the American Working Class, 1788–1850* (New York: Oxford University Press, 1984); Douglas Egerton, *Gabriel's Rebellion: The Virginia Slave Conspiracies of 1800 and 1802* (Chapel Hill: University of North Carolina Press, 1993); and Alan Taylor, *Liberty Men and Great Proprietors: The Revolutionary Settlement on the Maine Frontier, 1760–1820* (Chapel Hill: University of North Carolina Press, 1990). There has, though, been little attention to how religion mediated political ideologies and identities in the new republic. For a notable exception, see Jonathan D. Sassi, *A Republic of Righteousness: The Public Christianity of the Post-Revolutionary New England Clergy* (New York: Oxford University Press, 2001).

24. The Records of the Strawberry Baptist Association, 1787–1822, May 1794, LVA; *Minutes of the Goshen Baptist Association Holden at Glensoe's Meeting House, N. Fork., Pamunkey, in Orange County...1795* (Richmond, Va., 1795), 5, copy at VBHS; *Minutes of the North Carolina Chowan Baptist Association, holden at Sandy-Run Meeting-House...May, 1809* (Edenton, N.C., 1809), 5–6; *Minutes of the Ketocton Baptist Association, holden at Broad Run, Louden County, Virginia, August...[1809]* (Baltimore, Md., 1810), 13–16.

25. October 1, 1785, "Minutes of the Elkhorn Baptist Association, Kentucky, 1785–1805," in William Warren Sweet, ed., *Baptists: A Collection of Source Material: Religion on the American Frontier, 1783–1830*, vol. 1 (New York: Cooper Square, 1964), 419; Ketockton Baptist Association Minutes, 1793, 1794, VBHS; David

Thomas, *The Virginian Baptist: or, A View and Defence of the Christian Religion, as It is Professed by the Baptists of Virginia* (Baltimore, Md., 1774), 20; *Minutes of the Dover Baptist Association, Held at Grafton Meeting-House, York County Virginia, October 11th, 12th, 13th, 1806* (Virginia, 1807), 2, 4. Ellen Eslinger, in *Citizens of Zion: The Social Origins of Camp Meeting Revivalism* (Knoxville: University of Tennessee Press, 1999), argues that many Kentucky residents experienced political anxiety in the 1790s, which contributed to a general cultural unease that sparked Kentuckians' enthusiasm in the religious revivals that began in 1800; see chap. 5.

26. Quoted in Daniel Merritt, *Faith Flowing Freely: History of the Yadkin Baptist Association* (Elkin, N.C.: Nu-Line, 1990), 352; Flat Rock Baptist Church Records, September 1806, December 1806, NCBHC. See also Bryan Station Church, August 1804 and September 1804; and Marble Creek Church Records, Kentucky, 1787–1842, June 1, 1799, August 3, 1799, UK.

27. Roanoke District Association, 1815, 252; August 10, 1805, Minutes of the Elkhorn Baptist Association, Kentucky, in Sweet, ed., *Baptists: A Collection of Source Material*, 508. The Concord Association of Tennessee agreed, saying that such celebrations should be pious rather than the "frolic or vicians Rant usually practiced on that day." Concord Association Minutes, Tennessee, September 1814, 22, SBHLA.

28. John L. Brooke, "Ancient Lodges and Self-Created Societies: Voluntary Association and the Public Sphere in the Early Republic," in Ronald Hoffman and Peter J. Albert, eds., *Launching the Extended Republic: The Federalist Era* (Charlottesville: University of Virginia Press, 1996), 274; Minutes of the Tennessee Baptist Association, Holston, 1786–1850, 1805, 88, SBHLA; Ketocton Baptist Association Minutes, August 1815, 7, VBHS.

29. Portsmouth Baptist Association, May 1810, 4. For another example of the restriction of "worldly conversation" in the meetinghouse yard, see *Minutes of the Elkhorn Association of Baptists, Held at Cooper's Run, August 8, 1795 . . . until the 10th* ([Lexington, Ky.], 1795).

30. Portsmouth Baptist Association, May 1800, 12.

31. Roanoke District Association, 1812; General Meeting of Correspondence Minutes, Virginia, 1815, VBHS; Minutes of the Concord Association, Tennessee, 1812–1908, 1813, 16, SBHLA.

CHAPTER 6

1. The church declared that it "thought fit to Lay it aside Calling it no Bar amongst Brethren." Flat Rock Baptist Church, November 1788, January 1789, February 1789, April 1789, May 1789, NCBHC. Within a few months, the Elliots settled their dispute with the church and were received back into the membership; there is no indication that they were required to repent or "give satisfaction" for their previous conduct. Ibid., August 1789.

2. Numbers of African American converts are difficult to determine as they varied greatly across state and even locale. Robert G. Gardner estimated that by 1790

African Americans were nearly one-third of all Virginia Baptists (30.35 percent). Robert G. Gardner, *Baptists of Early America: A Statistical History, 1639–1790* (Atlanta: Georgia Baptist Historical Society, 1983), 101–110. Ellen Eslinger, in "The Beginnings of Afro-American Christianity among Kentucky Baptists," in Craig Thompson Friend, ed., *The Buzzel about Kentuck: Settling the Promised Land* (Lexington: University Press of Kentucky, 1999), found that relatively few blacks joined Baptist churches in Kentucky before the revivals that began in 1800 (203–206). In the churches sampled here, African Americans were the fast growing proportion of many churches. In Virginia and Kentucky, they were often between one-third and one-half of the members by 1790 and 1805, respectively. Slaves were smaller proportions of the membership in North Carolina and Tennessee. See Tables A.1 and A.2.

3. The relationship between slavery and evangelicalism is a crucial one to understanding the values of the evangelical sects and their position within southern society before the Civil War. As such, this topic has been analyzed in numerous scholarly works. In seminal works, Donald Mathews, in *Religion in the Old South*, and Rhys Isaac, in *The Transformation of Virginia*, find that evangelical churches offered a brief but significant challenge to the institution of slavery and racial hierarchies in the South. See also Larry M. James, "Biracial Fellowship in Antebellum Baptist Churches," in John B. Boles, ed., *Masters and Slaves in the House of the Lord: Race and Religion in the American South, 1740–1870* (Lexington: University Press of Kentucky, 1988), 37–57. Other historians, including Jewel L. Spangler, "Becoming Baptists: Conversion in Colonial and Early National Virginia," *JSH* 67 (2001): 243–286; and Christine Heyrman in *Southern Cross: The Beginnings of the Bible Belt* (New York: Knopf, 1997), dispute this claim, arguing that white evangelicals used their churches to extend their mastery over their slaves by adding another type of authority to monitor slaves' behavior, an authority invested with divine power. Randolph Scully proposes a model for reframing the debate, exposing the competing and contested meanings of black fellowship in " 'Somewhat Liberated': Baptist Discourses of Race and Slavery in Nat Turner's Virginia, 1770–1840," *Explorations in Early American Culture* 5 (2001): 328–371.

4. See, for instance, Saul Cornell, *The Other Founders: Anti-Federalism and the Dissenting Tradition in America, 1788–1828* (Chapel Hill: University of North Carolina Press, 1999); David Waldstreicher, *In the Midst of Perpetual Fetes: The Making of American Nationalism, 1776–1820* (Chapel Hill: University of North Carolina Press, 1997); Catherine Allgor, *Parlor Politics: In Which the Ladies of Washington Help Build a City and a Government* (Charlottesville: University of Virginia Press, 2002); Steven C. Bullock, *Revolutionary Brotherhood: Freemasonry and the Transformation of the American Social Order, 1730–1840* (Chapel Hill: University of North Carolina Press, 1996); Joanne B. Freeman, *Affairs of Honor: National Politics in the New Republic* (New Haven, Conn.: Yale University Press, 2001); John Lauritz Larson, *Internal Improvement: National Public Works and the Promise of Popular Government in the Early United States* (Chapel Hill: University of North Carolina Press, 2001); Richard R. John, *Spreading the News: The American Postal System from Franklin to Morse* (Cambridge, Mass.: Harvard University Press, 1996); and Simon P. Newman, *Parades and Politics of the*

Street: Festive Culture in the Early American Republic (Philadelphia: University of Pennsylvania Press, 1997).

5. James D. Essig, *The Bonds of Wickedness: American Evangelicals against Slavery, 1770–1808* (Philadelphia: Temple University Press, 1982), provides the most comprehensive study of this topic. Essig finds a vital movement during the revolutionary era that combined evangelical theology with a strain of republican ideology. Heyrman, however, argues that antislavery did not run very deeply in early evangelical churches and was one of the beliefs that white evangelicals were willing to sacrifice in order to secure greater respectability within southern society; see particularly Heyrman, *Southern Cross*, 24, 92–93, 138, and 155. Similarly, Jewel Spangler argues that antislavery was never a significant component of Virginia Baptists' beliefs or practices in "Salvation Was Not Liberty: Baptists and Slavery in Revolutionary Virginia," *ABQ* 13 (1994): 221–236. See also Edward R. Crowther, "Holy Honor: Sacred and Secular in the Old South," *JSH* 58 (November 1992): 632–635.

For analyses of Methodism and slavery in the late eighteenth-century South, see Donald G. Mathews, *Slavery and Methodism: A Chapter in American Morality, 1780–1845* (Princeton, N.J.: Princeton University Press, 1965); Dee E. Andrews, *The Methodists and Revolutionary America, 1760–1800: The Shaping of an Evangelical Culture* (Princeton, N.J.: Princeton University Press, 2000), chap. 5; Cynthia Lynn Lyerly, *Methodism and the Southern Mind, 1770–1810*, chap. 6; and John H. Wigger, *Taking Heaven by Storm: Methodism and the Rise of Popular Christianity in America* (New York: Oxford University Press, 1998), chap. 6.

6. Meherrin Baptist Church Minute Book, 1771–1837, Second Saturday and Sunday, June 1772; see also Third Saturday and Sunday, July 1772, LVA. Minutes of the Tennessee Baptist Association, October 1808, 37 (emphasis in original), SBHLA; The Records of the Strawberry Baptist Association, 1787–1822, May 1804, LVA. As Lyerly has argued, Methodists also incongruously combined efforts to moderate southern practices of slavery with antislavery in the late eighteenth and early nineteenth centuries; see Lyerly, *Methodism and the Southern Mind*, 140–145.

7. Concord Association Minutes, Tennessee, 1812, 12, SBHLA; Abbott's Baptist Church Minute Book, 1783–1874, Davidson, North Carolina, November 1807, NCBHC.

8. Zoar Baptist Church Minute Book, January 5, 1799, June 1, 1799, August 3, 1799, LVA. Unfortunately, the churchbook ends before it records the conclusion of the case. Cases of slaves bringing charges against their own masters were rare, but not unheard of. When John Lawrence tried to get his slave Nero to be disciplined for disobedience, Nero countercharged Lawrence with misconduct. Both were suspended. South Quay Baptist Church Minute Book, Nansemond County, Virginia, 1775–1827, August 1780, LVA.

9. Minutes of the Great Crossing Church, 1795–1813, November 1801, December 1801, SBTS. For examples of scholarship that argues that church discipline supported the system of slavery, see Heyrman, *Southern Cross*, 67–69, 301n57; and Spangler, "Salvation Was Not Liberty," 239–232.

10. Lyerly, *Methodism and the Southern Mind*, 48–49; James B. Taylor, *A History of Ten Baptist Churches of Which the Author Had Been Alternately a Member*, 2nd ed. (New York, 1827), 157–159. Taylor, recording the narrative many years later, clearly wanted to be faithful to Letty's original words because he found them to be so powerful when delivered to the church, but he noted his limitations, saying regretfully, "the style in which she spoke, I can only give a faint description of—I would give her own phraseology, of which I only recollect a part." Ibid., 157.

11. *Minutes of the Baptist General Committee, Held at Nuckols's Meeting-House, in the County of Goochland* (Richmond, Va., 1791), May 1791, 8, VBHS. The 1785 resolution was revisited (and reprinted) in the minutes of the 1791 meeting. *Minutes of the Baptist General Committee...1791*, 5, VBHS.

12. *Minutes of the Baptist General Committee, at their Yearly Meeting Held in the City of Richmond, May 8th, 1790* (Richmond, Va., 1790), 6–7, VBHS.

13. *Minutes of the Baptist General Committee...1791*, 5, 4, 8, VBHS. Twice during the minutes of the committee meeting, the representatives gave assurances that they understood the committee's narrow mission and would not attempt to usurp greater power. They answered the query about the original design of the General Committee, declaring it "was only to consider national grievances, and to take proper measures for redressing them." They repeated that theme in the circular letter, saying, "Look not upon us we beseech you, as your spiritual head. We disclaim all such power over the associations or churches. We desire you to view us, only as your political mouth, so speak in your case to the State Legislature, to promote the interest of the Baptists at large, and endeavor the removal of every vestige of oppression." Ibid., 4, 8.

14. Strawberry Baptist Association, May 1792. The Roanoke Association objected to the committee's

> strong remonstrances Against slavery, and the manner in which they have taken It up unanimously agreed to remonstrate, as christians, against oppression as we discover the same, and that we are heartily disposed to be under the influence of the spirit of humanity, yet nevertheless, we believe it would be a very great violation thereof (very little short of driving our children From us in a state of non age [dependency]) to emancipate our slaves promiscuously without means or visible prospects of their support. That tho' we are not unanimously clear in our minds whether the God of nature ever intended, that one Part of the human species should be held in an abject state of slavery to another part of the same species; yet the subject with us is so very abstruse and such a set of Complex circumstances attending the same, that we suppose the general committee nor any other Religious Society what ever has the least right to concern therein As a society, but leave every individual to act at discretion In order to keep a good conscience before God, as far as the Laws of our land will admit; and that it is the indispensable duty of marsters to forbear and suppress cruelty, and do that which is Just and equal to their servants. (Roanoke District Association Minute Book, 1789–1831, June 1790, LVA)

15. Ketockton Baptist Association Minutes, 1792, VBHS; *Minutes of the Baptist General Committee, Holden at Muddy-Creek Meeting-House: Powhatan County, Virginia* (Richmond, Va., 1793), 4 (emphasis mine).

16. John Leland, *The Virginia Chronicle: with Judicious and Critical Remarks, under XXIV Heads* (Fredericksburg, Va., 1790), 8, 10, 11.

17. Portsmouth Baptist Association, May 1796; *Minutes of the Kehukee Baptist Association, Holden at Parker's Meeting-House, on Meherrin, Hertford County, North-Carolina, September 1796* (Halifax, Va., 1796), 4 (emphasis in original); *Minutes of the Ketocton Baptist Association Held at Thumb Run, Fauquier County, Virginia, August 1796* (Dumfries, Va., 1796).

18. Portsmouth Baptist Association, May 26, 1792; May 25, &c. 17[9]3. Barrow may have engaged in some devious actions here to give his substitute query a public forum. The minutes from the 1794 meeting indicate that the representatives agreed that Barrow's substitute question was to be "expunged" from the official records. However, Barrow was assigned to prepare the minutes, and he neglected to remove his question. Portsmouth Baptist Association, May 24–26, 1794.

19. There were, of course, limits on these rights. They were only extended in their fullest sense to white men. Many women were not allowed to raise questions for debate or propose rules since some churches enjoined female congregants to keep silent in the churches, at least as far as church government was explicitly concerned. While there were not rules keeping African-American men from such activities, Baptist practices often did; in particular, churches typically held meetings of business on Saturdays, when slave members generally could not attend. There were, however, back-door opportunities to raise issues. It was quite easy to instigate a disciplinary investigation, for instance, which often led to a full church debate.

20. Forks of Elkhorn Baptist Church, January 1806, April 1806, SBTS. Palmer was later excommunicated for defending the antislavery actions of the minister. Ibid., August 1808; Waterlick Church, August 13, 1796; South Fork Baptist Church Minutes, December 19, 1807, July, Third Saturday, 1808, SBTS.

21. The majority of the churches sent word the following year that they rejected the plan, and the association agreed to drop it. Minutes of the Ketocton Baptist Association, August 1798, 3–4, VHS; Baptist Dover Association held at Bestland Meeting-House, Essex County, Virginia, October 14th, 1797, 4, VBHS; Carter Tarrant, *A History of the Baptised Ministers and Churches in Kentucky, &c. Friends to Humanity* (Frankfort, Ky., 1808), 15, 18, 47, copy at LC. Robert Carter was heavily influenced by Baptist antislavery beliefs as well as economic and political arguments when he decided to gradually manumit his 422 slaves; he eventually left the Baptist faith and became a Swedenborgian. Semple, *A History of the Rise and Progress of the Baptists in Virginia*, 134–135. For more on the Quakers and Methodists, see Jean Soderlund, *Quakers and Slavery: A Divided Spirit* (Princeton, N.J.: Princeton University Press, 1985); Hiram H. Hilty, *Toward Freedom for All: North Carolina Quakers and Slavery* (Richmond, Ind.: Friends United Press, 1984), 13–43; and Mathews, *Slavery and Methodism*, 3–26. For more on Baptists manumitting their slaves, see Tarrant, *A History*, 47.

22. Ronald Hoffman, "The 'Disaffected' in the Revolutionary South," in Alfred F. Young, ed., *The American Revolution: Explorations in the History of American Radicalism* (DeKalb: Northern Illinois University Press, 1976); "Diary of David Barrow of His Travel thru Kentucky in 1795," 5, NCBHC; Carlos R. Allen, Jr., ed., "David Barrow's Circular Letter of 1798," *WMQ* 3d ser., 20 (July 1963): 445.

23. Semple, *A History of the Rise and Progress of the Baptists*, 137; David Benedict, *A General History of the Baptist Denomination in America, and Other Parts of the World*, 2 vols. (Boston, 1813), 2:232–233; Frank M. Masters, *A History of Baptists in Kentucky* (Louisville: Kentucky Baptist Historical Society, 1953), 178; Joan Wells Coward, *Kentucky in the New Republic: The Process of Constitution Making* (Lexington: University Press of Kentucky, 1979), Table 1, 37; Table 6, 63.

24. Six of the sixteen antislavery votes came from the ministers, the seventh minister, David Rice, having resigned before the vote. Five of the remaining ten votes came from active laymen in Baptist and Presbyterian churches. Coward, *Kentucky in the New Republic*, 36–38, 45. See also Lowell H. Harrison, *Kentucky's Road to Statehood* (Lexington: University Press of Kentucky, 1992), 101–111; and Minutes of the Elkhorn Baptist Association, Kentucky, August 1791, in William Warren Sweet, ed., *Baptists: A Collection of Source Material: Religion on the American Frontier, 1783–1830* vol. 1 (New York: Cooper Square, 1964), 444. The following meeting was attended by many prominent emancipationists, including George Stokes Smith, William Hickman, and James Garrard, but the fifteen new representatives enabled enough of a shift that this meeting voted to "disapprove" of the memorial. Elkhorn Association, December 1791 in ibid., 447.

25. Coward, *Kentucky in the New Republic*, 107. Coward argues that both sides concealed their own concerns in this campaign. The antirevisionists employed fears of emancipation to discredit their opponents, and the emancipationists masked their own agenda with complaints of an aristocratic Senate. Coward, *Kentucky in the New Republic*, 107–109. For more on David Rice's leadership in these efforts, see Essig, *Bonds of Wickedness*, 84–88; and Harrison, *Kentucky's Road*, 108–109.

26. Only three members of Rollings Fork Church rejected this action. J. H. Spencer, *A History of Kentucky Baptists from 1769 to 1885*, 2 vols. (Cincinnati, Ohio: Baumes, 1885), 2:47–49, 1:183–184.

27. Ibid., 1:189; Minutes of the Elkhorn Association of Baptists, August 1807, 2, UK; "Minutes of the North-District Association of Baptists; Held... the first Saturday in October, in the year of our Lord one thousand eight hundred and six," (n. p.), 3, UK; Ellen Eslinger, "The Beginnings of Afro-American Christianity among Kentucky Baptists," in Craig Thompson Friend, ed., *The Buzzel about Kentuck: Settling the Promised Land* (Lexington: University Press of Kentucky, 1999), 203–206.

28. Allen, "David Barrow's Circular Letter," 445, 450. Whether as a representative or as a visitor, Barrow was frequently called upon by many associations in Virginia and Kentucky to aid in their work; they would request that he serve on committees, help to answer queries, or prepare association minutes. See, for instance, *Minutes of the Baptist General Committee... May 8th, 1790*, 5; Portsmouth Baptist Association, May 17[9]3, May 1794.

29. "North-District Association," [1806], 3; "Minutes of the North-District Association of Baptists; Held at Bethel Meeting House, in the County of Montgomery, State of Kentucky, Fifth, Sixth, Seventh and Eight[h] Days of October, 1805," (n. p.), 2, 5, SBTS; "North-District Association," 1806, 3, UK.

30. Tarrant, *A History*, 7; South Fork Baptist Church, December 19, 1807, July, third Saturday, 1808. For more on Barrow, see Essig, *Bonds of Wickedness*, 74–78.

31. Forks of Elkhorn Baptist Church, May 1806, June 1806, December 1806, September 1807, August 1808, January 1807, February 1807. For other members expelled for nonattendance for unnamed reasons, see ibid., July 1807, October 1807, May 1808, June 1808, and July 1808.

32. Minutes of the Baptized Licking-Locust Association, Friends of Humanity in Sweet, ed., *Baptists: A Collection of Source Material*, 566–569.

33. Ibid., 566–567, 568; Carter Tarrant, *The Substance of a Discourse Delivered in the Town of Versailles, Woodford County, State of Kentucky, April 20, 1806* (Lexington, Ky., 1806), 4–7, 32, 9; Tarrant, *A History*, 1, 42. See also Essig, *Bonds of Wickedness*, chap. 4; and Jonathan D. Sassi, *A Republic of Righteousness: The Public Christianity of the Post-Revolutionary New England Clergy* (New York: Oxford University Press, 2001).

34. Minutes of the Elkhorn Baptist Association in Sweet, ed., *Baptists: A Collection of Source Material*, 508.

35. Brief biographies of these (and other) ministers can be found in Spencer, *History of Kentucky Baptists*, 1:192–197, 1:191–192, 2:21–23, 1:189–190, 1:163, 1:190, 1:250; Sweet, ed., *Baptists: A Collection of Source Material*, 570–572.

36. March 15, 1808, *Kentucky Gazette and General Advertiser*, Kentucky Department for Library and Archives, Lexington; Benedict, *A General History*, 2:248; Gorin, comp., *Mt. Tabor Church Minutes*, August, Third Saturday, 1810; October, Third Saturday, 1810; August, Third Saturday, 1812; February, Third Saturday, 1814; and April, Third Saturday, 1814. See also April, Third Saturday, 1813, and April, Third Saturday, 1814. South Fork Baptist Church lost five men and ten women over slaveholding; by 1812, four of the women and three of the men had returned, with the men quickly returning to their positions of authority. See South Fork Baptist Church, July, Third Saturday, 1808; December, Fourth Saturday, 1811; February, Fourth Saturday, 1812; March, Fourth Saturday, 1812; April, Fourth Saturday, 1812; July, Fourth Saturday, 1812; Forks of Elkhorn Baptist Church, September 1807, November 1809, August 1812; and Spencer, *History of Kentucky Baptists*, 1:264.

37. Concord Association Minutes, Tennessee, September 1812, 12, SBHLA. See also Tennessee Baptist Association Minutes, 1802–1932, October 1808, October 1810, SBHLA; Forks of Elkhorn Baptist Church, January 1806, April 1806, May 1806. For the continuation of this pattern through the antebellum period, see Randy J. Sparks, *On Jordan's Stormy Banks: Evangelicalism in Mississippi, 1773–1876* (Athens: University of Georgia Press, 1994), 68–70; and Gregory A. Wills, *Democratic Religion: Freedom, Authority, and Church Discipline in the Baptist South, 1785–1900* (New York: Oxford University Press, 1997), 61–63.

CONCLUSION

1. Jean Friedman, *The Enclosed Garden: Women and Community in the Evangelical South, 1830–1900* (Chapel Hill: University of North Carolina Press, 1985); Stephanie McCurry, *Masters of Small Worlds: Yeoman Households, Gender Relations, and the Political Culture of the Antebellum South Carolina Low Country* (New York: Oxford University Press, 1995).

2. See Donald G. Mathews, *Religion in the Old South* (Chicago: University of Chicago Press, 1977); Blair A. Pogue, "I Cannot Believe the Gospel That Is So Much Preached: Gender, Belief, and Discipline in Baptist Religious Culture" in Craig Thompson Friend, ed., *The Buzzel about Kentuck: Settling the Promised Land* (Lexington: University Press of Kentucky, 1999), 229–230; Friedman, *The Enclosed Garden*; McCurry, *Masters of Small Worlds*; Janet Moore Lindman, "Acting the Manly Christian: White Evangelical Masculinity in Revolutionary Virginia," *WMQ* 3d ser., 57 (April 2000): 414–416; and Gregory A. Wills, *Democratic Religion: Freedom, Authority, and Church Discipline in the Baptist South, 1785–1900* (New York: Oxford University Press, 1997), 54–56. For contrasting views, see Cynthia Lynn Lyerly, *Methodism and the Southern Mind, 1770–1810* (New York: Oxford University Press, 1998); see also Randy Sparks, *On Jordan's Stormy Banks: Evangelicalism in Mississippi, 1773–1876* (Athens: University of Georgia Press, 1994).

3. Many scholars have studied the widened gap between black and white religious experiences in the antebellum era, which was marked by separate sermons for slaves, the development of a proslavery theology, and "brush arbor" churches where slaves could worship in secret. See Albert J. Raboteau, *Slave Religion: The "Invisible Institution" in the Antebellum South* (New York: Oxford University Press, 1978); and McCurry, *Masters of Small Worlds*, particularly chap. 4.

Selected Bibliography

PRIMARY SOURCES

Published

The Baptist Declaration of Faith: Revised and Adapted by Several District Associations of the United Baptists, in Virginia. Alexandria, Va., 1806.
Barrow, David. *Involuntary, Inherited, Perpetual, Absolute, Hereditary Slavery, Examined; Nature, Reason, Justice, Policy, and Scripture.* Lexington, Ky., 1808.
Benedict, David. *Fifty Years Among the Baptists.* New York, 1860.
———. *A General History of the Baptist Denomination in America, and Other Parts of the World.* 2 Vols. Boston, 1813.
Benningfield, Arland W., and Walter Lee Bradshaw, comps. "Shawnee Run Baptist Church Minutes 1799 through 1907, Mercer County, Kentucky." Louisville, Ky.: Benningfield, 1993.
Biggs, Joseph, and Jesse Read. *A Concise History of the Kehukee Association from Its Original Rise to the Present.* Tarboro, N.C., 1834.
Blair, John L., ed. "A Baptist Minister Visits Kentucky: The Journal of Andrew Broaddus I." *Register of the Kentucky Historical Society* 71 (1973): 393–425.
Burkitt, Lemuel, and Jesse Read. *A Concise History of the Kehukee Baptist Association from its Original Rise Down to Present Times.* Halifax, N.C., 1803.
Cain, Robert J., ed. *The Colonial Records of North Carolina*, Second Series, Vol. 10: *The Church of England in North Carolina: Documents, 1699–1741.* Raleigh: Department of Archives and History, 1999.
Cawthorn, C. P., and N. L. Warnell. *Pioneer Baptist Church Records of South-Central Kentucky and the Upper Cumberland of Tennessee, 1799–1899.* Galatin, Tenn.: Church History Research & Archives, 1985.

Clark, Walter, ed. *The State Records of North Carolina.* Winston and Goldsboro: State of North Carolina, 1895–1906.

Drake, Daniel. *Pioneer Life in Kentucky, 1785–1800.* Edited by Emmet Field Horine. New York: Schuman, 1948.

Edwards, Lawrence, ed. *Minutes of Davis Creek Church, 1797–1907.* Montevallo, Ala.: Times Printing, 1968.

Edwards, Morgan. *Materials towards a History of the Baptists.* 2 vols. Danielsville, Ga.: Heritage Papers, 1984.

Fithian, Philip Vickers. *Journal and Letters of Philip Vickers Fithian, 1773–1774: A Plantation Tutor of the Old Dominion.* Edited by Hunter Dickinson Farish. Charlottesville: University of Virginia Press, 1957.

Ford, Paul Leicester, ed. *The Works of Thomas Jefferson.* New York: Putnam's, 1904–1905.

Fries, Adelaide L. *Records of the Moravians in North Carolina.* Raleigh, N.C.: Edwards & Broughton, 1922.

Fristoe, William. *A Concise History of the Ketocton Baptist Association wherein a Description Is Given of Her Constitution, Progress and Increase.* Staunton, Va., 1808.

Gillette, A. D., ed. *Minutes of the Philadelphia Baptist Association, from A.D. 1707, to A.D. 1807.* Philadelphia, 1851.

Gorin, Sandra K., comp. *Mt. Tabor Church Minutes, Barren County, Kentucky. Vol. 1: November 5, 1798–December 1829.* [Beaver Creek] Glasgow, Ky.: Gorin Genealogical, 1994.

Ireland, James. *The Life of the Rev. James Ireland....* Winchester, Va., 1819.

Journal of the House of Delegates of Virginia. Williamsburg, Va.

Journals of the House of Burgesses. Williamsburg, Va.

Kaminski, John P., ed. *A Necessary Evil? Slavery and the Debate over the Constitution.* Madison, Wis.: Madison House, 1995.

Lancaster, Mary Holland, ed. *Minutes of Red River Baptist Church, 1791–1826, Robertson County, Tennessee.* Greenville, S.C.: n.d.

Leland, John. *The Virginia Chronicle: with Judicious and Critical Remarks, under XXIV Heads.* Fredericksburg, Va., 1790.

———. *The Writings of the Late Elder John Leland Including Some Events in His Life Written by Himself.* Edited by L. F. Greene. New York, 1845.

Madison, James. *The Papers of James Madison.* Edited by Robert A. Rutland, Charles F. Hobson, William M. E. Rachal, and Jeanne K. Snow. Charlottesville: University of Virginia Press, 1994–1999.

McBeth, Leon H. *Sourcebook for Baptist Heritage.* Nashville, Tenn.: Broadman, 1990.

The Middle District Association, South James-River... May, 1791. Richmond, Va., 1791.

Minutes of the Baptist Dover Association, Held at Hickory-neck Meeting-House, James City County, Virginia, October 12, 1799. Richmond, Va., 1799.

Minutes of the Baptist General Committee Held at Waller's Meeting-House, in Spottsylvania County, May 1799. Richmond, Va., 1799.

Minutes of the Baptist General Committee, at Their Yearly Meeting Held in the City of Richmond, May 8th, 1790. Richmond, Va., 1790.

Minutes of the Dover Baptist Association . . . in Essex County, Virginia, October, 1790. Richmond, Va., 1790.

Minutes of the Dover Baptist Association, Held at Grafton Meeting-House, York County, Virginia, October 11th, 12th, 13th, 1806. Richmond, Va., 1807.

Minutes of the Dover District Association, Held at Glebe-Landing, October 12, 1793. Richmond, Va., 1793.

Minutes of the Elkhorn Association of Babtists [sic] Held at Bryan's, Fayette County, State of Kentucky, August 9th, 10th, 11th, 1800. Lexington, Ky., 1800.

Minutes of the Elkhorn Association of Baptists Held at Cooper's Run, August 8, 1795. Lexington, Ky., 1795.

Minutes of the Elk-Horn Association of Baptists, Held at Marble Creek, August 7, 1794. Lexington, Ky., 1794.

Minutes of the Elk-horn Association of Baptists Held at South-Elkhorn, October 12, 1793. Lexington, Ky., 1793.

Minutes of the Elkhorn Association of Baptists, Held at Town Fork August 13, 1796. N.p., 1796.

Minutes of the Elk-horn Baptist Association Held at Tate's Creek, Madison County, August the 31st, 1792. Lexington, Ky., 1792.

Minutes of the Goshen Baptist Association Holden at Glensoe's Meeting House, N. Fork., Pamunkey, in Orange County . . . 1795. Richmond, Va., 1795.

Minutes of the Kehukee Baptist Association, Holden at Parker's Meeting-House, on Meherrin, Hertford County, North-Carolina, September 1796. Halifax, Va., 1796.

"Minutes of the Kehukey Baptist Association, 1769–1778." *Publications of the Kentucky Baptist Historical Society*, no. 3 (1913): 17–37.

Minutes of the Ketocton Baptist Association Held at Goose Creek, Loudon County, Virginia, August, 1795. Dumfries, Va., 1795.

Minutes of the Ketocton Baptist Association Held at Thumb Run, Fauquier County, Virginia, August 1796. Dumfries, Va., 1796.

Minutes of the Ketocton Baptist Association, Held at Happy Creek Meeting-House, in Frederick County, Virginia, August, 1801. Winchester, Va., 1801.

Minutes of the Ketocton Baptist Association, holden at Broad Run, Louden County, Virginia, August . . . [1809]. Baltimore, Md., 1810.

Minutes of the North Carolina Chowan Baptist Association, holden at Sandy-Run Meeting-House . . . May, 1809. Edenton, N.C., 1809.

Minutes of the United Baptist Association, Formerly Called the Kehukee Association, Holden at Davis's Meeting-House, Halifax County, North-Carolina, October, 1790. Edenton, N.C., 1790.

Minutes of the United Baptist Association Formerly Called the Kehukee Association, Holden at Flat-Swamp Meeting-House, Pitt County, North-Carolina, October, 1791. Edenton, N.C., 1791.

Minutes of the United Baptist Association, Formerly Called the Kehukee Association, Holden at Reedy-Creek Meeting-House, in Brunswick County, Virginia, May 1790. Edenton, N.C., 1790.

Minutes of the United Baptist Association, Formerly Called the Kehuky Association . . . in Pitt County, North-Carolina, October, 1789. Edenton, N.C., 1789.

Minutes of Two Sessions of the Baptist Middle-District Association, Holden at Salem and Spring Creek Meeting-House, in Chesterfield County. Richmond, Va., 1814.

Moore, John Trotwood, Mrs. *Dixon's Creek Baptist Church Minutes, 1799–1853.* Nashville: Tenn: Works Progress Administration, 1938.

Perry, William Stevens, D.D., ed. *Historical Collections Relating to the American Colonial Church.* Vol. 1: *Virginia.* Vols. 4–5: *Maryland and Delaware.* 1870–1878. Reprint, New York: AMS, 1968.

Proceedings of the Convention of Delegates . . . July, 1775. Richmond, Va., 1775.

Purefoy, Geo[rge] W. *A History of the Sandy Creek Baptist Association, from Its Organization in A.D. 1758, to A.D. 1858.* 1858. Reprint, New York: Arno, 1980.

Saunders, William L., ed. *The Colonial Records of North Carolina.* 10 vols. Raleigh, N.C., 1886–1890.

Semple, Robert B. *A History of the Rise and Progress of the Baptists in Virginia.* Richmond, Va., 1810.

Simpson, William S., Jr., ed. "The Journal of Henry Toler Part 1, 1782–1783." *Virginia Baptist Register* 31 (1992): 1565–1595.

———. "The Journal of Henry Toler Part 2, 1783–1796." *Virginia Baptist Register* 32 (1993): 1628–1658.

Sweet, William Warren, ed. *Baptists: A Collection of Source Material.* Vol. 1: *Religion on the American Frontier, 1783–1830.* New York: Cooper Square, 1964.

Tarrant, Carter. *A History of the Baptised Ministers and Churches in Kentucky &c. Friends to Humanity.* Frankfort, Ky., 1808. Rare Book Room, Library of Congress, Washington D.C.

———. *The Substance of a Discourse Delivered in the Town of Versailles, Woodford County, State of Kentucky, April 20, 1806. With Some Additions, and Miscelaneous [sic] Thoughts Connected with the Subject.* Lexington, Ky., 1806.

Taylor, James B. *A History of Ten Baptist Churches of Which the Author Had Been Alternately a Member.* 2nd ed. New York, 1827.

———. *Lives of Virginia Baptist Ministers.* 2nd ed. Richmond, Va., 1838.

Thomas, David. *The Virginian Baptist: or, A View and Defence of the Christian Religion, as It is Professed by the Baptists of Virginia.* Baltimore, Md., 1774.

Trabue, Daniel. *Westward into Kentucky: The Narrative of Daniel Trabue.* Edited by Chester Raymond Young. Lexington: University Press of Kentucky, 1981.

Van Schreeven, William J., comp. *Revolutionary Virginia: The Road to Independence.* 7 Vols. Edited by Robert L. Scribner. Charlottesville: Published for the Virginia Independence Bicentennial Commission by the University of Virginia Press, 1973–1983.

Virginia Gazette. Richmond, Va.: John Dixon & Thomas Nicolson, 1779–1780.

Virginia Gazette. Williamsburg, Va.: Alexander Purdie 1766–1775.

Virginia Gazette. Williamsburg, Va.: William Parks, 1736–1750.

Woodmason, Charles. *The Carolina Backcountry on the Eve of the Revolution: The Journal and Other Writings of Charles Woodmason, Anglican Itinerant.* Edited by Richard J. Hooker. Chapel Hill: Published for the Institute of Early American History and Culture at Williamsburg, Virginia, by the University of North Carolina Press, 1953.

Unpublished

John C. Hodges Library, University of Tennessee, Knoxville

Salem Baptist Church Minutes, Dekalb County, Tennessee, 1809–1908, microfilm.

Kentucky Historical Society, Frankfort

Duncan Papers.
Graves Creek Baptist Church Records, Henderson County, Kentucky [1803] 1807–1821, typescript.
Salt River Minutes, 1798–1864. In Fox Creek Church of Particular Baptists Record Book.
Six Mile Baptist Church Records, Kentucky, 1801–1816, typescript.
Stamping Grounds [McConnel's Run] Baptist Church Minutes, Kentucky, 1795–1843.

Library of Virginia, Archives, Richmond

Antioch [Raccoon Swamp] Baptist Church Records, Sussex County, Virginia, 1772–1837.
Berryville [Buck Marsh] Baptist Church Minute Book, Frederick County, Virginia, 1785–1803, 1803–1841.
Boar Swamp Baptist Church Minutes, Henrico County, Virginia, 1787–1828.
Briery Presbyterian Church Session Book, 1760–1840, Prince Edward County, Virginia.
Brock's Gap [Smith's Church and Linville's Creek] Baptist Church Records, Rockingham County, Virginia, 1756–1844, typescript.
Buck Mountain [Albemarle] Baptist Church Minute Book, Albemarle County, Virginia, 1773–1779, 1792–1811.
Chesterfield Baptist Church Records, Chesterfield County, Virginia, 1773–1788.
Chesterfield County, Virginia, Chancery Court Papers.
Chesterfield County, Virginia, Criminal Causes and Grand Jury Presentments.
Frying Pan Baptist Church Minute Book, Loudon County and Fairfax, Virginia, 1791–1828, microfilm.
Goose Creek Baptist Church Minute Book, Bedford County, Virginia, 1787–1821.
Goshen Baptist Church Records, Greene County, Pennsylvania, 1773–1802, microfilm.
Hanover Presbytery Records, 1755–1769, 1769–1785.
High Hills Baptist Church Book, Sussex County, Virginia, 1787–1845.
Ketoctin Baptist Church Minute Book, Loudoun County, Virginia, 1776–1890.
Meherrin Baptist Association Minutes, 1804–1825.

Meherrin Baptist Church Minute Book, Lunenburg County, Virginia, 1771–1837, 1842–1844.
Mill Creek Baptist Church Minutes, Botetourt County, Virginia, 1804 [1808]–1842.
Mill Creek Baptist Church Book, Frederick and Berkeley County, West Virginia, 1757–1857.
Mill Creek [Big Spring] Baptist Church Minute Book, Shenandoah and Page County, Virginia, 1798–1824.
Mill Swamp Baptist Church Records, Isle of Wight County, Virginia, 1777–1790, microfilm.
Morattico Baptist Church Records, Lancaster County, Virginia, [1764] 1778–1844, microfilm.
Mount Hermon [North Fork of Otter] Baptist Church Records, Bedford County, Virginia, 1804–1846.
North Fork Primitive Baptist Church Records, Loudon County, Virginia, 1784–1831.
Religious Petitions Presented to the General Assembly of Virginia, 1774–1802 microfilm.
Roanoke District Baptist Association Minute Book, 1789–1831. Pittsylvania County, Virginia.
Smith's Creek Baptist Church Minutes, Shenandoah and Rockingham, Virginia, 1779–1808, microfilm.
South Quay Baptist Church Minute Book, Nansemond County, Virginia, 1775–1827.
Strawberry Baptist Association Records, 1787–1822.
Tomahawk Baptist Church Records, Chesterfield County, Virginia, 1787–1842, 1842–1880, 1845–1856, microfilm.
Tussekiah Baptist Church Minute Book, Lunenburg County, Virginia, 1784–1826, 1883.
Upper King and Queen Baptist Church Minute Book, Upper King and Queen County, Virginia, 1774–1816.

North Carolina Baptist Historical Collection, Z. Smith Reynolds Library, Wake Forest University, Winston-Salem

Abbott's Baptist Church Minute Book, Davidson, North Carolina, 1783–1874, microfilm.
Barrow, David. "Diary of David Barrow of His Travel thru Kentucky in 1795," typescript.
Bethel Hill Baptist Church, Minute and Roll Book, Person County, North Carolina, 1803–1838, microfilm.
Cape Fear Baptist Association Minutes, 1806–1809, 1811–1814.
Chowan Baptist Association Minutes, 1806–1839.
County Line Primitive Baptist Association Minute Book, 1805–1904.
Flat Rock [Hunting Creek] Baptist Church Minutes, 1783–1820, microfilm.
Flatty Creek [Salem] Baptist Church Minutes, 1803–1816, Pasquotank County, North Carolina, microfilm.
Grassy Know Baptist Church, Iredell County, North Carolina, Minutes, 1804–1825, microfilm.

Lickfork Primitive Baptist Church Minute Book, Rockingham, North Carolina, 1786–1822, microfilm.
Newfound Baptist Church Minutes, Buncombe County, North Carolina, 1802–1836, 1872–1895, microfilm.
Red Banks Church Minute Book, Pitt County, North Carolina, 1791–1882, microfilm.
Reddies River Church Records, April 1798–1909, typescript.
Sandy Creek Baptist Church Minute Book, 1771–1845, microfilm.
Sandy Run Church Book, Mooresboro, North Carolina, 1782–1970, microfilm.
Well's Chapel [Bull Tail] Baptist Church Minutes, Sampson County, 1793–1985, microfilm.

North Carolina State Library and Archives, Raleigh

Bear Creek Baptist Church Minutes, Rowan County, North Carolina, 1792–1860.
Person County, North Carolina, Minutes, Court of Pleas and Quarter Session, 1796–1797.
Person County, North Carolina, State Docket and Court of Pleas and Quarter Session, 1802–1821.
Person County, North Carolina, State Docket, Superior Court, 1808–1838.
Person County, North Carolina, Trial and Appearance Docket, Superior Court, 1807–1836.
Person County, North Carolina, Trial Docket Court of Pleas and Quarter Sessions, 1792–1814.
Rutherford County, North Carolina, Minute Docket, Superior Court, 1807–1830.
Rutherford County, North Carolina, State Docket, County Court, 1783–1793, 1800–1813.
Rutherford County, North Carolina, State Recognizance Docket Superior Court, 1808–1821.
Rutherford County, North Carolina, Trial Docket County Court, 1785–1786, 1786–1787, 1792–1799.
Wheeley's Primitive [Upper South Hico] Baptist Church Minutes, Person County, North Carolina, 1790–1846, typescript.

Southern Baptist Historical Library and Archives,
Nashville, Tennessee

Concord Association Minutes, Tennessee, 1812–1908.
Cove Creek Baptist Church, Sherwood, North Carolina, 1799–1838, microfilm.
Brush Creek Primitive Baptist Church Minutes, 1802–1971, Smith County, Tennessee, microfilm.
Dandridge [French Broad] Baptist Church Minutes, Jefferson County, Tennessee, 1786–1940, microfilm.
Dumplin Creek Baptist Church Minutes, Jefferson County, Tennessee, 1797–1860, microfilm.

230 BIBLIOGRAPHY

Garrison Fork Baptist Church Minutes, Beech Grove, Tennessee, 1809–1993, microfilm.
Glen's Creek Baptist Church Minutes, Kentucky, 1801–1868, microfilm.
McCroys Creek Baptist Church Records, Davidson County, Tennessee, 1811–1816.
Mill Creek Baptist Church Minutes, Davidson County, Tennessee, 1797–1811 [1814].
Miller's Cove Baptist Church Records, Tennessee, 1813–1962, microfilm.
Spring Creek Baptist Church Minutes, Overton and Jackson Counties, Tennessee, 1802–1868, microfilm.
Tennessee Baptist Association Minutes, 1802–1932.
Tennessee Baptist Association [of] Holston Minutes, 1786–1850.
Tennessee Baptist Association [of] Stockton Valley Minutes.
Tom's Creek Baptist Church Record Book, Tennessee, 1808–1817, microfilm.

Archives and Special Collections, James P. Boyce Centennial Library, The Southern Baptist Theological Seminary, Louisville, Kentucky

Bethel Baptist Church Records, Christian County, Kentucky, 1816–1818.
Bethlehem Baptist Church, Washington County, Kentucky, Minutes, 1805–1871, typescript.
Brashear's Creek Baptist Church, Minutes, 1807–1818, typescript.
Burks Branch Baptist Church Minute Book, Kentucky, 1801–1872.
Church on the Twins [New Liberty] Minutes, [Baptist], Gallatin County, Kentucky, 1801–1838.
Forks of Elkhorn Baptist Church Minutes, Kentucky, 1788–1831.
Great Crossing Church Minutes, Kentucky, 1795–1813.
Long Run Baptist Church Minutes, Jefferson County, Kentucky, 1803–1817.
Mountain Island Church Minutes, Owen County, Kentucky, 1801–1836.
North District Baptist Association, Kentucky, 1805.
Richland [Little Beaver Creek] Baptist Church Minutes, Tennessee, 1791–1795, typescript.
South Fork Baptist Church, April 21, 1804 to October 1840, Larue County, Kentucky, microfilm.
Tate's Creek Baptist Church Minutes, Kentucky, 1798–1921.

Margaret I. King Library (Special Collections and Archives), University of Kentucky, Lexington

Bryan's Station Baptist Church Minutes, Fayette County, Kentucky, 1786–1901, typescript.
Elkhorn Association of Baptists Minutes, 1803, 1807.
J. Winston Coleman (1898–1983) Papers.
Licking Association of Baptists Minutes.
Lyle Family Papers, 1789–1944.

Marble Creek [East Hickman] Baptist Church Records, Kentucky, 1787–1842, typescript.
North District Association of Baptists Minutes, 1806, 1808.
Providence Baptist Church First Record Book, Clark County, Kentucky. Transcribed by George F. Doyle [1924].
Trabue Family Papers, 1700–1899.
Valentine Peers Papers, 1789–1826.

State Historical Society of Wisconsin, Madison, Microfilm

Boone's Creek Baptist Church, Minutes, Kentucky, 1795–1886.
Brier Creek Baptist Church, North Carolina, Minutes, 1783–1860.
Cashie Baptist Church Record Book, 1791–1832.
Eaton's Baptist Church Minutes, Rowan County, North Carolina, 1772–1787, 1790–1902.
Great Cohary Baptist Church Record Book, Sampson County, North Carolina, 1790–1855.
Jersey Baptist Church Record Book, Davidson County, North Carolina, 1784–1886.
Paw Paw Hollow [Formerly Fork of French Broad and Holston] Baptist Church Minutes, Sevier County, Tennessee, 1803–1880.
Sandy Run Baptist Church Record Book, Franklin County, North Carolina, 1773–1845.
Severn's Valley Baptist Church, Elizabethtown, Kentucky, 1788–1884.
Sinking Creek Baptist Church Minutes, Carter County, Tennessee, 1773–1963.
Yeopim Baptist Church Minutes, Chowan County, 1791–1882.

Tennessee State Library and Archives, Nashville

Cherokee Creek Baptist Church Minutes, 1783–1883, typescript.
Jefferson County, Tennessee, Court Minutes, 1792–1798.
Jefferson County, Tennessee, Order Book, 1801–1807.
Jefferson County, Tennessee, Quorum Minutes.
Mount Olivet Baptist Church Minutes, Wilson County, Tennessee, 1801–1975, microfilm.
Providence Baptist Church Minutes, Davidson County, Tennessee, 1813–1838. Transcribed by Anne E. Collins.
Saline Baptist Church Records, Stewart County, Tennessee, 1810–1964, microfilm.
Wilson Creek Primitive Baptist Church Records, Williamson County, Tennessee, 1804–1945, microfilm.

Wilson Library (Manuscripts Department), University of North Carolina, Chapel Hill

Brookes, Iveson Lewis, Papers, 1793–1865.
Drane, Robert Brent, Papers, 1851–1939.

Jackson and Prince Family Papers, 1784–1880.
Hamilton, William Southerland, Papers, 1778–1830.
Matrimony Creek Baptist Church Book, 1776–1814, North Carolina, microfilm.
Yadkin Baptist Church Minutes, Caldwell County, North Carolina, 1787–1946.

Virginia Baptist Historical Society, University of Richmond

Broad Run Baptist Church Book, Virginia, 1762–1872.
General Committee Minutes, 1789–1799.
General Meeting of Correspondence, Minutes, Virginia, 1808, 1810, 1814, 1815.
Hartwood Baptist Church Book, Stafford County, Virginia, 1775–1861.
Ketockton Baptist Association Minutes, 1792–1834.
Lower Banister [Riceville] Baptist Church Book, Pittsylvania, 1798–1845.
Middle District Baptist Association Minutes, 1791–1852.
New Hope Church Book, Patrick County, Virginia, 1798–1906.
Toler, Henry. Diary, 1782–1786.
Virginia Portsmouth Baptist Association Minutes, 1792–1815.
Waller's Baptist Church Records, Virginia, 1799–1818.
Waterlick Baptist Church Minutes, Shenandoah County, Virginia, 1787–1815, microfilm.
Williams, John. Journal, May 7, 1771–September 15, 1771.
Zoar Baptist Church Minutes, Berkeley County, Virginia, 1792–1801.

Virginia Historical Society, Richmond

Ayres Family Papers.
Baptist, Edward, Diary, 1790–1861.
Chappawamsic Baptist Church Minute Book, Stafford County, Virginia, 1766–1860.
Hickman, William. "A Short Account of My Life and Travels: For More than Fifty Years, a Professed Servant of Jesus Christ," 1828.
Hughes Family Papers.
Ketockton Baptist Association Minutes, 1798.
Virginia Portsmouth Baptist Association Minutes, 1793.

SECONDARY SOURCES

Ahlstrom, Sydney E. *A Religious History of the American People.* New Haven, Conn.: Yale University Press, 1972.
Allen, Carlos R., Jr. "David Barrow's Circular Letter of 1798." *WMQ* 3d Ser., 20 (1963): 440–451.
Allen, Jeffrey Brooke. "Means and Ends in Kentucky Abolitionism, 1792–1823." *Filson Club History Quarterly* 57(4) (Oct. 1983): 365–381.

———. "The Origins of Proslavery Thought in Kentucky, 1792–1799." *Register of the Kentucky Historical Society* 77(2) (Spring 1979): 75–90.
Alley, Reuben Edward. *A History of Baptists in Virginia*. Richmond: Virginia Baptist General Board, 1973.
Allgor, Catherine. *Parlor Politics: In Which the Ladies of Washington Help Build a City and a Government*. Charlottesville: University of Virginia Press, 2002.
Andrews, Dee E. *The Methodists and Revolutionary America, 1760—1800: The Shaping of an Evangelical Culture*. Princeton, N.J.: Princeton University Press, 2000.
Ayers, Edward L. *Vengeance and Justice: Crime and Punishment in the Nineteenth-Century American South*. New York: Oxford University Press, 1984.
Beeman, Richard R. *The Evolution of the Southern Backcountry: A Case Study of Lunenburg County, Virginia, 1746–1832*. Philadelphia: University of Pennsylvania Press, 1984.
Boles, John B. *Religion in Antebellum Kentucky*. Lexington: University Press of Kentucky, 1976.
———. *The South through Time: A History of an American Region*. Englewood Cliffs, N.J.: Prentice-Hall, 1995.
Boles, John B., ed. *Masters and Slaves in the House of the Lord: Race and Religion in American Society, 1740–1870*. Lexington: University Press of Kentucky, 1988.
Bolton, S. Charles. *Southern Anglicanism: The Church of England in Colonial South Carolina*. Westport, Conn.: Greenwood, 1982.
Bonomi, Patricia U. *Under the Cope of Heaven: Religion, Society, and Politics in Colonial America*. New York: Oxford University Press, 1986.
Boylan, Anne M. "Evangelical Womanhood in the Nineteenth Century: The Role of Women in Sunday Schools." *Feminist Studies* 4 (Oct. 1978): 62–80.
———. *The Origins of Women's Activism: New York and Boston, 1797–1840*. Chapel Hill: University of North Carolina Press, 2002.
Brant, Irving. "Madison on the Separation of Church and State." *WMQ* 3d Ser., 8 (1951): 3–24.
Braude, Ann. "Women's History Is American Religious History." In *Retelling U.S. Religious History*, edited by Thomas A. Tweed, 87–107. Berkeley: University of California Press, 1997.
Brekus, Catherine A. *Strangers and Pilgrims: Female Preaching in America, 1740–1845*. Chapel Hill: University of North Carolina Press, 1998.
Bridenbaugh, Carl. *Myths and Realities: Societies of the Colonial South*. Baton Rouge: Louisiana State University Press, 1952.
Brinsfield, John Wesley. *Religion and Politics in Colonial South Carolina*. Easely, S.C.: Southern Historical Press, 1983.
Brooke, John L. "Ancient Lodges and Self-Created Societies: Voluntary Association and the Public Sphere in the Early Republic." In *Launching the "Extended Republic": The Federalist Era*, edited by Ronald Hoffman and Peter J. Albert, 273–359. Charlottesville: University of Virginia Press, 1996.
Brown, Kathleen M. *Good Wives, Nasty Wenches, and Anxious Patriarchs: Gender, Race, and Power in Colonial Virginia*. Chapel Hill: University of North Carolina Press, 1996.

Brydon, G. MacLaren. "New Light upon the History of the Church in Colonial Virginia." *HMPEC* 10 (June 1941): 69–103.

———. *Virginia's Mother Church and the Political Conditions under Which It Grew*. Vols. 1 and 2. Richmond, Va.: Virginia Historical Society, 1947.

Buckley, Thomas E., S.J. *Church and State in Revolutionary Virginia, 1776–1787*. Charlottesville: University of Virginia Press, 1977.

———. "Evangelicals Triumphant: The Baptists' Assault the Virginia Glebes, 1786–1801." *WMQ* 3d Ser., 45 (Jan. 1988): 33–69.

Bullock, Steven C. *Revolutionary Brotherhood: Freemasonry and the Transformation of the American Social Order, 1730–1840*. Chapel Hill: University of North Carolina Press, 1996.

Bushman, Richard L. *From Puritan to Yankee: Character and the Social Order in Connecticut, 1690–1765*. New York: Norton, 1967.

Butler, Jon. *Awash in a Sea of Faith: Christianizing the American People*. Cambridge, Mass.: Harvard University Press, 1990.

Buza, Melinda S. "'Pledges of Our Love': Friendship, Love, and Marriage among the Virginia Gentry, 1800–1825." In *The Edge of the South: Life in Nineteenth-Century Virginia*, edited by Edward L. Ayers and John C. Willis, 9–36. Charlottesville: University of Virginia Press, 1991.

Bynum, Caroline Walker. "Women's Stories, Women's Symbols: A Critique of Victor Turner's Theory of Liminality." In *Anthropology and the Study of Religion*, edited by Robert L. Moore and Frank E. Reynolds, 105–125. Chicago: Center for the Scientific Study of Religion, 1984.

Bynum, Victoria E. *Unruly Women: The Politics of Social and Sexual Control in the Old South*. Chapel Hill: University of North Carolina Press, 1992.

Cashin, Joan E. *A Family Venture: Men and Women on the Southern Frontier*. New York: Oxford University Press, 1991.

Clinton, Catherine. "In Search of Southern Women's History." *Georgia Historical Quarterly* 76 (1992): 420–427.

———. *The Plantation Mistress: Woman's World in the Old South*. New York: Pantheon, 1982.

Clinton, Catherine, and Michele Gillespie, eds. *The Devil's Lane: Sex and Race in the Early South*. New York: Oxford University Press, 1997.

Coker, Joe L. "Sweet Harmony vs. Strict Separation: Recognizing the Distinctions between Isaac Backus and John Leland." *ABQ* 16 (1997): 241–250.

Conkin, Paul K. *Cane Ridge: America's Pentecost*. Madison: University of Wisconsin Press, 1990.

Cott, Nancy F. *Public Vows: A History of Marriage and the Nation*. Cambridge, Mass.: Harvard University Press, 2000.

Coward, Joan Wells. *Kentucky in the New Republic: The Process of Constitution Making*. Lexington: University Press of Kentucky, 1979.

Crismon, Leo T. "Virginia Baptist Ministers Who Migrated to Kentucky before 1800." *Virginia Baptist Register* 16 (1977): 757–771.

Crowther, Edward R. "Holy Honor: Sacred and Secular in the Old South." *JSH* 58 (1992): 619–636.

Curry, Thomas J. *The First Freedoms: Church and State in America to the Passage of the First Amendment.* New York: Oxford University Press, 1986.
Daniel, W. Harrison. "Virginia Baptists and the Negro in the Early Republic." *Virginia Magazine of History and Biography* 80 (January 1972): 60–69.
Daniels, Bruce C., ed. *Town and County: Essays on the Structure of Local Government in the American Colonies.* Middletown, Conn.: Wesleyan University Press, 1978.
Dayton, Cornelia Hughes. "Turning Points and the Relevance of Colonial Legal History." *WMQ* 3d Ser., 50 (1993): 7–17.
———. *Women before the Bar: Gender, Law, and Society in Connecticut.* Chapel Hill: University of North Carolina Press, 1995.
Delke, James A. *History of the North Carolina Chowan Baptist Association, 1806–1881.* Raleigh, N.C., 1882.
Drakeman, Donald. "Religion and the Republic: James Madison and the First Amendment." *Journal of Church and State* 25(3) (1984): 31–54.
Douglas, Ann. *The Feminization of American Culture.* 1977. Reprint, New York: Anchor, 1988.
Dreisbach, Daniel L. *Thomas Jefferson and the Wall of Separation between Church and State.* New York: New York University Press, 2002.
Eckenrode, H. J. *Separation of Church and State in Virginia: A Study in the Development of the Revolution.* 1910. Reprint, New York: Da Capo, 1971.
Ekirch, A. Roger. *"Poor Carolina": Politics and Society in Colonial North Carolina, 1729–1776.* Chapel Hill: University of North Carolina Press, 1981.
———. "Whig Authority and Public Order in Backcountry North Carolina, 1776–1783." In *An Uncivil War: The Southern Backcountry during the American Revolution*, edited by Ronald Hoffman, Thad W. Tate, and Peter J. Albert, 99–124. Charlottesville: Published for the U.S. Capitol Historical Society by the University of Virginia Press, 1985.
Epstein, Barbara Leslie. *The Politics of Domesticity: Women, Evangelism, and Temperance in Nineteenth-Century America.* Middletown, Conn.: Wesleyan University Press, 1981.
Eslinger, Ellen. *Citizens of Zion: The Social Origins of Camp Meeting Revivalism.* Knoxville: University of Tennessee Press, 1999.
Essig, James D. *The Bonds of Wickedness: American Evangelicals against Slavery, 1770–1808.* Philadelphia: Temple University Press, 1982.
Estep, William R. *Revolution within the Revolution: The First Amendment in Historical Context, 1612–1789.* Grand Rapids, Mich.: Eerdmans, 1990.
Finger, John R. *Tennessee Frontiers: Three Regions in Transition.* Bloomington: Indiana University Press, 2001.
Fliegelman, Jay. *Prodigals and Pilgrims: The American Revolution against Patriarchal Authority, 1750–1800.* New York: Cambridge University Press, 1982.
Fogleman, Aaron Spencer. "Jesus Is Female: The Moravian Challenge in the German Communities of British North America." *William and Mary Quarterly* 60 (2003): 295–332.

Fox-Genovese, Elizabeth. *Within the Plantation Household: Black and White Women of the Old South.* Chapel Hill: University of North Carolina Press, 1988.

Freeberg, Ernest A., III. "Why David Barrow Moved to Kentucky." *Virginia Baptist Register* 32 (1993): 1617–1627.

Freeze, Gary. "Like a House Built upon Sand: The Anglican Church and Establishment in North Carolina, 1765–1776." *HMPEC* 48 (1979): 405–432.

Frey, Sylvia R. *Water from the Rock: Black Resistance in a Revolutionary Age.* Princeton, N.J.: Princeton University Press, 1991.

———. and Betty Wood. *Come Shouting to Zion: African American Protestantism in the American South and British Caribbean to 1830.* Chapel Hill: University of North Carolina Press, 1998.

Friedman, Jean E. *The Enclosed Garden: Women and Community in the Evangelical South, 1830–1900.* Chapel Hill: University of North Carolina Press, 1985.

Gardner, Robert G. *Baptists of Early America: A Statistical History, 1639–1790.* Atlanta: Georgia Baptist Historical Society, 1983.

Gaustad, Edwin S. *The Great Awakening in New England.* New York: Harper, 1957.

Genovese, Eugene D. *Roll, Jordan, Roll: The World the Slaves Made.* 1974. Reprint, New York: Vintage, 1976.

Gewehr, Wesley M. *The Great Awakening in Virginia, 1740–1790.* Durham, N.C.: Duke University Press, 1930.

Goen, C. C. *Revivalism and Separatism in New England, 1740–1800.* New Haven, Conn.: Yale University Press, 1962.

Gorn, Elliot J. "'Gouge and Bite, Pull Hair and Scratch': The Social Significance of Fighting in the Southern Backcountry." *AHR* 90 (Feb. 1985): 18–43.

Greene, Jack P. "Independence, Improvement, and Authority: Toward a Framework for Understanding the Histories of the Southern Backcountry during the Era of the American Revolution." In *An Uncivil War: the Southern Backcountry during the American Revolution,* edited by Ronald Hoffman, Thad W. Tate, and Peter J. Alberts, 3–36. Charlottesville: Published for the U.S. Capitol Historical Society by the University of Virginia Press, 1985.

———. *Pursuits of Happiness: The Social Development of Early Modern British Colonies and the Formation of American Culture.* Chapel Hill: University of North Carolina Press, 1988.

Gundersen, Joan R. *The Anglican Ministry in Virginia, 1723–1766: A Study of a Social Class.* New York: Garland, 1989.

———. "Independence, Citizenship, and the American Revolution." *Signs* 13 (1987): 59–77.

Hamburger, Philip. *Separation of Church and State.* Cambridge, Mass.: Harvard University Press, 2002.

Harrison, Lowell H. *Kentucky's Road to Statehood.* Lexington: University Press of Kentucky, 1992.

Hatch, Nathan O. *The Democratization of American Christianity.* New Haven, Conn.: Yale University Press, 1989.

Hayden, Roger, ed. *The Records of a Church of Christ in Bristol.* [Bristol, U.K.]: Bristol Record Society, 1974.
Heyrman, Christine Leigh. *Commerce and Culture: The Maritime Communities of Colonial Massachusetts, 1690–1750.* New York: Norton, 1984.
———. *Southern Cross: The Beginnings of the Bible Belt.* Chapel Hill: University of North Carolina Press, 1997.
Hilty, Hiram H. *Toward Freedom for All: North Carolina Quakers and Slavery.* Richmond, Ind.: Friends United Press, 1984.
Hoffman, Ronald. "The 'Disaffected' in the Revolutionary South." In *The American Revolution: Explorations in the History of American Radicalism*, edited by Alfred Young, 273–316. DeKalb: Northern Illinois University Press, 1976.
Hoffman, Ronald, Thad W. Tate, and Peter J. Albert, eds. *An Uncivil War: The Southern Backcountry during the American Revolution.* Charlottesville: University of Virginia Press, 1985.
Huggins, Maloy Alton. *A History of North Carolina Baptists, 1727–1932.* Raleigh: General Board, State Baptist State Convention of North Carolina, 1967.
Hughes, Richard T., and C. Leonard Allen. *Illusions of Innocence: Protestant Primitivism in America, 1630–1875.* Chicago: University of Chicago Press, 1988.
Hutson, James H. et al. "Forum [on Jefferson and the Danbury Letter]." *WMQ* 3d Ser., 56 (October 1999): 775–824.
Ide, Arthur Frederick. *Woman in the American Colonial South.* Mesquite, Tex.: Ide House, 1980.
Isaac, Rhys. "Evangelical Revolt: The Nature of the Baptists' Challenge to the Traditional Order in Virginia, 1765–1775." *WMQ* 3d Ser., 31 (1974): 345–368.
———. "'The Rage of Malice of the Old Serpent Devil': The Dissenters and the Making and Remaking of the Virginia Statute for Religious Freedom." In *The Virginia Statute for Religious Freedom: Its Evolution and Consequences in American History*, edited by Merrill D. Peterson and Robert C. Vaughan, 139–169. Cambridge: Cambridge University Press, 1988.
———. *The Transformation of Virginia, 1740–1790.* Chapel Hill: University of North Carolina Press, 1982.
Isenberg, Nancy. "'Pillars in the Same Temple and Priests of the Same Worship': Woman's Rights and the Politics of Church and State in Antebellum America." *JAH* 85 (June 1998): 98–128.
Jabour, Anya. *Marriage in the Early Republic: Elizabeth and William Wirt and the Companionate Ideal.* Baltimore, Md.: Johns Hopkins University Press, 1998.
Jackson, Harvey H. "Hugh Bryan and the Evangelical Movement in Colonial South Carolina." *WMQ* 3d Ser., 43 (1986): 594–614.
James, Charles F. *Documentary History of the Struggle for Religious Liberty in Virginia.* 1899. Reprint, New York: Da Capo, 1971.
James, Larry M. "Biracial Fellowship in Antebellum Baptist Churches." In *Masters and Slaves in the House of the Lord: Race and Religion in American Society, 1740–1870*, edited by John B. Boles, 37–57. Lexington: University Press of Kentucky, 1988.

Joyner, Charles. "'Believer I Know': The Emergence of African-American Christianity." In *African-American Christianity: Essays in History*, edited by Paul E. Johnson, 181–201. Berkeley: University of California Press, 1994.

Juster, Susan. *Disorderly Women: Sexual Politics and Evangelicalism in Revolutionary New England*. Ithaca, N.Y.: Cornell University Press, 1994.

———. "'In a Different Voice': Male and Female Narratives of Religious Conversion in Post-Revolutionary America." *American Quarterly* 41 (1989): 34–62.

———. "Patriarchy Reborn: The Gendering of Authority in the Evangelical Church in Revolutionary New England." *Gender & History* 6 (1994): 58–81.

Kars, Marjoleine. *Breaking Loose Together: The Regulator Rebellion in Pre-Revolutionary North Carolina*. Chapel Hill: University of North Carolina Press, 2002.

Kay, Marvin L. Michael, and Lorin Lee Cary. *Slavery in North Carolina, 1748–1775*. Chapel Hill: University of North Carolina Press, 1995.

Kerber, Linda K. "'I Have Don...Much to Carrey on the Warr': Women and the Shaping of Republican Ideology after the American Revolution." *Journal of Women's History* 1 (1990): 231–243.

Kierner, Cynthia A. *Beyond the Household: Women's Place in the Early South, 1700–1835*. Ithaca, N.Y.: Cornell University Press, 1998.

———. "'The Dark and Dense Cloud Perpetually Lowering over Us': Gender and the Decline of the Gentry in Postrevolutionary Virginia." *JER* 20 (2000): 185–217.

Kroll-Smith, J. Stephen. "Tobacco and Belief: Baptist Ideology and the Yeoman Planter in Eighteenth-Century Virginia." *Southern Studies* 21 (1982): 353–368.

———. "Transmitting a Revival Culture: The Organization Dynamic of the Baptist Movement in Colonial Virginia, 1760–1777." *JSH* 50 (1984): 551–568.

Kulikoff, Allan. "The Origins of Afro-American Society in Tidewater Maryland and Virginia, 1700 to 1790." *WMQ* 3d Ser., 35 (April 1978): 226–259.

———. *Tobacco and Slaves: The Development of Southern Cultures in the Chesapeake, 1680–1800*. Chapel Hill: Published for the Institute of Early American History and Culture, Williamsburg, Va., by the University of North Carolina Press, 1986.

Lacey, Barbara E. "Women and the Great Awakening in Connecticut." Ph.D. diss., Clark University, 1982.

Lambert, Frank. *The Founding Fathers and the Place of Religion in America*. Princeton, N.J.: Princeton University Press, 2003.

Larkin, Jack. *The Reshaping of Everyday Life, 1790–1840*. New York: Harper & Row, 1988.

Larson, John Lauritz. *Internal Improvement: National Public Works and the Promise of Popular Government in the Early United States*. Chapel Hill: University of North Carolina Press, 2001.

Lebsock, Suzanne. *The Free Women of Petersburg: Status and Culture in a Southern Town, 1784–1860*. New York: Norton, 1984.

Lee, Jean Butenhooff. *The Price of Nationhood: The American Revolution in Charles County*. New York: Norton, 1994.

———. "The Problem of Slave Community in the Eighteenth-Century Chesapeake." *WMQ* 3d Ser., 43 (July 1986): 333–361.

Lefler, Hugh Talmage. "The Anglican Church in North Carolina: The Proprietary Period." In *The Episcopal Church in North Carolina, 1701–1959*, edited by Lawrence Foushee London and Sarah McCulloh Lemmon, 1–21. Raleigh: Episcopal Diocese of North Carolina, 1987.

———. "The Anglican Church in North Carolina: The Royal Period." In *The Episcopal Church in North Carolina, 1701–1959*, edited by Lawrence Foushee London and Sarah McCulloh Lemmon, 22–60. Raleigh: Episcopal Diocese of North Carolina, 1987.

Lemmon, Sarah McCulloh. "The Decline of the Church, 1776–1816." In *The Episcopal Church in North Carolina, 1701–1959*, edited by Lawrence Foushee London and Sarah McCulloh Lemmon, 61–93. Raleigh: Episcopal Diocese of North Carolina, 1987.

Levine, Lawrence W. *Black Culture and Black Consciousness: Afro-American Folk Thought from Slavery to Freedom*. New York: Oxford University Press, 1977.

Lindman, Janet Moore. "Acting the Manly Christian: White Evangelical Masculinity in Revolutionary Virginia." *WMQ* 3d Ser., 57 (April 2000): 393–416.

———. "A World of Baptists: Gender, Race, and Religious Community in Pennsylvania and Virginia, 1689–1825." Ph.D. diss., University of Minnesota, 1994.

Little, Lewis P. *Imprisoned Preachers and Religious Liberty in Virginia*. Lynchburg, Va.: Bell, 1938.

Lobody, Diane H. "'That Language Might Be Given Me': Women's Experience in Early Methodism." In *Perspectives on American Methodism: Interpretive Essays*, edited by Russell E. Richey, Kenneth E. Rowe, and Jean Miller Schmidt, 127–144. Nashville, Tenn.: Abingdon, 1993.

London, Lawrence Foushee, and Sarah McCulloh Lemmon, eds. *The Episcopal Church in North Carolina, 1701–1959*. Raleigh: Episcopal Diocese of North Carolina, 1987.

Loveland, Anne C. *Southern Evangelicals and the Social Order, 1800–1860*. Baton Rouge: Louisiana State University Press, 1980.

Lumpkin, William L. *Baptist Foundations in the South: Tracing through the Separates the Influence of the Great Awakening*. Nashville, Tenn.: Broadman, 1961. Reprinted in William L. Lumpkin and L. H. Butterfield, eds., *Colonial Baptists and Southern Revivals*. New York: Arno, 1980.

———. "The Role of Women in Eighteenth Century Virginia Baptist Life." *Baptist History and Heritage* 8 (1973): 158–167.

Lyerly, Cynthia Lynn. "Enthusiasm, Possession, and Madness: Gender and the Opposition to Methodism in the South, 1770–1810." In *Beyond Image and Convention*, edited by Janet L. Coryell et al., 53–73. Columbia: University of Missouri Press, 1998.

———. *Methodism and the Southern Mind, 1770–1810*. New York: Oxford University Press, 1998.

———. "Women and Southern Religion." In *Religion in the American South: Protestants and Others in History and Culture*, edited by Beth Schweiger and

Donald Mathews, 247–281. Chapel Hill: University of North Carolina Press, 2004.

Manis, Andrew M. "Regionalism and a Baptist Perspective on Separation of Church and State." *ABQ* 2 (1983): 213–227.

Mathews, Donald G. "Evangelical America: The Methodist Ideology." In *Perspectives on American Methodism: Interpretive Essays*, edited by Russell E. Richey, Kenneth E. Rowe, and Jean Miller Schmidt, 17–30. Nashville, Tenn.: Abingdon, 1993.

———. *Slavery and Methodism: A Chapter in American Morality, 1780–1845*. Princeton, N.J.: Princeton University Press, 1965.

Mathews, Donald G. *Religion in the Old South*. Chicago: University of Chicago Press, 1977.

McBeth, Leon. *Women in Baptist Life*. Nashville, Tenn.: Broadman, 1979.

McCoy, Drew R. *The Elusive Republic: Political Economy in Jeffersonian America*. Chapel Hill: Published for the Institute of Early American History and Culture, Williamsburg, Va., by the University of North Carolina Press, 1980.

McCurry, Stephanie. *Masters of Small Worlds: Yeoman Households, Gender Relations, and the Political Culture of the Antebellum South Carolina Low Country*. New York: Oxford University Press, 1995.

McGarvie, Mark Douglas. *One Nation Under Law: America's Early National Struggles to Separate Church and State*. DeKalb, Ill.: Northern Illinois University Press, 2005.

McLoughlin, William G. "Massive Civil Disobedience as a Baptist Tactic in 1773." *American Quarterly* 21 (Winter 1969): 710–727.

———. *Revivals, Awakenings, and Reform*. Chicago: University of Chicago Press, 1978.

Meade, William. *Old Churches, Ministers, and Families of Virginia*. Philadelphia: Lippincott, 1861.

Mercer, Jesse. *A History of the Georgia Baptist Association*. Washington, Ga., 1838; reprint, Washington: Georgia Baptist Association, 1980.

Merritt, Daniel. *Faith Flowing Freely: History of the Yadkin Baptist Association*. Elkin, N.C.: Nu-Line, 1990.

Mills, Frederick V. *Bishops by Ballot: An Eighteenth-Century Ecclesiastical Revolution*. New York: Oxford University Press, 1978.

Moore, R. Laurence. *Religious Outsiders and the Making of Americans*. New York: Oxford University Press, 1986.

———. *Selling God: American Religion in the Marketplace of Culture*. New York: Oxford University Press, 1994.

Nash, Gary B. *Quakers and Politics: Pennsylvania, 1681–1726*. Princeton, N.J.: Princeton University Press, 1968.

Newman, Simon P. *Parades and the Politics of the Street: Festive Culture in the Early American Republic*. Philadelphia: University of Pennsylvania Press, 1997.

Nobles, Gregory H. "Breaking into the Backcountry: New Approaches to the Early American Frontier, 1750–1800." *WMQ* 3d Ser., 46 (1989): 641–670.

Noll, Mark A. "Revolution and the Rise of Evangelical Social Influence in North Atlantic Societies." In *Evangelicalism: Comparative Studies of Popular Protestantism* in North America, the British Isles, and Beyond, 1700–1990, edited by Mark Noll, David W. Bebbington, and George A. Rawlyk, 113–136. New York: Oxford University Press, 1994.

Noll, Mark A., David W. Bebbington, and George A. Rawlyk, eds. *Evangelicalism: Comparative Studies of Popular Protestantism in North America, the British Isles, and Beyond, 1700–1990.* New York: Oxford University Press, 1994.

Norton, Mary Beth. "The Evolution of White Women's Experience in Early America." *AHR* 89 (June 1984): 593–619.

———. "Gender, Crime, and Community in Seventeenth-Century Maryland." In *The Transformation of Early American History: Society, Authority and Ideology,* edited by James A. Henretta, Michael Kammen, and Stanley N. Katz, 123–150. New York: Knopf, 1991.

———. "Gender and Defamation in Seventeenth-Century Maryland." *WMQ* 3d Ser., 44 (1987): 3–39.

Oakes, James. *The Ruling Race: A History of American Slaveholders.* New York: Vintage, 1983.

Otto, John Solomon. *The Southern Frontiers, 1607–1860: The Agricultural Evolution of the Colonial and Antebellum South.* New York: Greenwood, 1989.

Ownby, Ted. *Subduing Satan: Religion, Recreation, and Manhood in the Rural South, 1865–1920.* Chapel Hill: University of North Carolina Press, 1990.

Payne, Rodger M. "New Light in Hanover County: Evangelical Dissent in Piedmont Virginia, 1740–1755." *JSH* 61 (1995): 665–694.

Pestana, Carla Gardina. *Quakers and Baptists in Colonial Massachusetts.* Cambridge: Cambridge University Press, 1991.

Peterson, Merrill D., and Robert C. Vaughan, eds. *The Virginia Statute for Religious Freedom: Its Evolution and Consequences in American History.* Cambridge: Cambridge University Press, 1988.

Posey, Walter B. "Baptist Watch-Care in Early Kentucky." *Register of the Kentucky State Historical Society* 34 (October 1936): 311–317.

Prichard, Robert W. *A History of the Episcopal Church.* Harrisburg, Pa.: Morehouse, 1991.

Raboteau, Albert J. *Slave Religion: The "Invisible Institution" in the Antebellum South.* New York: Oxford University Press, 1978.

Ranck, George W. *The Traveling Church: An Account of the Baptist Exodus from Virginia to Kentucky in 1781 under the Leadership of Rev. Lewis Craig and Capt. William Ellis.* Louisville, Ky.: Baptist Book Concern, 1891.

Rennie, Sandra. "The Role of the Preacher: Index to the Consolidation of the Baptist Movement in Virginia from 1760 to 1790." *Virginia Magazine of History and Biography* 88 (1980): 430–441.

Rhoden, Nancy L. *Revolutionary Anglicanism: The Colonial Church of England Clergy during the American Revolution.* New York: New York University Press, 1999.

Richey, Russell E. *Early American Methodism.* Bloomington: Indiana University Press, 1991.

Ritchie, Carson I. A. *Frontier Parish: An Account of the Society for the Propagation of the Gospel and the Anglican Church in America, Drawn from the Records of the Bishop of London.* London: Associated University Presses, 1976.

Robinson, W. Stitt. *The Southern Colonial Frontier, 1607–1763.* Albuquerque: University of New Mexico Press, 1979.

Roeber, A. G. *Faithful Magistrates and Republican Lawyers: Creators of Virginia Legal Culture, 1680–1810.* Chapel Hill: University of North Carolina Press, 1981.

Rotundo, E. Anthony. "Body and Soul: Changing Ideals of American Middle-Class Manhood, 1770–1920." *Journal of Social History* 16 (1983): 23–38.

Rutman, Darrett B., and Anita H. Rutman. *A Place in Time: Middlesex County, Virginia, 1650–1750.* New York: Norton, 1984.

Ryland, Garnett. *The Baptists of Virginia, 1699–1926.* Richmond: Virginia Baptist Board of Missions and Education, 1955.

Salmon, Marylynn. *Women and the Law of Property in Early America.* Chapel Hill: University of North Carolina Press, 1986.

Sandlund, Vivien. "A Devilish and Unnatural Usurpation: Baptist Evangelical Ministers and Antislavery in the Early Nineteenth Century: A Study of the Ideas and Activism of David Barrow." *ABQ* 12 (1994): 262–277.

Sassi, Jonathan D. *A Republic of Righteousness: The Public Christianity of the Post-Revolutionary New England Clergy.* New York: Oxford University Press, 2001.

Schmidt, Leigh Eric. "'A Church-Going People Are a Dress-Loving People': Clothes, Communication, and Religious Culture in Early America." *Church History* 58 (1989): 36–51.

———. *Holy Fairs: Scottish Communions and American Revivals in the Early Modern Period.* Princeton, N.J.: Princeton University Press, 1989.

Schneider, A. Gregory. *The Way of the Cross Leads Home: The Domestication of American Methodism.* Bloomington: Indiana University Press, 1993.

Schweiger, Beth Barton. "Max Weber in Mount Airy; or, Revivals and Social Theory in the Early South." In *Religion in the American South: Protestants and Others in History and Culture,* edited by Beth Schweiger and Donald Mathews, 31–66. Chapel Hill: University of North Carolina Press, 2004.

Scott, Anne Firor. *The Southern Lady: From Pedestal to Politics, 1830–1930.* Chicago: University of Chicago Press, 1970.

Scully, Randolph. "'Somewhat Liberated': Baptist Discourses of Race and Slavery in Nat Turner's Virginia, 1770–1840." *Explorations in Early American Culture* 5 (2001): 328–371.

Seiler, William H. "The Anglican Church: A Basic Institution of Local Government in Colonial Virginia." In *Town and County: Essays on the Structure of Local Government in the American Colonies,* edited by Bruce C. Daniels, 134–159. Middletown, Conn.: Wesleyan University Press, 1978.

Sensbach, Jon F. "Before the Bible Belt: Indians, Africans, and the New Synthesis of Eighteenth-Century Southern Religious History." In *Religion in the Old South,* edited by Donald G. Mathews, 5–29. Chicago: University of Chicago Press, 1977.

Shepard, E. Lee. "'This Being Court Day': Courthouses and Community Life in Rural Virginia." *Virginia Magazine of History and Biography* 103 (1995): 459–470.
Smith-Rosenberg, Carroll. "Dis-Covering the Subject of the 'Great Constitutional Discussion,' 1786–1789." *JAH* 79 (1992): 841–873.
Sobel, Mechal. *Trabelin' On: The Slave Journey to an Afro-Baptist Faith*. 1979. Reprint, Princeton, N.J.: Princeton University Press, 1988.
Soderlund, Jean R. *Quakers and Slavery: A Divided Spirit*. Princeton, N.J.: Princeton University Press, 1985.
Spangler, Jewel L. "Becoming Baptists: Conversion in Colonial and Early National Virginia." *JSH* 67 (2001): 243–286.
———. "Salvation Was Not Liberty: Baptists and Slavery in Revolutionary Virginia." *ABQ* 13 (1994): 221–236.
Sparks, Randy J. *On Jordan's Stormy Banks: Evangelicalism in Mississippi, 1773–1876*. Athens: University of Georgia Press, 1994.
Spencer, J. H. *A History of Kentucky Baptists from 1769 to 1885: Including More than 800 Biographical Sketches*. 2 vols. Cincinnati, Ohio: Baumes, 1885.
Spruill, Julia Cherry. *Women's Life and Work in the Southern Colonies*. 1938. Reprint, New York: Norton, 1972.
Sweet, William W. "The Churches as Moral Courts of the Frontier." *Church History* 2 (1933): 3–21.
Taylor, Alan. *Liberty Men and Great Proprietors: The Revolutionary Settlement on the Maine Frontier, 1760–1820*. Chapel Hill: University of North Carolina Press, 1990.
Terry, Gail S. "Sustaining the Bonds of Kinship in a Trans-Appalachian Migration, 1790–1811: The Cabell-Breckinridge Slaves Move West." *Virginia Magazine of History and Biography* 102 (1994): 455–476.
Thorp, Daniel P. *The Moravian Community in Colonial North Carolina: Pluralism on the Southern Frontier*. Knoxville: University of Tennessee Press, 1989.
Turner, Victor. *The Ritual Process: Structure and Anti-Structure*. Chicago: Aldine, 1969.
Turner, Wallace B. "Abolitionism in Kentucky." *Register of the Kentucky Historical Society* 69(4) (Oct. 1971): 319–338.
Upton, Dell. *Holy Things and Profane: Anglican Parish Churches in Colonial Virginia*. New York: Architectural History Foundation; Cambridge, Mass.: MIT Press, 1986.
Vaughn, Steve. "Making Jesus Black: The Historiographical Debate on the Roots of African-American Christianity." *Journal of Negro History* 82(1) (Winter 1997): 25–41.
Waldrep, Christopher. "The Making of a Border State Society: James McGready, the Great Revival, and the Prosecution of Profanity in Kentucky." *AHR* 99 (June 1994): 767–784.
Waldstreicher, David. *In the Midst of Perpetual Fetes: The Making of American Nationalism, 1776–1820*. Chapel Hill: University of North Carolina Press, 1997.
Watson, Alan D. "The Anglican Parish in Royal North Carolina, 1729–1775." *HMPEC* 48 (1979): 303–319.

Wheeler, Robert. "The County Court in Colonial Virginia." In *Town and County: Essays on the Structure of Local Government in the American Colonies*, edited by Bruce C. Daniels, 111–134. Middletown, Conn.: Wesleyan University Press, 1978.

Wigger, John H. *Taking Heaven by Storm: Methodism and the Rise of Popular Christianity in America*. New York: Oxford University Press, 1998.

Wilentz, Sean. *Chants Democratic: New York City and the Rise of the American Working Class, 1788–1850*. New York: Oxford University Press, 1984.

Wills, Gregory A. *Democratic Religion: Freedom, Authority, and Church Discipline in the Baptist South, 1785–1900*. New York: Oxford University Press, 1997.

Wolfe, Margaret Ripley. *Daughters of Canaan: A Saga of Southern Women*. Lexington: University Press of Kentucky, 1995.

Woolverton, John Frederick. *Colonial Anglicanism in North America*. Detroit, Mich.: Wayne State University Press, 1984.

Wyatt-Brown, Bertram. *Southern Honor: Ethics and Behavior in the Old South*. New York: Oxford University Press, 1982.